ABC's *of* Murmuration

Collective Wisdom of Nature

ME *to* WE *to* US

Kathy J. Hagler, Ph.D.  Robin L. Graham

Copyright © 2024 by Kathy J. Hagler and Robin L. Graham

All rights reserved. No part of this publication may be reproduced, distributed, or transmitted in any form or by any means, including photocopying, recording, or other electronic or mechanical methods, without the prior written permission of the publisher, except in the case of brief quotations embodied in critical reviews and certain other noncommercial uses permitted by copyright law. For permission requests, contact the publisher at the address below.

www.ABCsofMurmuration.com

Printed in the United States of America

ISBN: 978-1-7375172-3-8 (Hardcover)
ISBN: 978-1-7375172-4-5 (Paperback)
ISBN: 978-1-7375172-5-2 (eBook)

Library of Congress Control Number: 2024921339

First Edition

10 9 8 7 6 5 4 3 2 1

DEDICATION

*With genuine gratitude and humility,
I dedicate this book to my sweet husband, Ken Hahn,
and all my dear friends in our lifetime murmuration.*

— Kathy

*For the joy of discovering the sacred human journey,
which we pass through together, and the interconnection with all.*

— Robin

*To Kristyn and Marissa,
the sensational, dedicated, and creative support team.*

To the ultimate wisdom of Nature, we are blessed.

*To the readers inspired to Embrace, Envision, Explore, and Engage
with greater purpose in their lives.*

— Kathy & Robin

CONTENTS

Preface.. vii
Glossary... ix
Introduction... xix

Chapter 1: Mirroring Nature's Path............................ 1
Chapter 2: Preparing for The Four-Path Journey............... 17

WALKWAY I: ME

Chapter 3: Why Me?.. 37
Chapter 4: How To Embark on The Journey of Me............... 65
Chapter 5: Integrating Mind, Body, and Spirit.............. 105
Chapter 6: Integrating The Power of Your Inner Adaptability... 129

WALKWAY II: WE

Chapter 7: The Strength of The Pack........................ 165
Chapter 8: Being Me And We: Autonomy and Mutuality......... 203

WALKWAY III: US

Chapter 9: Birds of a Feather Flock Together............... 235
Chapter 10: The Joy of Flying.............................. 259

MURMURATION

Chapter 11: Realizing Our Collective Legacy................ 289

Epilogue... 307
How-to Skills.. 313
Global Thought Leaders..................................... 317
PSYCH-K®—The Key to Sustainable Change..................... 321
About the Authors.. 323
Acknowledgments.. 325
Endnotes... 327

PREFACE

The year was 1784. At just 29 years old, Wolfgang Mozart had recently completed his *Piano Concerto No. 17 in G* and entered it into his log. No one had seen or heard it yet, but he was confident he could hear his melody floating in the air. Impossible! And yet, there it was again.

Imagine Mozart's astonishment when he overheard his composed piece echoing from the pet shop below. He wondered how his creation was being mirrored so perfectly. His curiosity led him downstairs, where he discovered a small starling gracefully lifting her melody—the very melody he had just finished creating—into the air. In that moment he realized, as you can too, that the wisdom embedded in nature could exceed even his most extraordinary imaginings. He bought the little bird, and his new songstress moved in with him that day.

Mozart and the starling soon became inseparable companions, united by their shared love for music. This remarkable partnership is well-documented and showcases Mozart's fascination with the starling's incredible mimicry, which brought him immense joy.

Now, we turn our focus to you. Are you ready to experience the joy of a partnership as demonstrated in nature? To explore the mesmerizing dance in the sky of a murmuration—the collective US? The invitation to this journey is not just about the starlings but about reaching the pinnacle of collective achievement, the ultimate success envisioned by those who dare to dream in harmony with nature.

GLOSSARY

A Note About Key Words: Throughout this book, we have highlighted glossary terms when they are first introduced or defined. Additionally, some terms are intentionally italicized throughout because they represent key concepts or terminology unique to this work. These distinctions emphasize their importance and reinforce their role as foundational ideas within the text.

The glossary is placed at the front of the book to provide quick and easy access to these key terms and concepts, helping you understand them right from the start. This placement is intended to enhance your understanding of the material as you progress through the chapters. Two pivotal terms essential to your journey in this book are **Walkways** and **Paths**, which we define as follows:

Three Walkways: ME. WE. US. These are the principal arteries through this book. These metaphorical routes represent the structured and intentional journey of personal and collective transformation. The Three Walkways—ME, WE, and US—illustrate the stages of individual growth, team collaboration, and community unity, guiding the journey from personal awareness to collective synergy and the wisdom of murmuration.

The Four Paths: Embrace. Envision. Explore. and Engage. These serve as dynamic and adaptable steps that guide individuals and groups in navigating the Walkways of ME, WE, and US.

30/30 Communication Strategy: A core practice in *Strategic Doing*™, where teams meet every 30 days to review progress, adjust action steps, and set new goals. This iterative process ensures accountability, agility, and continuous progress toward strategic objectives.

Activity Field/Energy of Doing: The energy generated within an individual—referred to as ME—that drives observable behaviors. It represents the core, foundational energy that powers action in a person.

Adaptability: The ability to adjust to new conditions, challenges, or environments, both in individuals and systems.

Amygdala: A part of the brain involved in processing emotions, particularly fear and pleasure, that plays a key role in memory formation.

Amygdala Hijack: A situation, trigger, or *Footlights of Consciousness* in which the amygdala overrides the rational brain, which then leads to an immediate and intense emotional response that is often associated with stress or fear.

Angular Alignment: The coordination of the direction or angle between multiple elements, often in reference to team dynamics or strategy alignment.

Art of Iterative Team Formation: The process of building and refining teams through repeated cycles of formation, feedback, and adjustment.

Attraction Zone: A conceptual area in which certain behaviors, ideas, or individuals are drawn together, often due to shared goals or mutual benefits.

Awareness Opportunities: Situations or moments in which individuals or teams can gain insights, increase consciousness, or become more mindful.

Brain Coherency: The harmonious functioning of different parts of the brain, which often leads to optimal cognitive performance and emotional regulation.

Brain Mapping: The study of brain structures and their functions—through the use of imaging techniques—to understand how different regions contribute to behavior and thought.

Brain Stem or Reptilian Brain: The oldest part of the brain responsible for basic survival functions like breathing, heart rate, and instinctual behavior.

Bummock: The submerged portion of a floating iceberg, used metaphorically to describe the hidden aspects of a situation or system.

Cannon-Bard Theory of Emotion: A psychological theory that proposes that emotions and physiological responses occur simultaneously, rather than one causing the other.

Cerebral Cortex or Complex Functioning: The outer layer of the brain associated with higher-order functions like thinking, planning, and decision-making.

Change Blindness: A phenomenon in which people fail to notice significant changes in their visual environment, which highlights the limits of human attention.

Collective Consciousness: The shared beliefs, ideas, and moral attitudes that operate as a unifying force within a society or group.

Collective Effectiveness and Growth: The enhanced ability of a group to achieve goals and develop over time through collaboration and shared learning.

Collective Intelligence: The ability of a group to solve problems and make decisions collectively, which regularly surpasses individual capabilities..

Collective Wisdom: The accumulated knowledge and insights that emerge from the collective experience of a group or community.

Confluence: The merging or coming together of different ideas, forces, or elements to create a unified whole.

Conscious Habits of Thriving: The deliberate practices and behaviors that contribute to sustained well-being and success.

Conscious Mind: The part of the mind that is aware of thoughts, feelings, and surroundings, and is capable of deliberate and intentional thinking.

Consciousness: The state in which an individual is aware of and able to think about their own existence, thoughts, and surroundings.

Context Field/Energy of Meaning and Purpose: A type of energy often communicated through the sharing of stories. This energy is intuitive and felt in the body. Shared knowledge and mutual support increase safety and deepen understanding of members within a group.

Convergent Whole Field/The Fourth Field: The unified outcome of all other fields—Activity, Relationship, and Context—which integrates their energies into a cohesive whole.

Covey's Habit Formation: The process of developing consistent, habitual behaviors through repeated practice, as popularized by Stephen Covey's principles.

Cross-Team Collaboration: The cooperative effort between different teams or departments to achieve a common goal.

Endogenous Control: The regulation of internal processes, such as attention or motivation, which originate from within the individual.

Entanglement: Particles can be "entangled," their fates intertwined regardless of distance. Einstein famously called this "spooky action at a distance."

Equilibrium: A state of balance or stability, often between competing forces or elements within a system.

Epigenetics: The study of how an individual's behaviors and environment can cause changes that affect the way their genes work. Unlike genetic changes, epigenetic changes are reversible and do not change DNA sequences, but they can change how the body reads a DNA sequence.

External Stimuli (Exogenous Control): External factors or influences that affect behavior or physiological responses.

Evolutionary Mindset: A way of thinking that emphasizes continuous growth, adaptation, and learning, inspired by evolutionary principles.

Fields of Energy: The concept that individuals or groups generate energy fields that can influence their environment and interactions.

Fight, Flight, Freeze, or Fawn: The four primary responses to stress or danger, driven by the autonomic nervous system.

Flock Logic: The principles governing group behavior, such as flocking, in which simple rules lead to complex social dynamics.

Global Impact: The influence or effect that actions, decisions, or products have on a worldwide scale.

Global Thought Leaders: Individuals who are recognized for their influential ideas and insights that shape global trends and practices.

Global Workspace: A theoretical framework in cognitive science that describes the brain's ability to integrate and process information from various sources to create a unified experience.

Grit: A personality trait characterized by perseverance and passion for long-term goals, often linked to success.

Human Fields of Energy (HFE): The various energetic fields generated by the human body, believed to influence health, well-being, and interactions with others.

Hummock: The visible portion of the iceberg—representing the conscious mind—where active thoughts and awareness reside.

Integrated Mindset: A holistic approach to thinking that combines various perspectives for congruent and effective adaptability, collaboration, and problem-solving.

Interconnected: Being linked or related to others, which emphasizes the web of relationships that connect individuals or systems.

Interdependent: A mutual reliance between individuals, groups, or systems in which each party depends on the other(s).

Internal Global Workspace: The internal cognitive system in which information is processed and made available to conscious awareness.

Leaderful: Leadership that is learned and practiced by all in a group. It is inclusive, shared, and important for collective decision making.

Leaderful Mindset: An approach to leadership that emphasizes the role of the influencer by emphasizing collaboration, empowerment, and shared responsibility.

Left Brain Hemisphere: The left side of the brain that is traditionally associated with logical thinking, language, and analytical processes.

Limbic System or Midbrain: A part of the brain involved in emotional regulation, memory, and motivation.

Limiting Subconscious Beliefs or Limiting Beliefs: Deep-seated beliefs that reside in the subconscious mind and often restrict personal growth or success.

Look Out to Look In or Looking Out/Looking In: A reflective practice that involves observing the external world to gain insights about an individual's internal state.

Mirror Neurons: Neurons that fire both when an individual acts and when they observe the same action performed by another, which plays a role in empathy and learning.

Mutuality: The quality of being shared or reciprocated, often in the context of relationships or agreements.

Murmuration: The phenomenon of synchronized movement of starlings, which symbolizes collective harmony and fluidity.

Neuroplasticity: The brain's ability to reorganize itself by forming new neural connections throughout life, which allows for learning and adaptation.

Oneness: The idea that all things are interconnected and unified, transcending individual differences.

Overcoming Toxic Beliefs: The process of identifying and challenging harmful or limiting beliefs that hinder personal growth and well-being.

Pathfinder Project: A strategic initiative designed to explore new directions, identify opportunities, and guide future actions or innovations.

Perception Blindness: A cognitive phenomenon in which an individual's perceptions differ from reality. It includes change blindness (obvious changes go unnoticed) and inattentional blindness (unexpected items are missed), and demonstrates the limits of visual awareness.

Plasticity: The capacity for an organism or system to change and adapt, particularly in response to environmental influences.

Presencing: A mindfulness practice that involves being fully present in the moment while employing the senses to access deeper insights and creativity.

Primitive, Brain Stem, or Reptilian Brain: The part of the brain responsible for basic survival instincts and autonomic functions, such as heart rate and breathing.

Priming: A psychological phenomenon in which exposure to one stimulus influences the response to a subsequent stimulus, often unconsciously.

Quantum Entanglement: A phenomenon in quantum physics in which particles become interconnected and the state of one instantly influences the state of another, regardless of distance.

Quantum Physics: The study of the fundamental principles governing the behavior of matter and energy at the quantum (atomic and subatomic) level.

Relationship Field/Energy of Interaction: The relationship energy field multiplies the contributions of individual energies. This is the Energy of Interaction, in which the exchange of energy occurs through communication.

Repulsion Zone: A concept that describes areas or situations in which individuals or forces are naturally repelled from one another, often due to conflicting interests or energies.

Right Brain Hemisphere: The right side of the brain, traditionally associated with creativity, intuition, and holistic thinking.

Rules of Civility: Established guidelines or norms that govern respectful and considerate behavior within a group or society.

Secure Base: A psychological concept in which an individual feels safe and supported by another, which enables them to explore and take risks.

Securer of Memories: The part of the brain, particularly the hippocampus, responsible for storing and retrieving memories.

Shinrin-Yoku: A Japanese practice, also known as "forest bathing," that involves immersing oneself in nature to promote mental and physical well-being.

Silent Navigator: An internal guide or intuition that directs decision-making without overt awareness, often based on subconscious processing.

Situatedness: The theory that the context or environment in which a person or thing is located influences behaviors, perception, and interactions.

Steward of Vital Functions: The part of the brain responsible for regulating essential bodily functions, such as breathing and heart rate.

Storer of Reactions: A concept or mechanism that enables or triggers responses, often in a biological or psychological context.

Subconscious Mind: The part of the mind that operates below the level of conscious awareness and influences thoughts, feelings, and behaviors.

Subconscious Thoughts: Thoughts that occur in the subconscious mind, often subconscious mind, which often influence behavior without conscious awareness.

Superpositioning: The theory that quantum entities can exist in multiple states at once until measured. Schrödinger's cat existing in a state of being both dead and alive until observed, illustrates this concept.

The Three P's (People, Practices, Place): A framework that emphasizes the importance of people, effective practices, and the right environment in achieving success.

Theory of Mind: The ability to understand that others have thoughts, beliefs, and perspectives different from an individual's own.[1]

Torchbearer in a Cave: A metaphor for leadership and exploration in which an individual illuminates the path ahead to guide others through uncertainty. It represents the responsibility to lead with vision and courage, and reveal new opportunities while navigating the unknown.

Unified Consciousness: A state in which an individual or group experiences a sense of oneness and alignment to transcend individual differences.

Vision of Murmuration: The collective vision of starlings emerges when individuals synchronize their actions and intentions to create harmony and shared purpose.

Walking a New Way: The practice of adopting new approaches, behaviors, or mindsets in response to changing circumstances or insights.

Whole-Brain State: A balanced and integrated use of both hemispheres of the brain as well as other areas with neuron functions, often associated with optimal cognitive function and creativity.

Whole System: A perspective that considers all parts of a system in order to recognize their interdependence and the impact of changes on the whole.

INTRODUCTION

I am because you are.
—Ubuntu

"A person is a person because of or through others." This phrase, rooted in the African philosophy of Ubuntu, reflects the idea that humans cannot exist in isolation.[2] The health, well-being, and success of the collective are amplified through each member's thriving, the magic of team collaboration, and the mysteries of successful gatherings, such as *murmuration*.

We wrote *The ABC's of Murmuration* to explore the hidden wisdom of nature, with the goal of revealing its true knowledge to guide us all toward a harmonious and sustainable existence. We believe that, by examining some of the principles that govern the natural world, we can identify the laws and structures that will guide us toward a more effective, compassionate, and balanced way of living, both now and in the future.

Nature provides us with a breathtaking example: murmuration. A mesmerizing display of collective intelligence seen in the synchronized flight of starlings, it exemplifies **adaptability**, unity, safety, and survival in the wild. Murmuration serves as a powerful metaphor for how we can align our own individual and collective behaviors to ensure a thriving future for humanity. The key to our survival lies in understanding the delicate balance between autonomy and affiliation. Moving from the singular brilliance of ME (yourself) to the supportive strength of WE (the best team), and finally to the **collective wisdom** and spirit of US (the best community) captures the spirit of this work. Murmuration is the new metaphor for thriving communities.

> *Once you've experienced the world from above,*
> *you'll never look at the ground*
> *the same way again.*
>
> —Unknown

The *ABC's of Murmuration* invites you to observe nature and other sentient-being experts who have mastered moving from individual brilliance to the supportive strength of a team to the collective wisdom of the whole community.

OUR GLOBAL EXPERTS

To explore murmuration as a paradigm for human collaboration, we called upon a group of experts from a wide variety of countries, industries, and specializations. Each of them contributed insight and wisdom to the chapters you will soon read (in approximately this order).

Jack Lowe and TDIndustries: an organization that murmurates like starlings, and that sees an *Evolutionary Mindset* as an entry point for employment.

Dr. Bruce H. Lipton and Duccio Locati: explain the importance of conscious choice in our lives. How being aware of the now, shifting limiting beliefs and adjusting perspectives, and connecting with others with kindness and respect, brings balance and harmony to our lives through the application of PSYCH-K®.

Ross Thornley: pioneer of *The AQai® Adaptability Quotient*. This framework provides valuable insights on building resilience and adaptability for individuals, teams, and entire organizations. It also has the ability to assess and report on the skill of adaptability, which supplies information that is critical for the growth of individuals and organizations.

Dr. Gary Cone: creator of the *Living in Choice* model. His work is designed to elevate the consciousness of each individual toward peace and joy.

Dr. Ed Morrison and Kathy Opp, creator of *Strategic Doing*™ and a *Strategic Doing*™ Fellow, respectively, show us how this model enables individuals to gather effectively, take action, and make meaningful improvements in areas critical to the aspirations and vision of organizations and communities.

Dr. Robert A. Cooke: founder of Human Synergistics, a management consulting company. Dr. Cooke's work provides tools to measure, change thinking and behaviors, and drive the improvements of organizational cultures. This work enables sustainability across all levels of an organization while also measuring the health of an organization.

Jon Berghoff: co-founder and CEO of *xchange*, he defines exponential outcomes for communities by choreographing conversations to unlock collective wisdom.

We are so grateful to each of these experts for their contribution to this book, and to the philosophy of murmuration that we are presenting to the world. More detailed biographies and links to expert websites can be found in the back of this book.

OUR VISION FOR YOU

It's worth mentioning that the starlings were our first global experts. To learn more about them, please read Lyanda Lynn Haupt's book, *Mozart's Starling*, a beautiful description of humans and nature. It was a large part of our inspiration.

With decades of combined experience in organizational transformation, personal growth, and leadership, the two of us bring a unique blend of wisdom and practical insights to this work. We hope our passion for fostering thriving communities, both professionally and personally, shines through each page. We also hope the *ABC's of Murmuration* will not only inspire you, but also equip you to step into your fullest potential as an individual and as part of a greater whole. Together, let us move from the brilliance of ME to the strength of WE and finally to the collective wisdom of US.

CHAPTER 1

MIRRORING NATURE'S PATH

We lie in the lap of an immense intelligence.
—Ralph Waldo Emerson

IMAGINE: AS THE DAY'S GOLDEN WARMTH FADES, REPLACED BY THE GENTLE EMBRACE OF TWILIGHT, AN EVERYDAY FIELD BECOMES AN AMPHITHEATER OF WONDER. There you are, front and center, heart open, eyes wide. A single starling, its wings slicing the air with intent, captures your attention. Soon, it's not alone. Like magnetized particles, others join and move together in a mesmerizing dance, their shimmering feathers catching the last light of day. The atmosphere thickens with energy, and resonates with a sound that feels like the universe's heartbeat growing louder. And then it blossoms: a murmuration, a symphony of starlings, each bird a note, together creating a living masterpiece against the canvas of the evening sky.

Their movements, delicate yet profound, recall the grace of ballet dancers. But what they're doing is more than just a dance. It's unity in motion. It's the power of individuals coming together, of finding balance in collaboration. This magical display speaks volumes about belonging. As these birds take to the sky and merge into one magnificent, fluid entity, they remind you of the power of unity. Not directed by a single lead bird yet perfectly coordinated through the *Leaderful Behavior* of each bird. They teach you the power of connectivity in ensuring safety and survival. Ultimately, you thrive when you find balance and harmony. Balance helps to avoid fear and anxiety. Harmony creates consistency and like mindsets.

In the skies above, the captivating murmuration of starlings leaves onlookers in wonder. The speed and synchrony of the birds' reactions in a murmuration take their breath away. But what they witness is not just nature's artistry; it's the culmination of individual effort and collective coordination. While you might assume individual birds are tracking every member of their massive flock, the truth is simpler and more profound. One incredibly interesting fact that has emerged from recent research is that the movement of a starling only affects the movement of the closest seven surrounding birds.[3] The closest statistical analogy is that of magnetism, where various particles align in a single direction as the metals become magnetized. Apparently, a similar thing occurs when a starling moves inside a murmuration. Starlings maintain their intricate formations by merging with nearby birds into a group of seven, later merging with other groups of seven to form a massive murmuration.

Starlings achieve synchronized flight by monitoring the movements of their closest neighbors

©2024 ABC's of Murmuration

Andrea Cavagna and colleagues at the University of Rome found that the starling groups "respond as one."[4] When a single starling changes direction or speed, the whole flock responds as if information has spread in real-time across the flock.

An awe-inspiring sight like the one described above prompts this reflection: Just like starlings, humans can create beautiful and harmonic patterns when they come together and allow growth and evolution to be paramount in their mindsets. In your life, these patterns manifest as families, communities, and organizational ecosystems.

Just as with human achievements, you see the result but often overlook the myriad moments of individual instinct, effort, and preparation that underpin such synchronized flights. These birds, through their daily endeavors—seeking sustenance, defending their flock, navigating environmental challenges—demonstrate unwavering dedication.

The next time the starlings' dance grabs your attention, remember the countless individual journeys and collective commitment that enable such a display. Let their resilience and dedication inspire you and reinforce the fact that behind every great spectacle, whether in nature or your own life, there's a story of persistence, preparation, adaptability, and passion.

AN INSPIRATIONAL TALE: A HUMAN MURMURATION STORY

Much like the first few starlings that begin to gather and gradually seek others to join their flight, the early days of what would become The Beatles started with a single, significant connection. In 1957, a young John Lennon met Paul McCartney at a local church fête. This meeting was not unlike the initial moments of a murmuration—one bird finding another, sensing potential, and sparking the beginning of something greater. John and Paul, both passionate about music, quickly realized that together they could create something neither could achieve alone.

When they began to play and write songs together, their collaboration became the nucleus around which others would eventually gather. George Harrison joined less than a year later, and eventually Ringo Starr in 1962. Each new addition to the group was like another starling joining the flight—adding new energy, direction, and depth to the growing formation. Just as a murmuration is not led by a single bird but instead is guided by the collective, the early Beatles found their rhythm through a shared understanding and mutual respect for each other's talents and musical assets.

LESSONS IN MURMURATION

Like the individual starlings that attune to nearby birds, individual humans need others to exist. Birds flock together for protection from predators. Humans can only thrive when in relationship with others. Each person is an individual, an entity that will be referred to as "ME." When a single ME partners with one ME or more, this book will refer to this entity as "WE." A WE can be a couple (two) or a group, such as a team or part of an organization. WE are part of something bigger too, and when combined, become the entity "US." In your professional lives, you are an employee (ME), part of a team (WE), and part of your organization (US). In your personal lives, you are an individual (ME) who is part of a nuclear family (WE), and who belongs to an extended family (US).

THE THREE WALKWAYS

ME = one starling; an individual

WE = a group of seven starlings; a couple, a team, a group[5]

US = a murmuration; groups of teams, a community

A symphony orchestra provides one of the most evocative human exemplifications of the delicate dance between the musical skill of the individual ME, the collaborative WE of the strings, woodwinds, brass, and percussion, and the collective US of the orchestra. Here, a multitude of individuals—each a ME—blend their instrumental voices to produce a rich tapestry of sound. Every musician infuses the music with their unique touch, all the while ensuring their performance aligns with the collective talents of the orchestra members and the amazing sound of the whole. As each musician tunes their instruments and then moves into the heart of the performance, a transformative resonance emerges. This combined force—the US—is much more powerful than just the sum of individual contributions. It's akin to a musical murmuration, where each note soars, dives, and weaves with its companions to create an auditory masterpiece. Embodying these principles, you can foster environments that resonate with unity in your communities and organizations, much like the mesmerizing harmony of a symphony orchestra.

©2024 ABC's of Murmuration

The *ABC's of Murmuration* has been written to artistically articulate human murmuration. Through this guide you will learn how every person, at each level of participation, can cultivate and contribute to a harmonious ME, WE, and US. Each participation level is built on three foundations—Awareness, Beliefs, and Connect—which guide and inform the choices of both individuals and collectives. These are the *ABC's*; the keys to unlocking collective wisdom.

In this framework, the word Connect was chosen instead of Connection because Connect is an action verb, which signals the importance of taking deliberate steps. Just as starlings must constantly and actively adjust to stay aligned with the flock, it should be emphasized that building harmony and community requires ongoing, conscious effort. It's not enough to simply exist within a connection; you must continuously Connect by acting as one. This active approach enables individuals to engage meaningfully and collaboratively rather than passively observing.

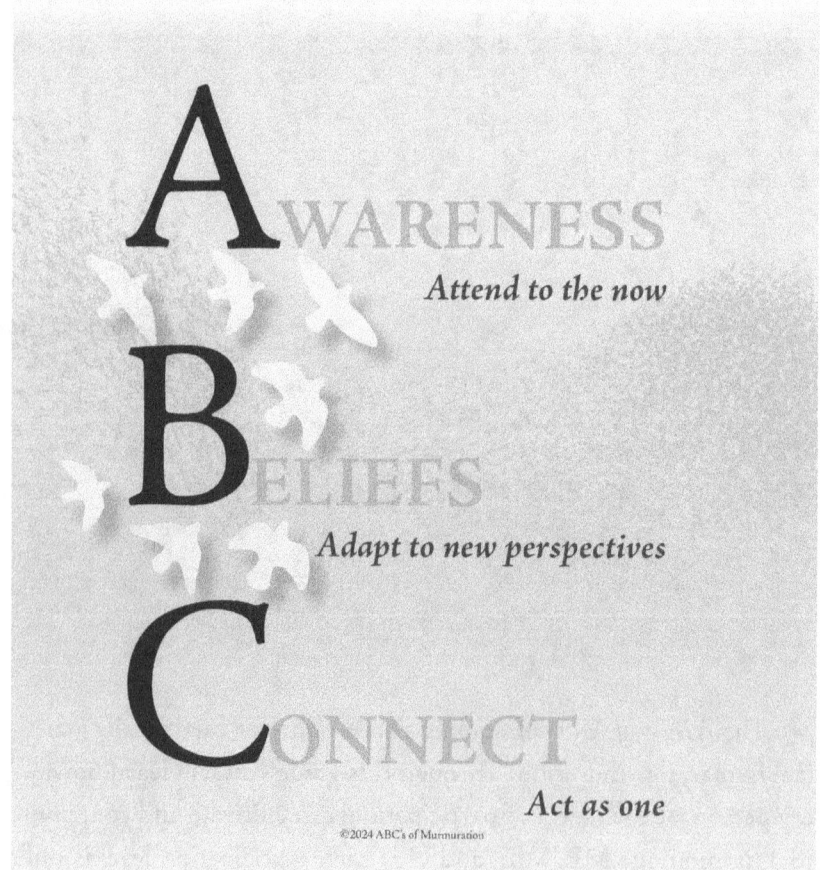

In the delicate and deliberate dance of murmuration, starlings offer a mesmerizing spectacle of Awareness, Beliefs, and Connect. You observe Awareness in the way starlings live in the now, the present moment, while listening and being acutely aware enough to mimic other living creatures and humans with pitch-perfect precision. You notice a change in perspectives or Beliefs when they receive clear messages from one of their team, which prompts immediate changes in direction. Their ability to STEP BACK and follow indicates trust in their fellow starlings. Of course, their ability to Connect is the most captivating. They seamlessly STEP UP to initiate, STEP BACK to follow, and, most amazingly, stay in their lane while flying flawlessly as they STEP TOGETHER in beautiful formations across the sky. As you observe their synchronized movements and tune into their intricate communication, you gain insight into a world where unity and collaboration reign supreme. The philosophy outlined in this book seeks to introduce this style of harmonious collaboration into your life at personal, professional, and communal levels.

Collective success hinges on each member embracing the spirit of murmuration: Awareness to the present moment, readiness to change perspectives and Beliefs while embracing new experiences—and perhaps even redrawing the canvas of their life around community. Nature, in its timeless wisdom, reveals the universe's grand design; its innate rhythms and habits. To embark on this transformative journey, you must evolve and embrace a growth mindset while mirroring the observation skills, inspiration, resilience, and adaptability of starlings. You must visualize success by painting a murmuration vividly in your mind. You must learn to mirror collective wisdom that has served starlings for centuries.

But why starlings? Nature showcases through starlings the essential role each individual bird plays to achieve murmuration. One starling starts the journey, then it builds relationships with others, and then the group of seven synchronizes. That first starling remains true to itself while merging into WE. To truly appreciate the magic of collaborative efforts, it's essential to understand how collaboration works at the level of one starling that, like you, is an individual with its own thoughts, feelings, and actions. Just like the starlings, your journey progresses from ME to WE and, subsequently, to US. Through the lessons, additional tools, and reflective exercises you'll find in the chapters to come, the individual (ME) evolves, explores relationships (ME into WE), and, ultimately, murmurates in synchronicity and, unity (the US).

WHY NATURE?

Look around. Whether it's the murmuration of birds, the meticulous logistics of a bee colony, the enduring stand of trees, or the dynamics of a community or workplace, nature outlines the blueprint for harmonious existence. Nature knows how to merge individual pursuits with collective insights. This essence of unity is something humans can learn from, mirror, and adopt. You can mindfully build spaces where shared purpose-driven Beliefs and intentional positive actions emerge without eroding the individuality of ME.

Nature adeptly steers entities—whether birds, bees, trees, or people—toward profound, purposeful bonds with others. It offers an ecological roadmap on how to gracefully navigate the journey from ME to WE to US. Murmuration attests to relationships of alignment and harmony.

The aspiration for this book is to foster a human unity, rich in harmonious habits, that uplifts and enlightens, far removed from the shadows of pain and discord in the world. In the mirror of nature's alliances, you will discover a blueprint for life—collective curious communities that resonate with purpose, wisdom, and harmony.

WHY MURMURATION?

The heart and soul of this book is the captivating dance of murmuration, a phenomenon that serves as an enlightening analogy for flourishing human connections and collaborations. Just as murmuration captures the synchronized ballet of vast starling flocks, it also paints the picture of how the individual vision by ME blends with the collective engagement of WE to culminate in a shared purpose that benefits all of US. The human equivalent of this murmuration promises a tapestry of resilience, responsiveness, optimism, open-mindedness, prosperity, and enduring unity.

As you dive into nature's mesmerizing display, this book will help you unearth insights that can illuminate the workings of thriving human communities—be it in workplaces or larger societal contexts. Watch for communities that thrive. Pay attention to the climate of their interactions, the sense of thriving, the sense of togetherness. Embark on this journey with us: feel the adrenaline, the meticulous strategies, the mutual respect, and the dedication that shapes this spectacle of advancement and growth—one starling, one individual, one team, one collective—at a time.

Delving into the mechanics of murmuration, every starling (ME) continually recalibrates its place in sync with its neighbors. Such coordination fosters a shared navigational guidance (WE), which lets the flock adeptly traverse its surroundings and counter challenges as a united entity (US). Inspired by this awe-inducing sight, you activate your Awareness with clear vision, facilitate flexibility and align your Beliefs, and harmoniously Connect with other humans to form community.

WHAT TO EXPECT FROM THIS BOOK

We have written *ABC's of Murmuration* to introduce you to the components of this philosophy and illustrate how you can use them to cultivate harmony in yourself, your teams, and your communities. The book is organized around the Three Walkways of ME, WE, and US, since murmuration begins with an individual, progresses to a small group, then expands to a larger entity. Our focus is on the inner work of ME, the relational work of WE, and the collective wisdom of US. We use these Three Walkways to illustrate the major avenues you will use to navigate nature's forests and spaces.

This chapter outlined your inspiration of murmuration and nature. The next chapter will introduce the framework of the Four-Path Journey, which takes the wisdom of nature and applies it to human interactions.

Chapters 3 through 6 focus on self-awareness of Walkway I, ME. Chapters 7 and 8 outline the components of advancing to Walkway II, WE. Finally, chapters 9 and 10 explore moving toward a unified US, Walkway III. For each of the Three Walkways, you will explore two things: why a deeper understanding of *interconnectedness* is beneficial and how you can cultivate that *interconnectedness* within yourself (ME), your groups (WE), and your world (US). The guidance offered here can be used in offices and places of faith, families and governing bodies, or anywhere humans benefit from collaborative harmony.

It's important to note that this book is intended to be read sequentially, as the chapters and Walkways build upon each other to guide you through a deeper process of transformation.

Our intention is that by Chapter 11, you'll find yourself standing in a field of wonder, witnessing the awe-inspiring dance of the starlings, letting this moment mark the beginning of your transformative journey. Just like these birds, you too are part of something larger; a beautiful pattern of collective harmony and building collective wisdom. This book is more than a guide; it's an invitation to explore the depths of ME, strengthen the bonds of WE, and embrace the vastness of US. Step into this journey of self-discovery and walking paths in unison and allow nature's wisdom to guide you toward a more connected and harmonious way of being.

Dive deep into a state of boundless compassionate curiosity and growth. Let your ever-evolving mindset guide you as you immerse yourself in the wonder of murmuration. Picture the journey as evolving, a new experience, beginning with ME, flowing into WE, and finally rushing forward into US. Life, in its essence, is a dance between solitude and togetherness. While every creature's innate drive leans towards survival and self-preservation, there's an undeniable truth: Living things thrive together. Nature beautifully showcases this dance and paints a vivid picture of what can be achieved when you transcend your individual goals and embrace the collective wisdom.

This book will also highlight various frameworks and skills that contribute to the evolution from ME to WE to US, referred to as the *ABC's of Murmuration Skills*. These approaches, including techniques like *Adaptability Quotient*®, PSYCH-K®, *The xchange Approach*, *Strategic Doing*™, and others, offer valuable insights into both personal and collective growth, much like the murmuration of starlings, which effortlessly adapt as a collective. While this book won't explore each skill or practice in great detail, it will introduce them as useful tools for navigating the challenges of collaboration, adaptability, and mutual support. For more detailed information on these skills and how to apply them, refer to the resource page at the back of the book.

Always remember, however, that ME and WE and US remain whole. It is the beauty of **quantum physics**: The quantum state allows the system to be in a few states simultaneously. ME, WE, and US remain intact, though entangled. A person (ME) enters a team (WE) and then becomes a community (US). The person, ME, remains in its own state.

IMPORTANT TIP: THE BALANCE OF INDIVIDUALITY AND UNITY

Harmonious communities arise when individuals gather around a shared mindset and vision. Imagine an environment where every member has a distinct voice and the chance to contribute meaningfully. Yet, finding **equilibrium** between the individual ME and the collective WE can be a nuanced journey. It's about ensuring each person blossoms within the group without diminishing their unique identity.

For a collective WE to truly thrive, every ME must retain their freedom to innovate, add value, evolve, and be accountable for their actions. This equilibrium means upholding one's individual essence while staying receptive and appreciative of the diverse strengths within the community. It's about coexisting with respect, openness, and a mutual recognition of your shared humanity.

With the evolution of the Three Walkways of ME, WE, and US as your map, you are positioned to affect profound and positive changes on your world. Let's embark on this journey together.

The story of The Beatles, much like a murmuration, is a testament to the power of connection and collaboration. Their journey from individual musicians to a harmonious collective serves as an inspiring reminder of what can be achieved when you come together with a shared purpose. As you continue exploring the concepts in this book, let The Beatles' early journey inspire you to find your place in the larger fields of life—where your unique contributions, when combined with those of others, create something truly extraordinary, such as the band's legacy in the field of music.

In mastering the *ABC's of Murmuration*, you'll harness the combined wisdom, creativity, and strength that connectivity offers. Remember, the odyssey toward unity and harmony begins with a single choice, and that is up to you. Embrace this journey and let murmuration light your path to a more intertwined and fulfilling existence.

How-to Skills: see pages 313–316 for more information
Leaderful Behavior
Strategic Doing™

CHAPTER 2

PREPARING FOR THE FOUR-PATH JOURNEY

*Nature often holds up a mirror
so we can see more clearly the ongoing processes
of growth, renewal, and transformation in our lives.*

—Mary Ann Brussat

THIS BOOK IS STRUCTURED AROUND THE THREE WALKWAYS OF ME, WE, AND US. This mirrors murmuration. Murmuration begins with an individual starling (ME), progresses to a small group of seven (WE), then expands to a large entity (US) of maybe up to a million! In addition, your work on the *ABC's of Murmuration* guides you down Four Paths.

On this Four-Path Journey, you will be part of conversations with **global thought leaders** who wisely unveil the potential of human murmuration as a guiding rhythm for the future. They offer you insights into the *what to, how to,* and *want to* (motivation) for creating compelling human murmuration in a complex world.

THE FOUR-PATH JOURNEY

EVOLVE *from* ME *to* WE *to* US

PATH I
Embrace
an *Evolutionary Mindset* to make a path for genuine alignment and harmony.

PATH II
Envision
Murmuration
With an inner eye, imagine murmuration as the vital light of change and love in the world.

PATH III
Explore
and Walk a New Way
Actively navigate the ABC's
AWARENESS:
Attend to the now
BELIEFS:
Adapt to new perspectives
CONNECT:
Act as one

PATH IV
Engage
in *Conscious Habits of Thriving*
STEP UP:
Initiate the first action
STEP BACK:
Allow others to STEP UP
STEP TOGETHER:
Embrace mutual trust and respect

©2024 ABC's of Murmuration

This chapter will outline the Four-Path Journey to enhance your understanding of murmuration. This is your introduction to these Four Paths, which you will travel again as you explore each of the Walkways of ME, WE and US.

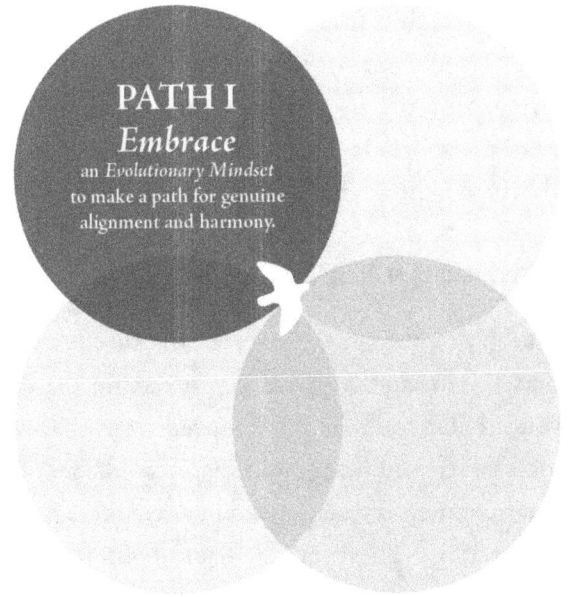

©2024 ABC's of Murmuration

PATH I

Embrace an Evolutionary Mindset

Setting forth on a new path demands that you evolve your thinking, feelings, and behaviors. While the initial challenge might seem daunting or even counterproductive, it's this very adaptability that has allowed nature to flourish against all odds. By aligning with nature's wisdom and lessons, we're inviting you (a ME) to adapt to new Beliefs that foster a mindset geared toward growth and change. An *Evolutionary*

Mindset requires that you learn how to shift *Limiting Beliefs* that are programmed in your subconscious. These automatic reactions do not have to happen. You can choose the Beliefs and behaviors that best suit your conscious intentions. You do not have to be driven by preprogrammed habits and thoughts. We will help you understand this and learn how to shift these Beliefs and live in choice. Preparing to embrace an *Evolutionary Mindset* means *Living in Choice*—being open to shifting your Beliefs and relinquishing the rigid behaviors programmed by these Beliefs. Let's start by examining some emotions, feelings, and behaviors that may hold you back from evolving.

EMOTIONAL READINESS

In the vast tapestry of human experiences, the **subconscious mind** has always acted as a guardian that seeks to protect and keep you safe. Yet the world you inhabit today is far removed from the wilderness of your ancestors. When you let age-old instincts like fear and limiting Beliefs dominate, you become ensnared in a relentless cycle of anxiety and defensive reactions. These include *fight, flight, freeze,* and *fawn*.[6]

Fight Response
Definition: The fight response is one of the first responses identified by Walter Cannon in his fight-or-flight theory. It is a physiological reaction that occurs in response to a perceived harmful event, attack, or threat to survival. It prepares your body to defend itself against the threat and mobilize energy and resources for physical confrontation.[7]

Flight Response
Definition: The flight response is the second element of the fight-or-flight mechanism. It occurs when you react to a threat by fleeing, or attempting to escape the situation, to avoid confrontation and potential harm.[8]

Freeze Response

Definition: The freeze response manifests as immobility. It is a reaction to specific stimuli commonly observed in prey animals. This reaction is seen in traumatic situations where the individual feels overwhelmed and unable to respond to the threat by either fighting or fleeing. In humans, freezing behavior might involve a physical halt or a mental "shut down" as a reaction to overwhelming stimuli.[9]

Fawn Response

Definition: The fawn response is a term introduced by Pete Walker, a psychotherapist who specializes in complex trauma. It describes a reaction where you attempt to appease or please others in order to avoid conflict, criticism, or further trauma. It involves a loss of personal boundaries and a hyper-focus on others' needs over your own.[10]

In order to embrace an *Evolutionary Mindset* and make a path for genuine alignment, each ME (you) must recognize all four of these responses and their triggers, and begin the work of choosing how you want to respond instead. Avoid being driven by the programmed reactions coming from your subconscious. They are instincts ingrained in you from times long past, which were created to cope with danger you seldom face in modern life. They linger because they are programmed in your cells. You must learn to override this programming.

Look to the starlings to find lessons in adaptability and resilience. They've built patterns and helpful habits—a *collective consciousness*—that offer them protection amidst nature's unpredictability. They are not prisoners to the reactions of fight, flight, freeze, or fawn. Instead, their dance in murmuration becomes a north star, a shining example that offers new lessons to individual starlings to move with synchronicity toward survival.

Your ultimate aspiration? To transcend and evolve from mere survival to find fulfillment, peace, and purpose. While your subconscious and its limiting Beliefs might anchor you in fear, your *consciousness* yearns to break free from these chains and chase harmony. As you venture into the subsequent chapters, you will become equipped with the wisdom of starlings, which will help you identify and overcome fear-based triggers and harmoniously align with the natural world around you. Are you ready to evolve?

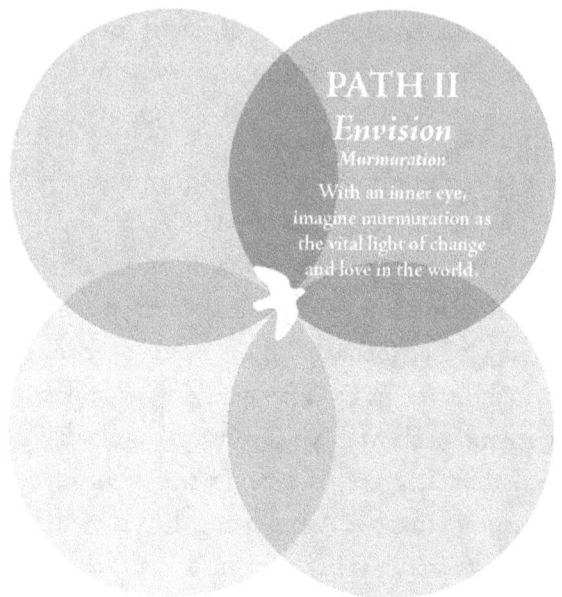

©2024 ABC's of Murmuration

PATH II

Envision Murmuration

Nature's ultimate quest is harmony and survival—shared goals for every life form nurtured by nature. With this understanding, anchor your journey to the powerful imagery of murmuration, see it in your mind's eye, hear the murmurs, attune to the communication. Remember, this phenomenon is a beacon of resilience, responsiveness, optimism, open-mindedness, prosperity, and enduring safety for starlings and humans. Your modern world is echoing a plea for such harmony.

To walk this path, embed your vision in the authentic lessons of nature. Follow the lessons of Awareness to the now, change Beliefs to shift to new perspectives, and Connect with others for harmony—all the while keeping murmuration as your north star. As you do this, embracing nature becomes imperative, for it holds sobering secrets for your communities, societies, economies, and your very essence. As William Wordsworth so aptly said, "Come forth into the light of things, let Nature be your teacher." Allow the insights, convictions, and connections intrinsic to murmuration to be the wind beneath your wings, just like the starlings.

If an immersive practice will help you imagine murmuration as the vital light of change and love in the world, you can follow the ancient Japanese tradition called **shinrin-yoku** or forest bathing. All this requires is spending time in the woods, focusing on relaxing and engaging your senses. It involves being calm and quiet in nature, observing your surroundings, and breathing deeply. It is both a mindfulness practice and an eco-antidote to your possible obsession with technology and society's ever-increasing fast pace. The importance of the natural world to humans' physical and mental health has for centuries been recognized by many cultures. It can help you on your journey with PATH II.

In coming chapters, we'll explore other ways to use your inner eye to see murmuration as a paradigm for positive change in the world.

PATH III

Explore and Walk a New Way

This path is where you begin to actively navigate the *ABC's of Murmuration*. As you learn to appreciate your mind, body, and spirit in Walkway I, you notice that the mindset of ME is responsible for each individual's ability to evolve and envision. Your body and spirit explore new behaviors that actively display the *ABC's* and *Walk a New Way*. **Let's quickly review the *ABC's*:**

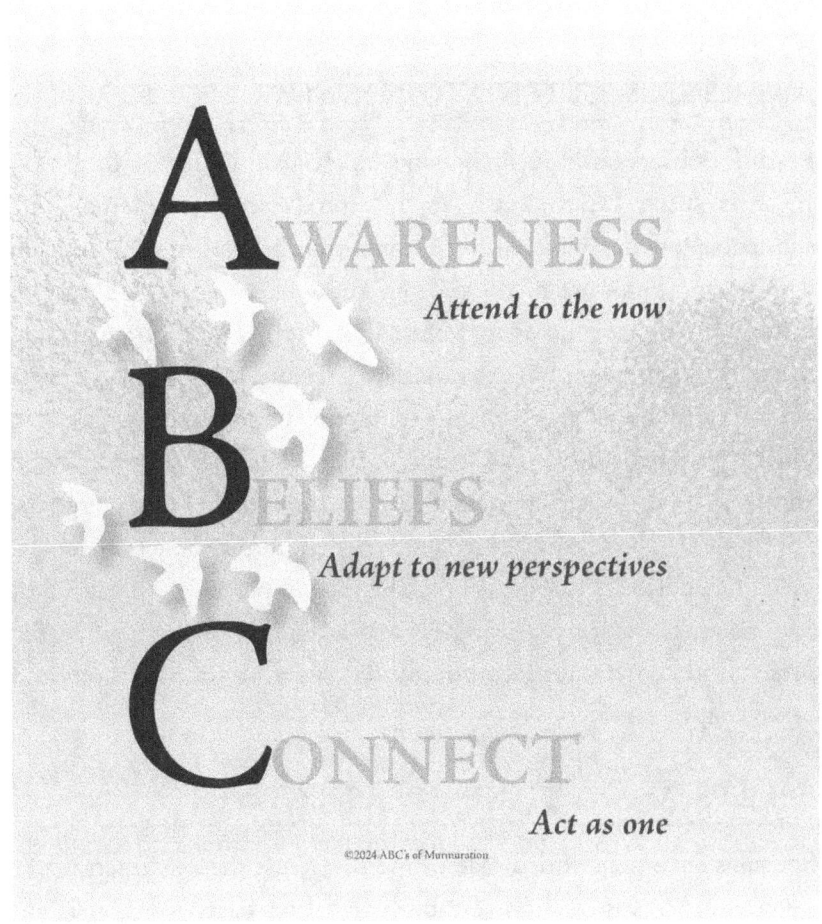

Walking a New Way on an unfamiliar path takes courage and curiosity. As always, you can glean wisdom from the ways of the starlings and let their natural behaviors be your guide. Let's examine the *ABC's* from the lessons found in starling murmuration.

One thought leader, Ross Thornley, whose work on adaptability has been foundational, provided the background needed to explain this major skill of the starlings: adaptability. According to Thornley, adaptability involves being aware of changes, re-evaluating decisions, exploring new ways to approach challenges, and ensuring alignment within a group. These are all essential aspects of adaptability, which are as crucial to human success as they are to the starlings' synchronized movements.[11]

AWARENESS: ATTEND TO THE NOW

Starlings observe and identify dangers, food, and sleeping locations. In their space, external dangers like predators can emerge quite suddenly. Put yourself in the position of the observer starling and you will see and be aware of the danger. You will develop the ability to instantly recognize and adapt your thinking and behaviors; to attend to the now. You might have to unlearn a previous lesson. This signifies your need to use all your senses and develop a more keen Awareness. Once a potential threat is identified, like a hawk to a starling, you and your team must respect and react to the signal. Team members, not immediately aware of the danger, depend on the reactions of the individual who sees it. Mistakes can happen. A perceived threat might be a misinterpretation. Awareness and attending to the now, to the present moment, requires continuously evaluating your decisions and being adaptable.

BELIEFS: ADAPT TO NEW PERSPECTIVES

Starlings have generational habits and they trust their instincts. Over generations, starlings have established habits based on consistent factors in the environment. These habits build trust and consistency within the murmuration. But the world is constantly changing and, like all living beings, these birds must adapt. Major shifts in the environment (e.g., a hurricane destroying a roosting place) challenge established habits or instincts. When environmental changes arise, small groups within the murmuration might explore new areas for gathering food or rest in the evening. Such exploration requires curiosity into the potential of new opportunities and environments. True adaptability means recognizing and responding with resilience to these shifts, for the birds and also for you.

Changing Beliefs and adapting to new perspectives also happens for starlings as they join to form groups of seven. They choose to see things differently as they bond with another ME and form a WE. Along with environmental shifts, the newly formed WE—the relationship, the result of the bonding—encourages each starling to adapt to new perspectives. For you, the drive to belong, to become a WE, also encourages you to adapt to new perspectives. It will help you assess your habits and thinking, then shift your Beliefs as you walk PATH III.

CONNECT: ACT AS ONE

When an unexpected event stuns a starling (like a bright light), it could disrupt the entire murmuration. However, the starlings are prepared to adapt and demonstrate a collective and cohesive response to disruption. It shows you how the birds are linked and in sync, yet one bird can impact the whole.

Like starlings, you have the capability to respond creatively instead of reacting instinctively. Global thought leader Jon Berghoff's *xchange Approach* introduces a key skill called *Pause, Notice, and Choose* to help you navigate disruptions. Even though you are wired to react instantly, there are many moments when pausing, noticing, and deliberately choosing your response is most beneficial.[12] This approach shifts you from *reaction* to *creation*. Think about how the words reaction and creation use the same letters—moving the "C" to the front symbolizes consciously choosing your response in any given situation.

Acting as one isn't just about responding to change or events as a harmonious unit, it's also about acknowledging the strengths and challenges of the individuals who make up the group. Just as bees and ants have different roles within their colonies, starlings also have diverse roles within their murmuration. It's essential to support those who might need more assistance, whether they're new, tired, or overwhelmed. And just as essential is to allow strong individuals to leverage their strengths and shine on behalf of the collective. The murmuration is the US, the cumulative effect that is observable when the starlings act as one. As Helen Keller wisely said, "Alone we can do so little; together we can do so much."

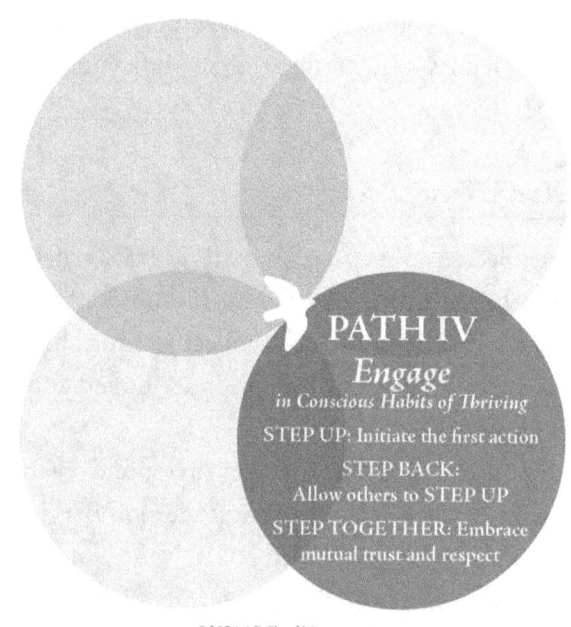

©2024 ABC's of Murmuration

PATH IV

Engage in Conscious Habits of Thriving

As you walk down the paths, it's imperative to understand the rules. To cultivate habits that will help you thrive as a ME, enable you to support a WE, and position you to collaborate with an US, you need to have a clear picture of how all the elements of a successful murmuration interact. PATH IV is about conscious habits that support all Three Walkways—ME, WE, and US. These behaviors allow the murmuration's crescendo to reach its peak as thousands unite and create a vast synchronized canvas in the sky that flows seamlessly from ME to WE to US.

These conscious habits or behaviors mirror the methods starlings use to make decisions in flight. Equipped with panoramic vision that provides an almost 360° view of their area, they can see and respond to virtually everything around them, including their fellow murmurators. *Their flight is a dance based on three habitual transformative behaviors, each aligned with human values:*

STEP UP: Initiate the first action
Guided by intuition and alertness, the forerunner starling surges vertically, usually toward the middle, upon sensing danger.

STEP BACK: Allow others to STEP UP
A key lesson to learn in forming trusting teams, the forerunner gracefully descends and follows, and allows another bird to STEP UP into a *leaderful* approach.

STEP TOGETHER: Embrace mutual trust and respect
Each starling is adept at sensing peril, yielding the navigation initiative when appropriate, and fostering a profound connection with the group, harmonizing collectively. They each stay in their own lane. They STEP TOGETHER with trust and respect.

STEP UP
Initiate the first action

STEP BACK
Allow others to STEP UP

STEP TOGETHER
Embrace mutual trust and respect

©2024 ABC's of Murmuration

Starlings aren't partaking in an aimless dance. They rally for protection, sustenance, and warmth; a shared strategy that ensures the collective can survive and thrive. In the same way you, too, must cultivate conscious habits that are rooted in purpose, whether it's for personal growth, to strengthen team dynamics, or to contribute to a thriving community. By aligning your actions with your intention, you create a ripple effect that not only benefits yourself but also supports the collective. PATH IV reminds you that thriving isn't accidental; it's the result of mindful choices, cooperation, and the consistent practice of behaviors that nurture both individual and communal well-being.

WHERE TO BEGIN?

As you consider each of the Four Paths—EMBRACE, ENVISION, EXPLORE, ENGAGE—a thought emerges: if surviving and thriving are the shared pursuits of every being, then isn't journeying together, in harmony, the wiser choice? Indeed, it is. Yet, the road to genuine human connection has often been paved with tales of trepidation and tribulations. Many times, connections seem difficult. It might feel easier to walk the paths alone. True connection serves as a linchpin for enduring prosperity, stability, and growth, but can be challenging to cultivate. So it is important to remember that building this intricate web of relationships—even within yourself as mind, body, and spirit—is a marathon, not a sprint. You can learn to journey with others, but you cannot do so on an accelerated timeline.

As you contemplate the journey from ME to WE to US, you are reminded that true harmony and collective success can only emerge through conscious collaboration over time. They are the result of your persistence, preparation, adaptability, and the passion to evolve. Just as nature finds its rhythm through time and practice, so too must you find your way through the Four-Path Journey. This journey is about more than just individual growth; it's about aligning your personal goals with the larger vision of collective success, the human murmuration.

Nature did not find its rhythm overnight. As you find your way from the singular brilliance of ME to the supportive strength of WE, and finally to the collective spirit of US, your spotlight will first shine on the foundational work: the internal work necessary for ME. You will find the first of those lessons in Walkway I, ME, Chapters 3 through 6.

Lao Tzu once said, "If you are depressed, you are living in the past. If you are anxious, you are living in the future. If you are at peace, you are living in the present."[13] Might the starlings be signaling a shift, heralding a move toward peace and harmony?

As you venture into this transformative journey, center yourself with the three guiding questions listed below, which are based on the *ABC's of Murmuration*. ***Allow these questions to illuminate the path ahead and assist you in pivoting toward these possible actions:***

AWARENESS: What knowledge, skills, or motivations might need to be shifted to help me gain a deeper understanding of being present?

BELIEFS: What limiting Beliefs, present in my life right now, should I set aside to be able to shift my current perspectives and EMBRACE, ENVISION, EXPLORE, AND ENGAGE?

CONNECT: What expansive Beliefs and behaviors would support me in becoming part of a WE relationship as well as expanding successfully into the collective US?

Remember, every journey starts with a single step. Let's ensure yours is grounded in introspection, purpose, and clarity.

YOUR TURN: MOMENT OF REFLECTION

Recall the last instance when you felt a strong emotional reaction or were "triggered" while interacting with someone. When might you have felt the urge to fight, flee, freeze, or fawn? What was your immediate reactive behavior? Using this fundamental framework, unpack this experience:

1. **WHAT**: Can you identify the specific trigger? What did it feel like? What did it look like to others?

2. **WHEN & WHERE**: When and where did this happen?

3. **WHY**: What might be the underlying reason or programmed memory that caused your behavioral or verbal reaction?

4. **HOW**: Describe your behavior or reaction.

5. **WHO**: Were there any witnesses to this interaction? Did they offer feedback or comments?

6. **WHAT DO I WANT INSTEAD?** Now, take a moment to consider: Is this reaction a recurring pattern for you? Have you responded this way before? Name the habit or belief that could be the cause of this reaction. What response or choice could you have "created" instead?

Understanding these moments, examining them through a structured lens, and recognizing patterns can be the first step toward being Aware of what is happening to you right now, in this moment, so you can shift your Beliefs and Connect with others in a meaningful way.

Chapter 2: Preparing for The Four-Path Journey

How-to Skills: see pages 313–316 for more information

The xchange Approach

Pause, Notice, and Choose

Global Thought Leaders: see pages 317–320 for more information

Ross Thornley

Jon Berghoff

WALKWAY I: ME

An Invitation to Step Up

CHAPTERS 3 - 6

CHAPTER 3

WHY ME?

You wander from room to room hunting for the diamond necklace that is already around your neck.

—Rumi

WHAT KNOWLEDGE DO YOU NEED ABOUT YOURSELF TO BE ABLE TO FLOW FROM ME TO WE TO US AND MURMURATE LIKE STARLINGS? This journey inward to understand the self is the most profound of all. You most often search externally for what might already be nestled deep within. You are reminded of the truth in Rumi's words, which suggest that perhaps the essence of ME you are trying to comprehend has always been present. Perhaps what you have been looking for externally is hidden within your subconscious Beliefs, thoughts, and feelings.

What are the biggest and boldest steps you can take, as an individual ME, to grasp the subconscious and conscious intricacies of your Beliefs, thoughts, feelings, emotions, and behaviors? Is there a pivotal layer of self-awareness, an elemental essence of ME, waiting to be unveiled? What intention can that essence of ME set while reading this chapter? What information will help ME know what I really want? What knowledge do I need to discover or realize the essence of ME?

Throughout this chapter, you will discuss the importance of ME in the larger system of the murmuration. We start here because each ME must understand and accept itself before it can progress to participating in WE. ME is the elemental entity of murmuration. Like an individual starling, its distinct and separate existence can join with other things, but full participation is mandatory to create community. To move from ME to WE to US, the ME must be consciously Aware and present, able to shift limiting Beliefs, and motivated to Connect.

First, let's explore how ME begins the journey down PATH I. Embracing an *Evolutionary Mindset* to make a path for genuine alignment and harmony.

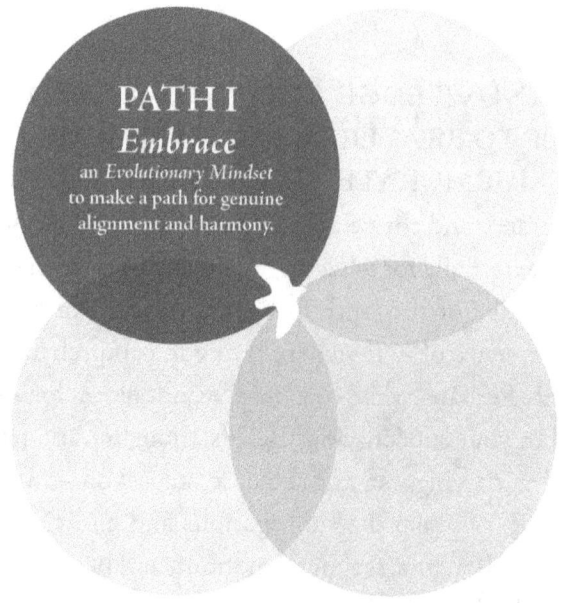

©2024 ABC's of Murmuration

PATH I

Embrace an Evolutionary Mindset

To embrace an *Evolutionary Mindset*, ME must become self-aware. Visualize the subconscious mind as a vast storehouse of the history of ME. It holds ingrained Beliefs, reoccurring thoughts, feelings, and emotions about ME and the world. This storehouse of history is analogous to a database of information on a computer. These are programmed into the ME computer, the mind, even before birth. In the formative years, ME stores this information and uses those programs throughout life.

According to expert Dr. Bruce H. Lipton, 70 percent of these thoughts are negative and redundant, and are created from limiting Beliefs. The other 30 percent are initiated from supportive Beliefs that can deliver abundance.[14] They behave seamlessly and automatically, the software embedded in the mind. These programs have become habits and are positioned to react when triggered.

Now, let's look at becoming self-aware and breaking free of these stored limiting subconscious habits that limit ME from making conscious choices. Shinzen Young, author and mindfulness teacher, explains subconscious habit repositories as those that can be tapped through increased *Awareness across three distinct domains:*[15]

WHAT I SEE AND HEAR: A sense of what you see and hear from the multitude of sounds around you and the embedded images in your mind

WHAT I TOUCH: The physical sensations you experience and your internal interpretation of the sensation

WHAT I FEEL: Susceptibility to impressions, emotional states, and the resultant responses or reactions

Embracing these *Awareness opportunities*, you open the door to a deeper understanding of the self, which allows ME to make choices instead of just reacting. Cultivating self-awareness invites ME to embrace an *Evolutionary Mindset* that harmonizes with what is really wanted, the choices of an authentic ME. Let's dig deeper into Young's system of self-understanding.

WHAT I SEE AND HEAR

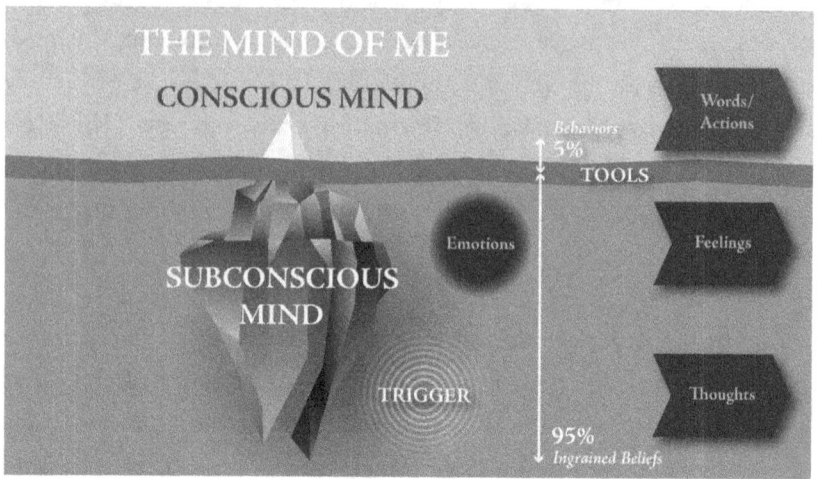

©2024 ABC's of Murmuration

THE MIND OF ME: ICEBERG MODEL
This graphic illustrates the conscious mind (5 percent) as the tip of an iceberg above water, while the subconscious mind (95 percent) lies beneath, driving thoughts, feelings, and emotions that influence behaviors (words and actions).

To understand the subconscious habits of ME and begin making more conscious and intentional choices, it helps to understand where the things ME sees and hears are housed, or where they live in the mind and body. So imagine a vast and majestic iceberg being a mirror to the different parts of your mind. Here are the sections of the picture:

CONSCIOUS: THE PEAK ABOVE

The tip of the iceberg, known scientifically as the *hummock*, symbolizes the *conscious mind*. Research reveals that this active, alert segment of your mind accounts for just 5 percent of your thinking capacity.[16] It captures the present moment, the now. Current actions, words, and observable behaviors of ME live in the now. It's the part of the mind that determines, "What do I really want?" The conscious mind has its limitations, however. It is in charge of short-term memory. It handles merely one to three events simultaneously, and processes just 40 bits of information every second.

SUBCONSCIOUS: THE EXPANSE BENEATH

Venturing below the water's surface, you find the iceberg's vast and submerged part, the *bummock*, which is the vast subconscious. While the conscious mind is a mere 5 percent of your mental capacity, your subconscious is in control with 95 percent!

The subconscious plays three pivotal roles:

STEWARD OF VITAL FUNCTIONS: Oversees indispensable bodily functions such as heartbeat, respiration, digestion, and walking.

SECURER OF MEMORIES: Analogous to a computer's hard drive, it safely stores your software of past Beliefs, thoughts, emotions, and experiences. Memories that signal abundance and those that signal limitations and fear are stored here.

STORER OF REACTIONS: Acting as the system software, it guides your reactions based on stored experiences; its chief objective chief objective is to ensure your safety and survival. It is the most ancient of systems and it is meant to protect ME. It is critical as a system to the starlings and to ME! Its processing power is unparalleled. It juggles thousands of tasks simultaneously, and processes an astounding 40 million bits of information each second.[17]

Recognizing these aspects of your mind, the iceberg model emerges as one of the most valuable visuals because it allows ME to continuously envision the complex inner world with clarity and intention.

Turn your attention to the interplay between your conscious mind (with its 5 percent of decision-making capability) and the subconscious forces (with its 95 percent of capability).

Have you ever deliberately set a goal, like losing 10 pounds, only to find a voice within yourself cautioning, doubting, or even obstructing your path to success? It's a dance between your conscious mind's vision and wishes and the often-resistant tug of your subconscious. Your internal monologue may say things like, "You know you have tried this before and it didn't work. You gained 10 pounds instead!"

These voices, triggers, or tugs from your subconscious engage within you in two major ways. First, they come as a sensation. These sensations come from your Aristotelian senses of sight, touch, sound, color, and taste. Remember, you heard the voice inside, the Securer of Memories, that told you you had tried before! The other set of triggers come in the form of feelings. Perhaps from the Storer of Reactions, which has an emotional characteristic and immediately solicits a knee-jerk reaction of fight, flight, freeze, or fawn. Imagine trying to move forward while 95 percent of your internal force is demanding you move backward, through voices in your head and knee-jerk reactions. It's no wonder such endeavors can feel so draining and exhausting.

WHAT I TOUCH AND FEEL

Deep within the corridors of your subconscious, your sensations and feelings stand firm like ancient trees, that cast shadows over the ground of what ME is thinking. It's an ever-active forest in there, what some liken to the "monkey mind;" thoughts forever hopping from branch to branch. When a sensory trigger—be it a familiar scent, a haunting tune, or even a fleeting touch—brushes against the mindscape of ME, your subconscious swiftly reaches into its vast repository. It picks out Beliefs that resonate with that stimulus and weaves them into your thoughts and, possibly, becomes a trigger that activates your behavior, the behavior of ME.

Imagine this: A past experience, the last Thanksgiving dinner your mother prepared, has sown the seed (through smells) of a particular experience and habitual belief. When faced with a similar situation, this belief fuels your thoughts and kindles the emotion of fear and grief (linked to your mother's death). Your subconscious perceives her death as a reminder of your own mortality. This reaction stems from your fundamental nature, which is wired for survival. Thanksgiving and its smells have been coded in your software as habitually sad and fearful for you.

Emotions, the heart of your feelings, transform this basic fear into a dynamic force. This "e-motion," or energy in motion, then intensifies the fear, which drives it to the forefront of your mind. This energy then manifests in the present moment through your behaviors, words, or actions. Thanksgiving then becomes a trigger for emotional stress. Your heart hurts. You have been triggered by your senses and the Securer of Memories, and that has been magnified by your subconscious feelings of fear and loss. This subconscious activity makes Thanksgiving dinner very uncomfortable.

Think of words you might speak at the dinner table as the notes of the melodies that give voice to your deep-seated feelings. Perhaps you would say, "This is a very sad occasion for me." These words become the music that sets the climate of the dinner for you and others. The actions or reactions that follow choreograph the collective dance. It may not be harmonious like the murmuration of starlings.

When orchestrated by fear and/or grief, your reactions tend to follow the familiar patterns of fight, flight, freeze, or fawn. Though these responses happen in a blink, they're tailored to the individual and the perceived danger. Emotional intelligence experts call this event an *amygdala hijack*. Your *amygdala*, an integral part of your brain, is stirred by unsettling emotions. Like a conductor taking center stage, it commands your attention by orchestrating a symphony of feelings and emotions that crescendo into observable reactions from you. Hence, you tend to avoid Thanksgiving celebrations; your words and actions create the dance that brings your e-motions to the table; you may flee the scene, leaving the turkey dinner and the relatives behind.

NAVIGATING FEAR: THROUGH THE SENSES
By Kathy Hagler

Let me take you back to a moment from my past, a harrowing encounter that taught me about the profound impact of fear on my ability to think clearly and consciously. It's important to remember that your subconscious mind automatically drives an astounding 95 percent of your thinking, feelings, and actions.

Several years ago while residing in Los Angeles, I unexpectedly came face-to-face with three burglars in my home. The sheer terror of that encounter prompted a visceral need to escape. So the very next day, I found myself on a plane to Houston, where I hoped to find solace with my dear friend, Liz. I believed a change of scenery and the presence of my friend would bring the comfort I so desperately needed.

When I reached Houston I checked into my hotel. Eager to wash away the stress, I ran a warm bath. As I began to let go of the tension, a sound yanked me back: the unmistakable noise of a key turning in a lock.

"It must be Liz," I thought, relief flooding over me. "Hi, Liz!" I called out, but my greeting was met with unnerving silence.

Curiosity nudged me out of the bath, and I cautiously approached the room, only to find myself face-to-face with an unfamiliar man, his intent made clear by the gun he pointed at me. I noticed my heart raced and my body immediately froze. (This was an automatic behavioral reaction to this experience.) As the seconds passed, a familiar voice cut through the thick air of tension. Liz was outside, knocking persistently.

"I know you're in there! Undo the deadbolt. Stop with the games and let me in."

I desperately wanted to to cry out for help, cry out for help, but my voice was held captive by fear. Sensing my heightened anxiety, the intruder made a snap, subconscious decision. He shoved me against the wall to clear his way out. He bolted past a bewildered Liz and disappeared. His fear of being caught overcame his plan to attack.

Notice that when the man held the gun to my head, my body froze. It was a behavioral reaction to the experience. Also notice that when Liz knocked at the door, his subconscious told him to throw me across the room and run out. His fear of being caught overcame his plan of attack. These raw moments shed light on the power of the subconscious. When fueled by deep emotions like fear, instinct overrules conscious decisions. This experience allowed me to better navigate my emotions and work toward deeper self-awareness.

FEAR'S SPECTRUM: FROM PARALYSIS TO TRANSFORMATION

Since PATH I is all about embracing an *Evolutionary Mindset* to move ME toward alignment and harmony, addressing fear is crucial. This one emotion can prevent ME from learning to make conscious and intentional choices.

Fear, while universally experienced, differs vastly in its intensity and impact. At one end of the spectrum, you have the immobilizing terror I felt in that hotel room. At the other, subtler fears manifest, such as the hesitation in expressing an unpopular opinion for fear of backlash. Over time, your subconscious, with its habitual responses to information, automates your reactions to these fears. You react.

Regardless of its severity, fear acts as a curtain by shrouding your present experience and pulling you into your subconscious habits, which detaches you from the reality of the moment. It can prevent you from being in the NOW and truly enjoying experiences. It can block you from progressing down PATH I toward personal evolution.

Amidst an onslaught of fight, flight, freeze, or fawn reactions, you often find yourself ensnared in the clutches of amygdala hijacks. It's easy to assume that you become a mere puppet to such overpowering emotional responses. Yet, it is entirely within your grasp to regulate these reactions and choose different responses. Daniel Goleman, in his work on emotional intelligence, emphasizes the importance of mastering your impulses as a key life skill.[18] Using these insights, I've confronted my hotel room anxieties head-on by always remembering to secure the deadbolt, and embrace caution without cowering from fear. A situation that could have kept me perpetually at home actually became a gift. I am careful where I drive and park, I lock my house, and when I get on an elevator I pay attention at all times. The gifts from difficult experiences are meant to teach you lessons rather than curtail your growth and joyful experiences. Pay attention and learn.

The goal isn't to eradicate subconscious fears, but rather to let them serve as your internal alarm systems. Instead, you must focus on comprehending and effectively managing them. Doing so paves the way to profound self-awareness and equilibrium. This newfound knowledge becomes a lever that aids in personal growth and promotes positive change.

Your subconscious, which brims with Beliefs, thoughts, and feelings, serves as a compass that steers the direction of your life. Exploring the influential role of your subconscious is just the beginning. As you progress, you uncover the complex interplay between subconscious Awareness and conscious attention. This intricate relationship forms the core of your next exploration.

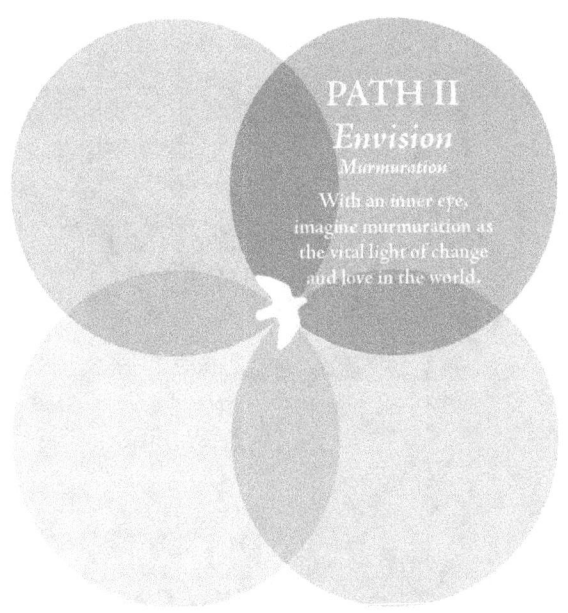

©2024 ABC's of Murmuration

PATH II
Envision Murmuration

PATH II invites you, each individual ME, to embrace murmuration as the internal dance of mind, body, and spirit. ME is also invited to envision murmuration as the external mindset or vision of Connection with others. It is imperative to attain internal harmony within the mind, body, and spirit, and also achieve external harmony in order to murmurate. Let's dive into what that means for ME.

Each ME gets triggered. These triggers often disrupt internal harmony, which pulls attention away. Triggers come from your ingrained habits. Let's look at the relationship between your triggers and habits. How are triggers and conscious attention intimately linked? A subtle shift in energy, like an 'aha moment,' a sudden realization or comprehension, bridges the gap between Awareness of a trigger in your subconscious and your conscious attention. As the esteemed psychologist William James described, this initial spotlight of attention to your conscious mind is like the *Footlights of Consciousness*.

Footlights of Consciousness

Footlights of Consciousness flashed in Max's subconscious

Max's subconscious thoughts

Max's Awareness of Belief takes hold and he decides to shift mindset

©2024 ABC's of Murmuration

FOOTLIGHTS OF CONSCIOUSNESS

This graphic illustrates Max's Footlights of Consciousness journey. He becomes Aware of his subconscious trigger and consciously attends to it. He Connects with Sam by expressing appreciation for the gift of tickets.

Imagine a theater stage. Dancers linger in the shadows, anticipating their performance. Suddenly, the footlights illuminate one dancer, who captivates your gaze. A cascade of **subconscious thoughts** and emotions, seemingly independent of your will, swiftly pull you into a not-so-positive reaction, similar to Max in the graphic. Seated amidst the audience, your mind moves from submerged emotions and thoughts to an overt behavior.

However, unlike Max, you lean over to your companion and remark with emotion, "I can't believe I'm seeing this type of show again. I despise such shows; I've never enjoyed them."

Your behavior, as spoken words, manifests your current conscious state. It sets the climate for the evening: chilly!

This showcases the domino effect between a triggered thought from your past—your feelings located in the subconscious, your Storer of Memories—and your discernible behavior in the present. It's a visceral "been there, done that" reflex response that is anchored in a previous, perhaps less favorable, experience. It is a replay of a memory, spurred by your past subconscious Awareness of a similar unpleasant situation.

As your ingrained patterns activate and amplify over time, they become your habits. They persistently tread the same course and intensify unless you purposefully choose to *Walk a New Way*.

Habits create your thoughts, which evolve into your feelings. They then are transformed into e-motions or energy in motion. You have a habit that gets triggered, a thought occurs, a feeling follows, and words or actions come next. These emotions are your *Footlights of Consciousness*, and materialize into words or actions. At this point, you basically stand at the crossroads, choosing either to let your subconscious habits drive your words and actions or to seize control of your emotions, with your attention, and divert your course. You must disrupt the habit loop. To envision both the harmony of internal murmuration and the potential harmony of murmurating with others, you must break the habit loop of allowing limiting Beliefs to drive your words and reactions.

Your focused attention acts as a beacon or a spotlight, the *Footlights of Consciousness*, that begins to illuminate your subconscious mind's habits. Within moments, the relationship between Awareness and attention culminates in words or actions that may or may not be your intended and conscious choice. It is literally up to you.

Why is it most often a subconscious decision? The mechanism of attention operates on dual controls. It reacts spontaneously, swayed by past inner Beliefs and triggers, or **external stimuli (exogenous control)**. You possess the power to direct your attention purposefully **(endogenous control)**. Your power of choice enables ME to navigate by *Walking a New Way*. Only you can choose to control your behaviors.

©2024 ABC's of Murmuration

PATH III

Explore and Walk a New Way

As ME begins down PATH III, your focus shifts to action. This path is about active exploration and learning to *Walk a New Way* by living out the *ABC's of Murmuration* every day. Let's look at why this is important to your growth, one letter at a time.

AWARENESS
Attend to the now

BELIEFS
Adapt to new perspectives

CONNECT
Act as one

©2024 ABC's of Murmuration

AWARENESS: ATTEND TO THE NOW

Each starling must attend to the now. Each starling must be completely present and conscious to be a harmonious participant in murmuration. Likewise, Awareness is a secret weapon of ME. Awareness is the instrument of consciousness that pierces through the mind's subconscious secrets. The only reality you have is each instance in time, each single occurrence of something in that moment of time.

Attention to Awareness orchestrates the seamless interplay of your mind, body, and spirit, and grants your conscious self the freedom to direct your actions and make a conscious choice. This metamorphosis transforms not only your personal journey, but also the story you portray to those around you. It changes the collective dance.

Thought leader Ross Thornley uses the *Jam Jar* metaphor to explain how you can become trapped by your subconscious Beliefs, thoughts, feelings, and emotions of the past. Imagine living inside a jam jar, where everything that shapes your behavior is displayed on a large, clear label on the outside.[19] Others can easily read this label—perhaps it says "Strong Grape Jam, Spoiled"—but from inside the jar, you're completely unaware of how you're being perceived. This metaphor illustrates how unconscious patterns can define you to others, even when you're not aware of them. Remember that every time you use a past program in your subconscious, you are robbed of your precious time in the present moment. Many thoughts based on the past stem from fear and drain you of your energy. Awareness requires that you pay attention to the now.

BELIEFS: ADAPT TO NEW PERSPECTIVES

Each starling in a murmuration must remain open to input from those around it and be able to make immediate shifts in order to remain in harmonious formation. For ME, it is the realization that you have the knowledge and skills to shift your perspectives, disrupt the habit loop, and make a conscious choice to *Walk a New Way*.

By acknowledging and honing this amazing skill, you will find secrets that shed light on hidden Beliefs, feelings, emotions, and behaviors of ME. As these Beliefs and feelings become more apparent, it is essential to ask yourself: What commitment will I, or ME, make to observe and name Beliefs, thoughts, feelings, and behaviors as they are happening? How will I shine a light on them and bring them out in the open, and expose them for what they are: my past! Is there an elemental essence of ME waiting to be discovered? What is hiding in my subconscious mind? What do I want? How can I free myself from unwanted thoughts and emotions? Will the real ME please stand up and be counted?

Understanding yourself isn't about changing who you are. It's about finding out who is the authentic and genuine ME. Asking questions will uncover this authentic ME—under all the pain and limiting Beliefs—and the answers unearthed will begin to pave the way forward and illuminate the life the real ME wants to live.

To begin cultivating Awareness in ME, ask:

1. **WHAT** brings forth my strongest emotions, both limiting and expansive emotions?
2. **WHAT** are those emotions? What past Beliefs and habits call them forward?
3. **WHEN AND WHERE** did I pick up these Beliefs and emotional habits that now influence my reactions, regardless of my choice? Which ones prevent me from making my own choices?
4. **WHY** do certain thoughts and feelings prevail in my mind and end up guiding my actions?
5. **HOW** can I gain control and consciously navigate away from reactive, limiting emotions that result in misplaced behaviors?
6. **WHO** am I, both in the silent dialogue with my inner self and in the stories others tell of me?
7. **WHO** am I to others? How do I appear to them?

By confronting these questions, you begin to understand the intricate makeup of the inner ME. ME must find the will to persist in addressing limiting Beliefs even when conflict or difficulties are encountered. First, a commitment must be made to *Walk a New Way*. Next, the passion of an envisioned murmuration followed by persistence and the ability to pursue your new plan are the critical elements of your success.

CONNECT: ACT AS ONE

Integrate mind, body, and spirit to mobilize conscious actions and embrace a renewed path of acting as one. If you can begin to envision your inner self, mind, body, and spirit acting as one murmuration striving for harmony, you can truly understand the importance of Connecting externally with others. In the words of G.I. Gurdjieff, "If you help others, you will be helped, perhaps tomorrow, perhaps in one thousand years, but you will be helped. Nature must pay off the debt. It is a mathematical law and all life is mathematics."[20]

ME must learn to break the poverty consciousness that comes from limiting Beliefs and leave behind this programming to see the world as a place of abundance. First, however, you must learn to love ME and appreciate the abundance in ME. From this mindset of Connecting mind, body, and spirit in harmony, all else flows. The more you Connect with the inner ME, the more you Connect with others and act as one, in harmony.

Learning to forgive yourself and others is important as you move toward acting as one, both internally and externally. When you choose to not hold onto limiting Beliefs and instead rise above them, there is a consciousness shift; a decision to let go of your programmed habits of the past. The path to inner and external *oneness* is always your choice.

When presented with a situation, remember the skill that was discussed earlier: *Pause, Notice, and Choose*. Take a moment to pause and breathe deeply, and notice how this situation and information resonates within you. If fear is present, then know that subconscious habits are in play. Ask, "What do I want instead?" Courage is the trait that is needed for the mind, body, and spirit to move forward as one. Forgiveness of yourself and others is nothing more than choosing to let go.

You learn to behave like the starlings. You move from a harmonious ME to WE with a few others, and then this small group moves into the US; the murmuration that provides harmony for safety and security.

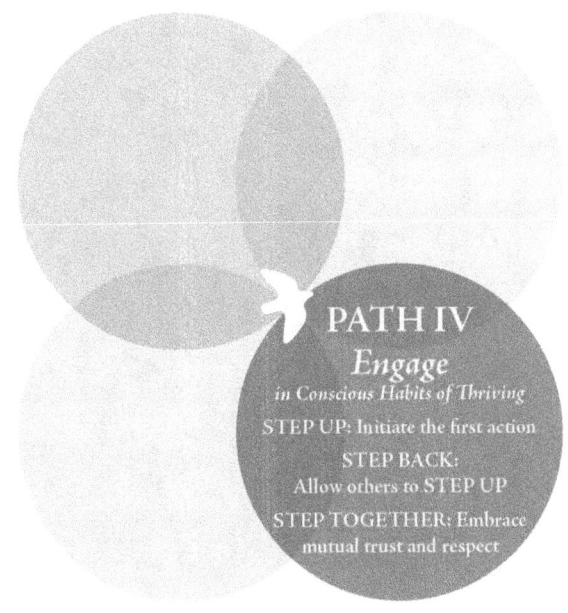

©2024 ABC's of Murmuration

PATH IV

Engage in Conscious Habits of Thriving

The last path, PATH IV, is focused on interpersonal collaboration and interaction. For you (a ME), this means using the self-knowledge

Chapter 3: Why Me?

gained on the previous three paths to become a harmonious contributor and ally. It means learning the dances of STEP UP, STEP BACK, and STEP TOGETHER to mirror murmuration in your life.

PATH IV invites you to engage in *Conscious Habits of Thriving* by adopting the habits of the starlings. To understand how this unfolds, let's examine each action.

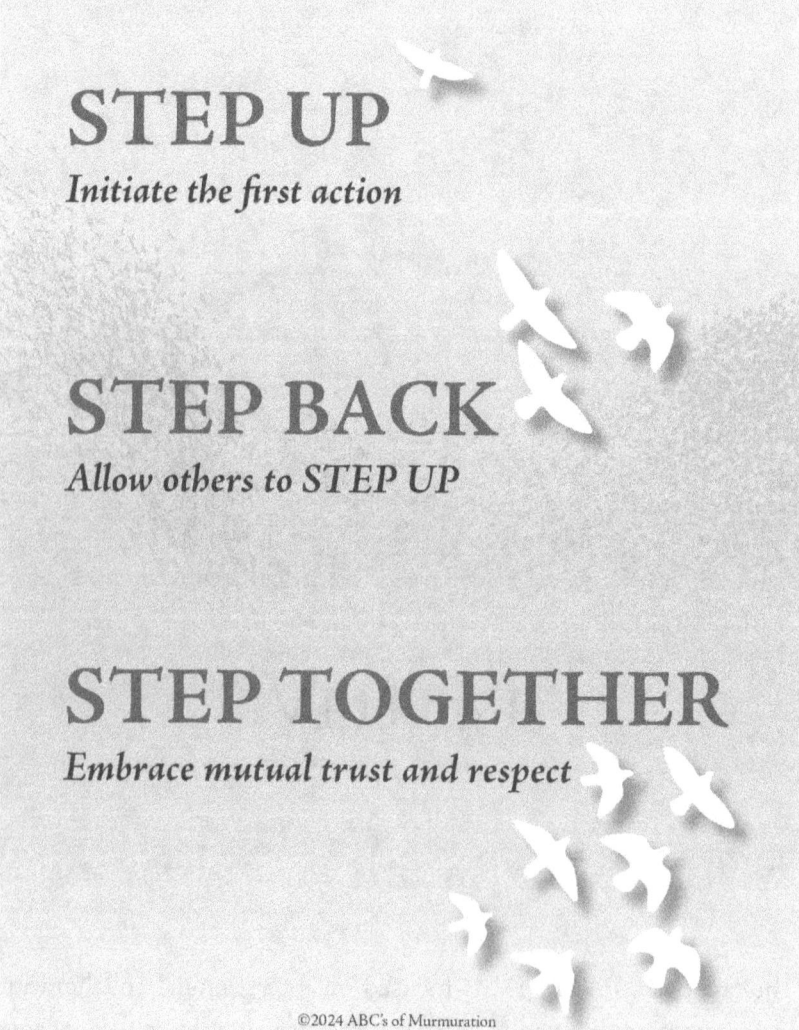

STEP UP
Initiate the first action

STEP BACK
Allow others to STEP UP

STEP TOGETHER
Embrace mutual trust and respect

©2024 ABC's of Murmuration

STEP UP: INITIATE THE FIRST ACTION

Every murmuration begins with a single starling taking action. A single ME making conscious decisions. For each ME, STEPPING UP encompasses wielding the power of choice, which affects both your internal equilibrium (mind, body, and spirit) and you external rapport (interaction and perception of others and their state of mind). It also means recognizing that the ingrained subconscious constraints of your mind can be intercepted. You can remold your knee-jerk reactions by pausing, noticing, and choosing your path.

STEPPING UP requires paying close attention to the following:

- Awareness of the subconscious Beliefs and deeply seated habits dwelling within you
- Attendance to illuminating these patterns
- Acknowledgment that they can be disrupted by your conscious intent and choice

Through this book, the aim is to arm you with skills and practices to intentionally disrupt your ingrained, **limiting subconscious Beliefs** and break the chains of toxic habits that hinder your growth and harmony. You will be introduced to the formidable power of personal choice and intention, which are housed in your conscious mind. It's here, within this realm, that you employ skills like paying attention, adapting to new perspectives, and responsibly acting as one in harmony with others by letting go of liming Beliefs. Empowered, ME can make the conscious choice to *Walk a New Way* while maintaining a heightened sense of Awareness of the now.

STEP BACK: ALLOW OTHERS TO STEP UP

In the journey of self-awareness and understanding your subconscious, you can look to The Beatles as an example of how adaptability and shared leadership—knowing when to STEP UP and when to STEP BACK—can lead to success.

The Beatles' journey serves as a powerful example of how leadership within a group is not static but fluid, much like the starlings' murmuration. Different members of the band STEPPED UP to lead at various times, which demonstrated an intuitive understanding of when to take the lead and when to STEP BACK. This dynamic approach to leadership was key to their collective success.

John Lennon, often seen as the early leader of the group, played a crucial role in guiding the band through its formative years. However, as The Beatles evolved, leadership became a shared responsibility. Paul McCartney STEPPED UP during pivotal moments, particularly after the death of their manager, Brian Epstein, which allowed the band to remain focused and innovative. George Harrison, once considered the "quiet Beatle," emerged as a significant creative force and brought new influences into the band's music. Ringo Starr, with his steady rhythm and easy-going nature, helped maintain the group's cohesion during challenging times.

This leaderful approach—where each member knew when to lead and when to follow—mirrors the concepts explored in this chapter related to understanding the essence of ME. Just as The Beatles' members had to confront their own Beliefs, emotions, and roles within the group, you too must explore your own subconscious, uncover your potential, and decide when it's time to STEP UP or STEP BACK. The Beatles' story reminds you that true leadership is about being self-aware and knowing how to contribute to the collective good so the entire group thrives together.

It was The Beatles' behavior that indicated when STEPPING UP and STEPPING BACK was happening. It is also your behavior, the behavior of ME, that indicates to others where you are in your ability to adapt to your subconscious mind.

STEP TOGETHER:
EMBRACE MUTUAL TRUST AND RESPECT

One of this book's experts, Dr. Gary Cone, conceptualized the *Living in Choice* model that supports the creation of your habit, to STEP TOGETHER. To intentionally *Live in Choice*, Dr. Cone suggests specific states of mind for thoughts, feelings, and emotions. This chart represents both the abundant and the reactive limiting state of mind in your subconscious. You can choose, however, to be reactive and limited or abundant in your thoughts, feelings, emotions, and, consequently, behaviors. The choices you make are your responsibility. Remember that choice is the power of your 5 percent conscious mind. You can choose to embrace your responsive and proactive behaviors to STEP TOGETHER and embrace mutual trust and respect.[21]

To prepare you for a more in-depth look at choice, the following graphic represents the *Living in Choice* model, and highlights the different states of mind and their impacts on your behaviors. Before you are able to understand how to STEP TOGETHER and embrace mutual trust and respect, you are basically left alone to wander on a path to learn lessons. Remember, you can make choices. Each ME can choose *oneness*, trust, and respect. It's critical that you choose to be proactive while learning the three lessons in each area of thoughts, feelings, and emotions. Pause, study the chart, and notice the difference between proactive and reactive Beliefs. Which do you choose? It is your choice.

EMCS® Living in CHOICE
Levels of Responsibility

COURAGE
Affirming, empowered, feasible, constructive, strong, active, positive, engaged, excited, imaginative, possible, feasible

WILLING
Intentional, optimistic, enthusiastic, prepared, courageous, adequate, creative, playful, active, invigorated, answerable, worthwhile, responsible

NEUTRAL
Trust, satisfied, interested, fascinated, welcomed, needed, essential, tuned in, appreciated

ANTAGONISM
Hides inadequacy, feels attacked, annoyed, combative, indignant, bothered, counter-active, burdened, opposing

PRIDE/INDIFFERENCE
Belligerent, demanding, scornful, pessimistic, immobilized, numb, unfeeling, stagnant, destructive, disconnected, rigid, detrimental

ANGER/RESENTMENT
Hides behind "You hurt me and that gives me the right to protect myself," confused, incensed, over-wrought, wounded, hysterical, wrathful, fuming, furious, abused, unappreciated, rejected, numb, offended, hurt & used

EMOTION

ACCEPTANCE
Harmonious, forgiving, adaptable, worthy, open, amused, approachable, deserving, choosing to, owning

REASON
Wise, understanding, bold, proud, daring, protected, selfless, thoughtful, motivated, considerate, understanding

LOVE
Reverent, benign, revelatory, risking, trusting, caring, knowing, pleasurable, secure, respectful, giving, responsible

DESIRE/HOSTILITY
Blaming, "Someone else is responsible for me not getting what I want.", Frustrated, picked on, sarcastic, trapped, mean, deprived, withholding, vindictive

FEAR
Anxious, escape, "Something will be taken away from me," avoids, uncared for, trapped, disappointed, frightened, threatened, overlooked, unacceptable, unwelcome, defeated

GRIEF
Regretful, despondent, tragic, self-blaming, victim, depressed, unacceptable, morose, melancholy, defeated, deserted

FEELING

JOY
Serenity, whole, exuberant, fulfilled, energetic, complete, unencumbered

PEACE
Perfection, bliss, harmony, trust, thoughtfulness, nurturing, complete

ENLIGHTENMENT
Pure, sincere, ineffable, aware, respectful, appreciating, powerful

SHAME
"I won't survive," humiliation, cowardice, betrayed, disgraced, self-blaming, dishonored, bad (embarrassed), doubtful

SEPARATION/GUILT
Self-destructive, non-entity, "God does not love me, therefore, I am unlovable," lost, ruined, condemned, ineffectual, conquered

APATHY
Waiting to succumb, resigned, hopeless, takes no responsibility for cause, uncared for, insignificant, powerlessness, distrustful & suspicious

THOUGHT

| PRO-ACTIVE | REFLEX/ | RE-ACTIVE |
| *State of Mind* | BELIEF | |

Copyright 2003 • Gary Cone Corp. Inc. • Living in Choice Levels of Responsibility is used in the Energy Matrix Clearing Systems

WHY WOULD YOU WANT TO *WALK A NEW WAY?*
By Kathy Hagler

Let's illustrate the answer to this WHY question by telling a story. While on a business trip, I had an illuminating experience. Habitually, I'd use hotel mornings for writing, creating breakthroughs in my thinking. But this day was different. As I sat down for breakfast, I found myself next to a businessman discussing workplace relationships with a colleague on the phone. This sparked an immediate response within me. Although a part of me was hesitant, driven by my past habits and subconscious fears, I felt a compelling urge to reach out. This is a great example of how past Beliefs and thoughts can also drive an automatic reaction from you.

Embracing the mantra to *Walk a New Way*, I overcame my inhibitions, stood up, walked to his table, and introduced myself. This simple act transformed my perceptions of what was proper. It forged a meaningful connection and emphasized the profound impact of interpersonal harmony. We enjoyed an amazing conversation about hiring practices. For example, after I introduced myself and confessed that I overheard part of his discussion, I asked if he would be willing to have a conversation with me about hiring practices. He happily engaged in a conversation with me. After carefully STEPPING UP to begin the conversation, I quickly STEPPED BACK to provide him space to respond, if he was so inclined. The result was a STEPPING TOGETHER around best hiring practices, and a new relationship was formed.

Such interactions reinforce the intrinsic human need for connection that is rooted in our survival instincts. Consider the starlings: for them, the art of murmuration is a dance of unity and survival. Likewise, humans thrive when they exist harmoniously within a community.

In Carter Phipps' book, *Evolutionaries: Unlocking the Spiritual and Cultural Potential of Science's Greatest Idea*, he captures this sentiment that humans who live the longest strike a balance between being individually creative and being a cooperating member of an innovative society.[22]

Your mind, body, and spirit converge in this harmonious dance, guiding you from the shadows of fear to the luminous present. This transformative and revealing light unveils a new path; one of personal growth, harmony, and genuine connections.

Nature's profound wisdom inspires this dance. It emphasizes your immense capacity for personal evolution and the nurturing of deeper relationships. Consider the rewards when an individual (ME) elevates another (WE). It's akin to the unfolding of a rosebud, which reveals the magnificent bloom nestled within. Always remember, while you are distinctively individual, you also play an indispensable role in the grand tapestry of life. So, how do you intentionally create the habits that consistently form the bones of your own existence?

In Chapter 3, you've journeyed through the intricate layers of ME—your mind, body, and spirit. By uncovering the dynamics between your conscious and subconscious minds, you've gained insights into ME as the core of murmuration. This chapter has highlighted the importance of self-awareness, the need to address and transform limiting Beliefs, and the ultimate power of conscious choice.

As you prepare to move forward, remember that each moment of Awareness and each conscious decision contributes to your personal growth and harmony. Now, let's take these insights and practices to the next level as you explore Chapter 4, where you will deepen your understanding of how to activate your internal dynamics to influence the world around you.

YOUR TURN: MOMENT OF REFLECTION

Your intuitive mind connects ME with the external world. This realm harnesses intuition, spirituality, and other facets to paint a canvas of boundless possibilities for ME in multiple *fields of energy*, including WE, US, and the universe. As the esteemed Rumi once said, "Beyond ideas of wrongdoing and right doing, there's a field. I'll meet you there…the world is too full to talk about."[23]

Reflect on your understanding of the subconscious and conscious mind, the parts of the iceberg both above and below the waterline.

1. **WHAT HAVE YOU NOTICED ABOUT YOUR MIND FROM THIS READING?** Can you pause and notice when you are conscious, in the now? Can you pause and notice when you are subconscious, being driven by your programmed habits of the mind?

2. **CONSIDER A RECENT EVENT WHERE YOU CONSCIOUSLY CHOSE A DIFFERENT BEHAVIOR** than your subconscious insisted upon, or *Walked a New Way*. Jot down answers to these questions:

    a. Can you recall the exact moment, the Awareness, the moment the *Footlights of Consciousness* lit the stage of your mind and instructed your next behavior?

    b. Dive deep into your emotions and the steps you undertook to pay attention and challenge the deeply rooted habit in your subconscious. What was this habit? What behavior did it loudly suggest to you?

c. What did you do next?

   d. Did the behavior change?

   e. What new behavior did you choose?

3. **CONSIDER ROSS THORNLEY'S *JAM JAR* METAPHOR.** It was introduced to illustrate how individuals can be trapped by their own subconscious thoughts, feelings, and emotions. In this metaphor, you're inside the jam jar, unaware of how your internal state is presented to the outside world. While you can't see the label from inside, others can easily read it. It might say something like "Stuck in the Past, Needs Fresh Perspective." This label reflects how others perceive you, based on your subconscious habits and behaviors.

4. **RECALL TIMES WHEN YOU STEPPED UP, STEPPED BACK, STEPPED TOGETHER** and think about your jam jar's label. What did it say in each instance?

How-to Skills: see pages 313–316 for more information
Footlights of Consciousness
Jam Jar
Living in Choice Model
Pause, Notice, and Choose

Global Thought Leaders: see pages 317–320 for more information
Gary Cone
Bruce H. Lipton
Ross Thornley

CHAPTER 4

HOW TO EMBARK ON THE JOURNEY OF ME

*Every cell in your body
is eavesdropping on your thoughts.*

—Deepak Chopra

THE JOURNEY INWARD IS PROFOUND. Imagine ME as a whirling murmuration powered by the internal starlings of mind, body, and spirit. They are programmed to perform the dance of life with ME, just as starlings are programed for their life-giving murmuration.

Your cells are programmable, according to cell biologist Dr. Bruce H. Lipton. You can quite literally transform the components of your body by changing how you think and what you perceive both internally and externally. Often, you look externally for improvements when the key may be nestled deep within. This truth is encapsulated in Dr. Lipton's work. This research has shown that your cells are like computer chips. They are programmed from outside their structure and also deep within your system. You are the driver of your own biology, and experts agree that you have the ability to shift your Beliefs from limiting habits stored in your subconscious to self-enhancing ones.[24]

In this chapter, you will explore how you, as an individual ME, can chart the course of your mind, body, and spirit; your internal life-giving murmuration.

THE GLOBAL WORKSPACE OF ME

Life's true harmony unfolds when your mind, body, and spirit move in alignment, which gives birth to a dynamic, *internal global workspace* that is constantly evolving. Think of the *global workspace* as a theater of mental functioning. A bright spotlight of attention directs your eyes toward the stage and secures your Awareness, your consciousness. The rest of the theater is in the dark subconscious. However, your mind, body, and spirit bind together the broadcast of the whole performance, the front of the house, including the stage (conscious), and the back of the house (subconscious).[25]

VISUALIZING THE INTERNAL PATHS

The components of your mind, body, and spirit are like *interconnected* paths that constantly shape and influence one another. Imagine a dense forest with long, winding trails, each one uniquely formed by the natural landscape. This mirrors the personal journey of ME, where mind, body, and spirit follow twisting, interconnected paths through your internal world. In essence, this internal journey is a reflection of your own murmuration—a synchronized movement that Connects every part of you.

This internal murmuration flows like a *confluence* of energy that guides ME toward WE, and eventually to US. As you find harmony within yourself, that internal balance extends outward, strengthening your connection with others. In turn, this external harmonization between WE and US reciprocates, which fuels the internal harmony of ME. It's a cycle of growth and connection. The more aligned and in harmony you are internally, the more you contribute to the collective strength of WE and US. And the more harmonious the collective becomes, the more it nourishes your internal balance of mind, body, and spirit.

This reciprocity represents the dynamic nature of your personal and collective journeys. Just as a murmuration of starlings thrives through synchronized movement, your internal and external worlds thrive through the balance of ME, WE, and US.

ME: MIND, BODY, AND SPIRIT

In his book, *The 7 Habits of Highly Effective People*, Stephen Covey described a Venn Diagram with **habit formation** habit formation serving as the common thread that connects the key areas of *what to*, *how to*, and *want to*.[26] Your mindset represents the *what to*, your skillset represents your behaviors that are the *how to*, and your motivation represents your *want to*.

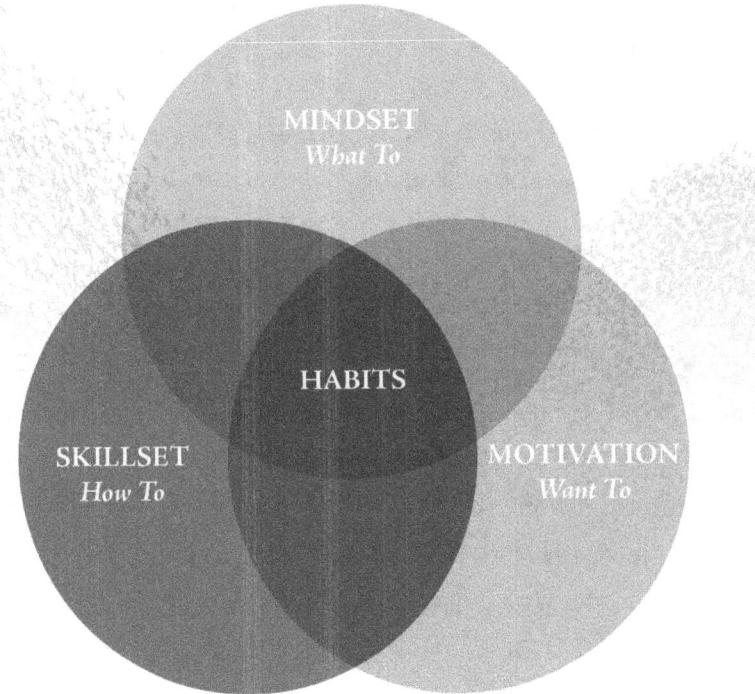

Your personal murmuration journey always begins by turning inward and focusing on the ME:

- The *what to* and *why*, articulated by the mind, set your course toward forming conscious habits.

Chapter 4: How to Embark on The Journey of Me   67

- The *how to*, exemplified by the body, manifests as the tangible skillsets and behaviors of your repeated and habitual endeavors.
- The *want to*, anchored in the spirit, provides your motivation to walk the new path of your choosing.

Your mind, the mind of ME, is a mysterious, powerful influencer. It directs the *what to* do. Your mind STEPS UP to navigate. It sets your compass on the conscious habits of murmuration, the promise of oneness. You follow the mind to align the body and spirit. Next, ME instinctively knows that the reach of mind, body, and spirit is strengthened by others. It must extend to the collective WE. The body of ME, the behaviors, represent the *how to* do things like initiate the behaviors to Connect with others. Much like starlings, the habitual behavior of STEP UP, STEP BACK, STEP TOGETHER solidifies the WE. Your spirit, the spirit of ME, *wants to* be part of WE and *wants to* move to the unity of ONE. Therefore, it directs your mind to adopt new Beliefs that will assure your evolution from ME to WE to US. Alignment of mind, body, and spirit is occurring.

Each ME, its mind, body, and spirit, must consciously choose how to evolve. **Follow these steps to create an *Evolutionary Mindset:***

- Awareness: Consciously live in the present, the now
- Beliefs: Unlearn habitual and limiting behaviors and implement new supporting ones
- Connect with others
- Choose to boldly *Walk a New Way*
- Learn the conscious habits: STEP UP, STEP BACK, STEP TOGETHER

In following these steps, you should remain ever mindful that this is more than a mere personal journey. This map reflects the intricate dance of your mind, body, and spirit, which murmurate together and cast their influence in moment-by-moment interactions with others. This molds interpersonal relationships and sends resonant waves into the wider world. Little did you realize that your very survival depends on the habits, thoughts, emotions, and behaviors of each ME, their internal global workspace, and their ability to murmurate like starlings.

ME is not only navigating its own course but also illuminating the way for others. It aids them in finding their paths and encourages them to join the grand murmuration. This moves the ME to WE to US. And as you can easily see, it is also US to WE to ME. It is in *oneness* with resolve and clarity that you forge ahead on this enlightening odyssey, taking each path with mindfulness and intention. Let's embrace an *Evolutionary Mindset*.

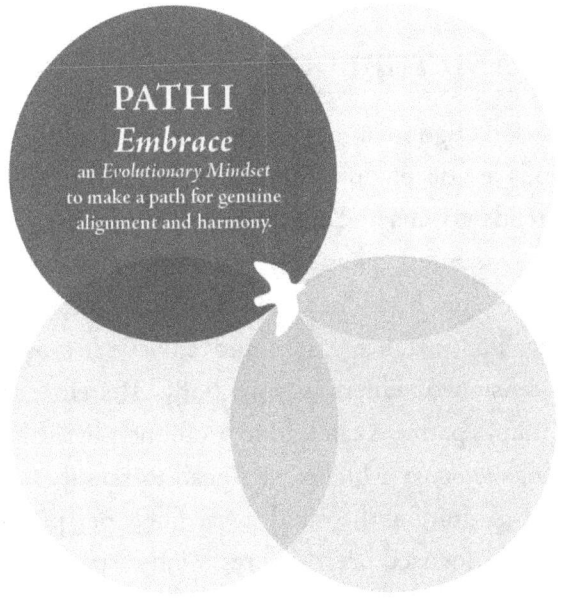

©2024 ABC's of Murmuration

PATH I

Embrace an Evolutionary Mindset

THE MIND

Just as pathways in a forest guide you through nature's maze, your subconscious mind directs your life's trajectory based on deeply entrenched Beliefs. As you've learned in previous chapters, the subconscious mind steers 95 percent of your actions; you just have to sit back and watch! However, this raises a critical question: Is conscious direction even possible with only 5 percent steering capability? If your subconscious mind and its limiting Belief paths control so many of your actions, how can you consciously, intentionally create a united community of your mind, body, and spirit that will thrive? It seems overwhelming, but striving for this alignment fosters personal growth and influences broader evolutionary opportunities.

THE MIND AND THE BODY

This process of alignment begins with understanding that your mind and body are deeply interconnected. What your mind believes, your body tends to enact. Your thoughts—whether conscious or subconscious—manifest physically through your actions, habits, and behaviors. The body becomes a reflection of your mind's programming. For instance, stress and anxiety in your mind can manifest as tension or illness in your body. Therefore, consciously shifting the mind's patterns can lead to profound physical changes. To embrace an *Evolutionary Mindset*, you need to recalibrate the body's responses by first guiding the mind toward new perspectives. By the use of your body, focused breathing techniques specifically, you also can guide your mind toward new perspectives. The mind and body are interconnected paths in your global workspace.

As the mind sets the path, the body follows it, through both actions and behaviors. By installing the *ABC's of Murmuration* into your mental framework, you provide the body with a clear map for *what to* do and *how to* act. Your mind's Awareness, in harmony with your body's actions, begins to create a unified direction for your personal growth.

THE MIND, THE BODY, AND THE SPIRIT

The key to creating harmony between the mind, body, and spirit lies in embracing an *Evolutionary Mindset*. To do this, you need to follow these steps based on the *ABC's of Murmuration*:

AWARENESS: Attend to the now

Recognize and Attend to:

- Identifying what a trigger feels like in your mind, then your body and spirit
- Paying attention to key past-triggering Beliefs in your mind; start by writing them down
- Keep a "trigger journal" to track triggers, noting where you sense them first (mind, body, or spirit), and identify the corresponding habits that are keeping you stuck

Understand:

- Inherent Beliefs from your past that are causing underlying knee-jerk reactions in the mind, body, or spirit. Write these down.
- Habits that have been created through knee-jerk reactions. Your brain forms neural circuits that reinforce habits solidifies them through repetition. Write these down. Are these habits in the mind, body, or spirit?

Question:

- Stop and ask, "Why do I feel this way?"
- "Why did I behave that way?"
- "Is this really what I want?"

BELIEFS: Adapt to new perspectives

- Recognize and Identify: The habitual Beliefs lodged in your subconscious. Refer to your notes.
- Dive Deep: Consciously explore the emotion, understanding its possible roots and the past Beliefs that have been programmed into a habit.

- Question: Stop and ask, "Where does this limiting feeling originate from?" Reflect on your past events that caused these emotions.
- Shift Perspective: Determine if the Belief is still relevant. Ask yourself, "What do I want instead? What is my new perspective? How can I unlearn the past Belief?"

CONNECT: Act as one

- Intentionally Connect: Allow and encourage your mind, body, and spirit to choose new Beliefs and perspectives by consciously communicating your choices to yourself and others, using both words and actions. Writing these down and discussing them with close friends help bring them into your consciousness.
- Communicate: Use present-moment conscious activities, such as your words and actions, to unlock and express emotions, which brings them forward into observable behavior. Read over them often. Create new habits.

By implementing these steps, you can effectively integrate the *ABC's of Murmuration* into the daily life of your mind, body, and spirit. This begins to foster a harmonious alignment of all three—essential for the personal growth of ME. This is a process that takes time and repetition; Don't expect immediate results. But with dedication and discipline, these practices can help you harness the conscious mind of ME to act with Awareness of the now, release limiting Beliefs, and shift your mindset.

EXAMPLE OF SHIFTING YOUR MINDSET (WANT TO)

Imagine your partner reveals they've lost their wedding ring. This news, appearing as an immediate, bright *Footlight of Consciousness*, could trigger an immediate raw emotional response that mirrors your deep-seated subconscious Beliefs. Such a knee-jerk reaction, visible to others, might typically reinforce a habitual response and—perhaps unintentional—look of disgust.

To prevent this reaction, the *ABC's of Murmuration* provide a conscious solution: Be aware of the present moment, the *Footlight of Consciousness*; shift your habitual Beliefs by changing your perspective; and become connected to another's situation and reality. (This takes practice!)

Old Way: Reaction Driven by Limiting Beliefs

- **Spouse**: "I cannot find my wedding ring."
- **You**: "What? Again? You just lost it two weeks ago!"
- **Body Reaction**: Your face scrunches up like a prune, a reflex that shows your underlying subconscious belief and visible disgust.

EXAMPLE OF SHIFTING YOUR BEHAVIOR (HOW TO)

Transforming the Response: To preempt the instant build-up of emotional steam and visceral reaction, and foster a healthier interaction, remember *The xchange Approach* of *Pause, Notice, and Choose*.

New Way: Embrace an *Evolutionary Mindset*

- **Be Aware and *Pause***: Acknowledge the immediate moment.
  - Put your "car in neutral"
  - Ask in your mind: "Did they do it on purpose?"
- **Challenge Your Belief and *Notice*.**
  - Adopt a new perspective: "I know there's a lot on my partner's mind."
  - Intentionally relax your facial muscles.
  - Immediately embrace a mindset of seeing yourself as a *Torchbearer in a Cave* who shines light in the dark on a possible path toward a better outcome.

EXAMPLE OF SHIFTING YOUR SPIRIT (WANT TO)

- **Connect and *Choose*:**
    - Decide to accept your partner's busy mindset and STEP BACK.
    - Ask them to suggest possible locations for the ring and follow their lead.
    - Breathe deeply and ease your body's tension.

As you continue forward—pausing to notice your mind and its emotions, the knee-jerk reactions of your body, and your behavior of saying things you might regret or exposing your feelings through physical movements—you must focus on making conscious choices. In other words, focus on the question, "What do I want instead?" When you are too close to a situation, or too deeply involved in it, it can be hard to have an objective or complete perspective of your mindset and physical reactions. But when you embrace an *Evolutionary Mindset* and explore the *ABC's*, you begin to evolve in ways that allow you to choose. Your spirit *wants to* STEP BACK and adopt new perspectives so that your physical behaviors are your choice. You can choose to behave in a conscious way that leads to *what you want instead*, a peaceful co-existence, your chosen "end in mind."

Once you have some mastery of making conscious choices by utilizing the mind, body, and spirit, you can move forward. Let's forge ahead to PATH II and adopt even more of the elements of murmuration.

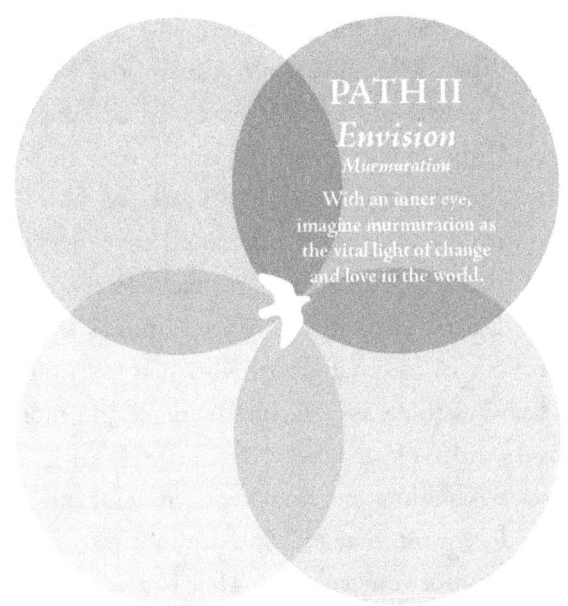

©2024 ABC's of Murmuration

PATH II
Envision Murmuration

THE MIND, BODY, AND SPIRIT

How do you use your inner eye to visualize murmuration? Start by envisioning a beautiful red rose. See it as clearly as possible. Now, with your senses, smell its fragrance. It's remarkable that you can experience the rose within, even though there is no actual rose in front of you. In the same way, it is crucial to hold the ***vision of murmuration*** in your mind's eye, just like the rose. You must see its collective cohesion and unity, and physically feel the security in its breadth and depth.

Remember that the journey from ME to WE to US is a river of opportunities. When ME moves into a team, the ME does not go away. When ME moves into a larger group, an US, the ME does not go away. The ME becomes part of the murmuration. Murmuration is emblematic of unity. Murmuration indicates, as with the starlings, that WE are stronger together. Understand that for ME, surviving or continuing to live is human nature itself. Every aspect of your personality is derived from this. In your mind's eye, see ME in murmuration with its internal global workspace of mind, body, and spirit. ME is always there as ME, but stronger and more resourced when in concert with WE or US.

Therefore, by holding murmuration in your mind's eye and asking, "What do I want instead?" you are motivated by your spirit, your *want to*, to secure your survival. That is being surrounded by a community that forms a safe environment for ME, WE, and US. A ME can contribute talent and energy to promote the success of the whole, the US.

In science, there is the concept known as emergent properties. These are qualities not seen in one part of a system that become apparent when the parts of that system interact. The whole of murmuration has characteristics and power that the individual ME could never have alone. When you visualize murmuration in your mind's eye, remember that it is bigger, better, and safer together.

Knowing this, you are ready to progress to PATH III and begin to actively navigate the *ABC's of Murmuration* in your daily life.

©2024 ABC's of Murmuration

PATH III
Explore and Walk a New Way

THE SPIRIT

How do you consciously navigate the Awareness of the now, shift your Beliefs, and Connect to others? ME does this by being adaptable and open to messages and needs, both internal and external. Just like starlings, adaptability of mind, body, and spirit is key.

New paths can be exciting, and require your conscious mind's attention, your body's courage, and your spirit's flexibility to embrace new experiences and *unlearn* limiting subconscious Beliefs. It takes personal resilience to reroute (by unlearning your old route) and redefine your thinking trajectory, while you continuously strive to consciously choose your way. This also encompasses harmoniously

Connecting with your environment. You must learn a new way as well as learn to listen to your *want to*, the desire of your spirit.

To do this, encourage ME to draw inspiration from the starlings' murmuration in nature. Then decide to follow the *ABC's* with your mind (*what to*), your body and skills (*how to*), and your spirit and motivation (*want to*):

AWARENESS: Attend to the now
- Be aware of your current surroundings and environment and engage your five senses
- Ask yourself, "What do I really want in this moment?"

BELIEFS: Adapt to new perspectives
- Reflect on your Beliefs
- Question, "What could I/should I do in this moment?"

CONNECT: Act as one
- Connect your mind, body, and spirit as one
- Ponder, "What will I do, and how will I do it to achieve the results I want in this moment?"

WALK A NEW WAY:
A FURTHER EXPLORATION OF SPIRIT

Your spirit emits waves of desire, intention, and intuition, which propels human evolution and your fervent yearning to transform and elevate. This internal compass, rooted deep within, becomes the foundation for lasting habits.

The spirit represents the *want to*, the heart's desire, a potent driving force. Your *want to*, or motivation, is driven by your life's values, or what ME loves about life. It is about heart. It bridges your current and desired states to facilitate habit formation and transformation. All of these practices require ME to remain fluid and willing to adapt to unexpected or new inputs. According to Ross Thornley, the *AQai*®

Adaptability Quotient expert, true adaptability requires creating new pathways, akin to laying fresh snow for skiers. The analogy captures the essence of adaptability. Just as skiers carve out new trails on untouched snow, you have the power to forge new paths in your life, or *Lay New Snow*. This process hinges on a conscious decision-making practice we've discussed before—*Pause, Notice, and Choose*. Let's revisit this skill from a fresh perspective:

PAUSE
- **STEP UP** and ask yourself, "What do I really want now?"
- **STEP BACK** to understand your immediate *want to*, your intention. This is like a skier surveying the landscape to decide where to lay the first tracks on fresh snow.

NOTICE
- Ask yourself, "What could I/should I do?"
- Contemplate potential actions. Imagine a skier considering the best route down the slope by weighing the risks and rewards.

CHOOSE
- Ask yourself, "What will I do?"
- If you decide to make a change, break free from habitual routes and deliberately choose a new path, much like the skier venturing away from the well-trodden paths to experience the thrill of creating new tracks.

Step Up and Lay New Snow: (Do It!)
Actively and decisively shape your surroundings with intention and Awareness. Just as a skier gracefully navigates the slope and leaves a unique trail behind, you too leave your mark on the world with each new pathway you take in your journey. Congratulations!

Much like starlings adjusting their trajectories in a mesmerizing dance, the spirit pilots your path and harmonizes personal aspirations with shared dreams. This internal heartbeat of evolution, motivation, or *want to* powers the *ABC's of Murmuration*, and redirects you from a ME-focused narrative toward a WE-centric symphony, which moves US closer to collective consciousness.

WALK A NEW WAY:
A FURTHER EXPLORATION OF MIND AND BODY

As you redefine your mind's defensive subconscious patterns of thought and emotion (*what to*) into conscious, physical, and behavioral frameworks of choice (*how to*), the evolutionary spirit of *want to* nudges you toward making intentional conscious decisions, growing, participating in purposeful activities, and cleaning up past experiences that limited you. Emulating starlings, your triad of mind, body, and spirit can cultivate synergy, enhance engagement, enrich communication, and streamline collective goals. They can do this at the same time they are forming new habits. Yet remember that navigating this transformative landscape demands introspection into your subconscious and understanding its protective, survival instincts. Your work on ME is exciting and evolutionary!

It takes courage to spotlight your ideas, shift your perspective, and amplify your voice, with commitment being the key. As Justice Sonia Sotomayor said, "I think it's important to move people beyond just dreaming into doing. They have to be able to see that you are just like them, and you made it."[27] This commitment requires courage to see, in your mind's eye, murmuration as your goal, and to infuse its essence and possibilities into your life's rhythm.

WANT TO: A COMMON MISSING LINK
IN HUMAN MURMURATION

Most of the time, in each ME, the missing link in the mind, body, and spirit murmuration is the *want to*, or the spirit. New habits are not formed without the motivation, the *want to*. To follow your spirit, your *want to*, you must listen to your intuition and:

Pause
STEP BACK and pause, and determine when and where to navigate. Allow others to STEP UP in their own space and mirror the choreography of murmuration.

Notice
Consciously be aware that when moving into WE, those who have been with you in the past might choose a different path. Pay attention when making the shifts to new paths so that others do not feel tossed aside. Remember compassion, wisdom, and personal power, as you let others know your intentions for new paths and possible changes to the current relationships. You need to learn to change directions without leaving pain in your wake.

Choose
You must learn how to shed the barriers created by your limiting Beliefs. In addition, you are better served by forging connections with others. Individual triumphs will amplify collective milestones, just like collective milestones amplify individual triumphs.

In summary, the *ABC's of Murmuration* chart shows a transformational journey. It urges you to explore the subconscious mind of ME—aligning mind, body, and spirit as one—and commit to WE and then US. This sculpts an environment of collective prosperity. The spirit, with its thirst for growth, guides you toward self-actualization. Harnessing this intrinsic motivation and *want to* becomes an important part in the pursuit of lasting change, growth, and enlightenment.

It is the spirit that houses your intuitive, spiritual essence; the nucleus of your aspirations and yearnings for growth. It's your innate urge, your *want to*, to evolve, to emerge better. Such a desire is central to habit formation and path sculpting. When driven by profound motivation, the *want to*, you harness this desire to navigate obstacles and stay the course in your own growth expedition.

From the complexities of the subconscious mind, let's shift focus to the tangible realm of *body*, where your Beliefs manifest visibly.

Making your path means walking over the same area many times. The next phase suggests that you must work hard to consciously make your new paths the chosen habits you will follow, the behaviors you will adopt. These are the habits that starlings have used to successfully murmurate.

UNCHARTED TERRITORY

When lost, you typically look at a map to figure out where you are and how to get to your chosen destination. This works well, assuming there is a map of the territory in which you find yourself and you know your destination. However, this is not always the case. At this time in human history, you are venturing into uncharted territory, whether you know it or not. And as an individual ME, you may find yourself covering ground that your predecessors never even knew existed. When you look to them for guidance, they often come up short. Not knowing exactly where you are, you find yourself unsure of which way to go, and eventually the uneasy feeling that you are lost presents itself.

The beauty of being lost is the same thing that makes it scary: it asks you to look within yourself to find the way. If you have no map, you must go on instinct and rely on your inner compass to show which way to go. This can be scary because so much seems to be riding on it. You fear you might go too far in the wrong direction or become paralyzed and make no progress at all. Yet, this is the very challenge you need in order to develop your ability to trust yourself. You are also learning to trust that the universe will support and guide you. We may believe this intellectually, but it is only through experience that it becomes ingrained knowledge. Learning to tolerate being lost and trusting that you will be guided, you begin your journey. You *Walk a New Way*.

You are learning to feel your own way rather than following an established path, and in doing so you learn to trust yourself. It is this trust that Connects you to the universe and reminds you that no matter how lost you feel as you journey, on the inner level you are already home.

PATH IV

Engage in Conscious Habits of Thriving

THE BODY

How do you take steps to initiate action, allow others to STEP UP, and embrace mutual trust and respect? You effectively shift your physical state through Awareness and presence.

The connection between your mind and body means that your thoughts directly influence your bodily responses and reactions. As was stated at the very beginning of this chapter, your cells hear everything your mind says. If you are consumed by worry, fear, or doubt, your body reacts as though these threats are real. Being fully conscious and present—living in the NOW—is essential. Only then can you actively have the necessary behavior to STEP UP, STEP BACK, and STEP TOGETHER, and engage in conscious behavioral choices rather than reactionary habits.

To adopt behavioral habits that support collective thriving, it's essential to understand the interconnectedness of your mind and body. Just as repeated use carves a path through a forest, habitual actions shape both your physical and mental states. Through repeated and intentional actions, your body follows the directives of your mind, and vice versa. This reciprocal relationship helps you adopt new behavioral habits.

Jack Lowe, Jr., former CEO of TDIndustries, said this about his behavioral habits around *Servant Leadership:* "Our company promoted safety, diversity, and valued opinions at every level. *Servant Leadership* emphasized listening and valuing others' opinions. The company emphasizes collaboration over a strict hierarchy. We were recognized as a top employer for 25 years in a row."[28]

A LIVING EXAMPLE: TDINDUSTRIES AND THE FOUR-PATH JOURNEY

Servant Leadership is a foundational principle for fostering unity and collaboration. This style of leadership emphasizes putting the needs of others first, empowering employees, and creating an environment in which every member of an organization is encouraged to be a leader. This approach not only transforms individuals but also cultivates a thriving, collaborative environment, much like a murmuration. Basically, TDIndustries knows *what to* do, *how to* do it, and that they *want to* thrive. And thrive they have for eight decades.

Founded in 1946, the construction and technology corporation stands as a testament to the power of creating unity, collaboration, safety, and security. The company provides commercial and industrial services such as air conditioning, electrical, and plumbing systems, primarily through general contractors. Lowe, TDIndustries' retired CEO, emphasized the critical role of *Servant Leadership* throughout his tenure at the helm. For him, it was more than just a philosophy; it was a lived ethos that framed every decision, interaction, and strategy. He named it "leaderful" at TDIndustries.

Evolving to a Leaderful System

HIERARCHICAL SYSTEM
"It's About ME"
Authority, Autocratic Control, Blaming, Concealment, Control Contests, Disconnected Sectors, Self-Serving, Territoriality

HARMONIC SYSTEM
"It's About US"
Accountability, Aligned Responsiveness, Collaboration, Collective Wisdom, Dialogue, Impactful Influence, Mutual Engagement, Support

©2024 ABC's of Murmuration

PATH I: *Embrace* an Evolutionary Mindset

Lowe saw synchrony in nature, particularly in the behavior of starlings during murmuration. He equated this to companies, notably TDIndustries, that resonate harmony. Just as starlings take turns leading and following, Lowe believed leaders should do the same: leading, or STEPPING UP when necessary, but also STEPPING BACK to allow others to STEP UP. This harmonious, flexible dynamic fostered a culture of persistence, preparation, passion, and adaptability.

PATH II: *Envision* Murmuration

TDIndustries' journey with *Servant Leadership* began in the late 1960s and quickly became integral to the organization. The company envisioned a culture of collective cohesion in which every employee was a leader. This vision was more than just lip service; it was actively practiced. If profitable executives didn't embrace this ethos, they were shown the door. The collective good was paramount.

PATH III: *Explore* and Walk a New Way

TDIndustries conducted regular trainings and meetings, not just for operational decisions, but also to delve deep into the heart of *Servant Leadership*. The company emphasized internal promotion, and held a firm belief that everyone, regardless of rank, was a leader and deserved to have a voice in the company. This approach encouraged employees to attend to the present moment, adapt to new perspectives, and Connect as one unified entity. And they were all extremely loyal to the purpose and goals of the company. After all, they helped create them. They were leaderful.

PATH IV: *Engage* in Conscious Habits of Thriving

TDIndustries adopted habits that supported collective thriving. As a 100-percent-employee-owned company, every member had a stake in their success. They embraced the principles of STEPPING UP to initiate actions, STEPPING BACK to allow others to lead, and STEPPING TOGETHER to foster mutual trust and respect.

SERVANT LEADERSHIP PRINCIPLES

As demonstrated by TDIndustries, the principles of *Servant Leadership* are not just theoretical concepts but practical, actionable strategies that can transform an organization. Their commitment to these principles has created a thriving, collaborative environment in which every member is empowered to be leaderful. Below is a graphic that highlights the key elements and benefits of *Servant Leadership*, a framework that can work in any group, from corporations to families, community groups to governmental bodies.

10 Pillars of Servant Leadership

1 PURPOSE-DRIVEN
Inspires leaderful growth of others toward compelling mission

2 PROACTIVE LISTENING
Heartfelt, open communication

3 COMPASSION
Understands and responds to others perspectives

4 RESTORATIVE ACTIONS
Promotes healing behaviors

5 SELF-AWARENESS
Knows and shares strengths and limitations

6 LEADERFUL MINDSET
Encourages without command and control

7 VISIONARY
Adopts possibility awareness and actions

8 ANTICIPATORY ADAPTABILITY
Foresees challenges and opportunities

9 RESPONSIBLE MANAGEMENT
Promotes sustainability through teams

10 COMMUNITY BUILDER
Prioritizes culture of belonging

©2024 ABC's of Murmuration

CONSCIOUS HABITS OF THRIVING FOR ME

STEP UP: Initiate the first action
- Embrace a decisive mindset, but not as an authority
- Adapt through conceptualization, foresight, and expansive thinking—in the spirit of *Laying New Snow*
- Share information openly
- Steward the space for healthy challenges

STEP BACK: Allow others to STEP UP
- Recognize STEPPING BACK as the first step toward WE
- Foster personal growth
- Grant autonomy
- Recognize excellence
- Walk side by side in authentic relationships

STEP TOGETHER: Embrace mutual trust and respect
- Actively promote evolved Beliefs and aligned behaviors
- Bond in trust
- Embrace vulnerability
- Nurture relationships

In order to create thriving habits like those of the starlings, let's review the triad of *what to/why to*, *how to*, and *want to* and how they form the crucible in which habits are nurtured and honed. From this elevated vantage point, you aim to craft the perfect balance that empowers the global workspace of mind, body, and spirit to deftly choreograph the *Conscious Habits of Thriving* in murmuration: STEP UP, STEP BACK, STEP TOGETHER.

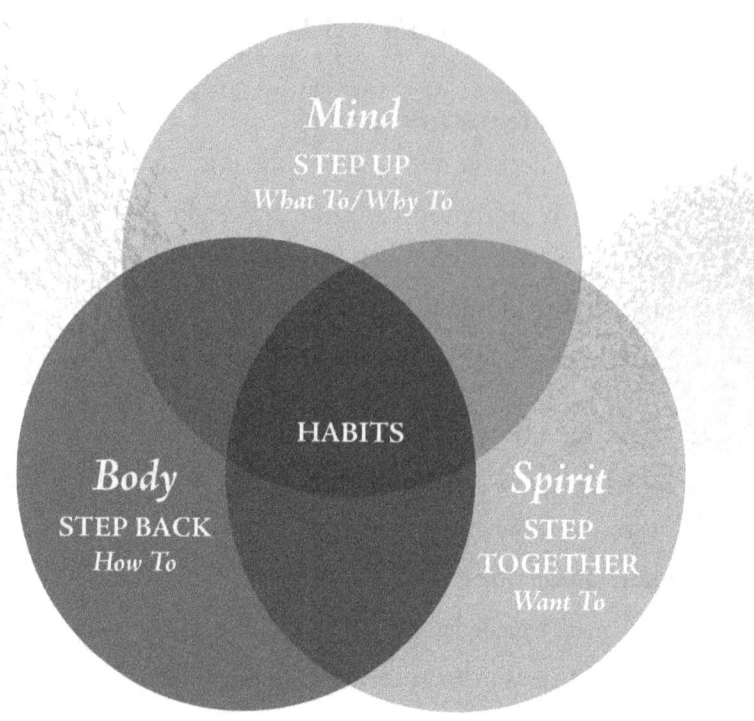

Top Circle
What to/Why to: *Mind* (STEP UP: Initiate the first action)

Left Circle
How to: *Body* (STEP BACK: Allow others to STEP UP)

Right Circle
Want to: *Spirit* (STEP TOGETHER:
Embrace mutual trust and respect)

ADOPT CONSCIOUS HABITS OF THRIVING: THE MIND

To truly embrace conscious habits that support collective thriving, it's essential to understand the role your mind plays in this process. Your body, mind, and spirit are deeply interconnected, and by harnessing the power of embodied consciousness, you can align your actions with your aspirations. Let's explore your emotions and how they relate to habit formation.

Your emotions serve as messengers from your subconscious, encapsulate the energy of past Beliefs, ideas, and feelings. They convert feeling from the subconscious into action. This Awareness signals that you need to pay attention to and identify your conscious intentions, your *want to*. It is at that point you need to make a choice to either STEP UP, STEP BACK, or STEP TOGETHER, your *how to*. When your thoughts align with your consciously chosen intentions, and those align with your behaviors, you experience harmony. Conversely, misalignment brings disharmony. However, if you do not consciously choose the correct action between taking the initiative, giving another space, or coming together as one, there will also be disharmony.

Let's look at these definitions:

A SUBJECTIVE EXPERIENCE (THE MIND) —
The personal lens through which you perceive a feeling. Your personal perception of a feeling, your *Footlight of Consciousness*, your radiant beam. It is your spotlight of Awareness, a heightened sense.

A PHYSIOLOGICAL RESPONSE (THE SPIRIT) —
The sensory experience a feeling induces within your body. The physical sensation it stirs, like a quickened heartbeat, tight throat, or tense stomach.

A BEHAVIORAL RESPONSE (THE BODY) —
Your instinctive actions when ensnared by specific emotions, be it fight, flight, freeze, or fawn. The actions prompted by feelings. There is either an unintended subconscious reaction and behavior or the creation of an intentional conscious response.

Emotions also hold these distinctions:

- **Inherent and Universal:** Innately woven into our being
  Examples: Anger, fear, joy, sadness, disgust

- **Swift and Instinctual:** Arising spontaneously

    Examples: Happiness, surprise, wonder
- **Valuable:** Key to your survival instincts

    Examples: Anticipation, trust

Yet every emotion—be it fear, serenity, or contempt—holds significance. Let your past be a foundation for pursuing what you want and need from life and not what you want to avoid at all costs. Use the skill of *Pause, Notice, and Choose* to walk your path consciously.

Emotions can render your subconscious Beliefs into behavioral trajectories that are inadvertently expressed through your body in words and reactions, and aimed indiscriminately at others. A well-worn path in nature, crafted by repetitive movements, mirrors *how* your body, guided by the subconscious mind, molds your behavioral path. Disruptive behavior can happen again and again as the well-worn path of your reaction. Again, *Pause, Notice, and Choose* your responses. Otherwise your subconscious Beliefs will transform into habits.

HOW HABITS FORM

Habits form through a process known as the habit loop. This three-step process, first identified by researchers at MIT, involves a cue, a routine, and a reward. The cue triggers your brain to initiate a behavior, the routine is the behavior itself, and the reward is a benefit received from the behavior that reinforces the habit loop. Over time, this cycle becomes more automatic as the brain begins to associate the cue with the reward directly, which makes the behavior more unconscious and ingrained. To alter these patterns, it's essential to disrupt the loop by changing the routine or the reward. As Charles Duhigg explains in *The Power of Habit*, understanding this loop is crucial to habit modification and personal growth.[29]

ADOPT CONSCIOUS HABITS OF THRIVING: THE BODY

Your body, intricately synchronized with the mind and spirit, is a profound instrument in the deliberate and visual sculpting of your reality. Your present-day actions and behaviors offer a vivid behavioral glimpse into your internal sanctum (whether intended or not!). This is immediately perceptible to those around us because it is reflected in your facial expressions, posture, and words. Remember the *Jam Jar* and how others see the label.

In essence, as you STEP UP, your words and actions emerge as palpable pictures of your innermost Beliefs, feelings, and emotions. They represent the tangible state of your consciousness, which directs your experiences and leaves an indelible impact on others. When you intentionally STEP BACK and STEP TOGETHER, your behavior creates a pivotal thread in the tapestry of your conscious evolution.

As you consciously elevate your Awareness—this time by scrutinizing and analyzing your behaviors—you open up a realm of possibilities. This proactive conscious reflection empowers you to recalibrate your actions, which lets them them echo your ever-evolving mind and spirit. By intentionally substituting counterproductive habits with those that mirror your internal progression, you refine your body and transform it into an adept conduit for conscious creation. This ensures that the ME journey along PATH IV harmonizes seamlessly with your internal aspirations. And as these aspirations are steered by a purposively chosen vision of murmuration, your consciousness acquires the relentless compass of murmuration by which to navigate.

In this dynamic dance of consciousness, your body isn't merely a passive bystander that responds solely to the mind's directives or the spirit's yearnings. Instead, your body evolves as an engaged collaborator, a strong member of the *oneness*, in the conscious creation process that symbolizes your voyage through varying consciousness realms. It does not just highlight your individual metamorphosis; it also amplifies the collective rhythm and resonance of your unified existence.

THE INTERSECTION OF EMOTIONS AND BODY

The intricate relationship between your body and emotions has interested many scholars throughout the years. The **Cannon-Bard Theory of Emotion** suggests that your physiological response and your experience of an emotion are simultaneous events.[30]

Yet some theorists argue that your body's reaction to a situation preceded your emotional experience, which suggests that your choice to STEP UP, STEP BACK, or STEP TOGETHER is driven by your body. We lean toward this universal consensus: Emotions find expression within both your mind and body. And, unfortunately, in many cases, the *Jam Jar* gives others a front-row seat to your emotions as they observe your body's reactions. Many times, this is about missing the cue to STEP BACK or STEP TOGETHER.

To genuinely appreciate your body's role in conscious evolution, you must cultivate a keen sensitivity to your physical actions, habits, and reflexes.

Essential reflections include:

- Do your actions mirror your thoughts and the emotions you choose, or those chosen by subconscious, limiting Beliefs?
- Are your actions nourishing your growth journey and enhancing the well-being of your community?
- Do your actions genuinely resonate with your core values and ideals?
- Are you in the *Jam Jar* of your choosing?
- Again, take a moment to ask yourself: "What do I really want now?

A NEW PATH FOR SYLVIA

Here is a short, fictional story that illustrates how easy it is to default to subconscious action, and how important it is to both ME and WE to intentionally choose actions that resonate with your core values.

Sylvia, a dedicated consultant, enjoyed years of close collaboration with Simplex Jewelers. She formed deep friendships with Marjorie, the owner, and Louise, an employee. Shared lunches and social events made their bond strong. However, Sylvia's relocation for a new job led to a natural drift.

FIVE YEARS LATER

Marjorie invited Sylvia for a Christmas reunion:

Marjorie: "Sylvia, join us for Christmas! Louise will be here, too."

Sylvia: "I'd love to! See you on December 22."

However, Sylvia later discovered that Louise had been feeling "ghosted" by her absence. A surprised Sylvia realized her unintentional neglect had hurt Louise deeply.

STEPS TO RECONNECT

- **STEP UP:** Act responsibly and initiate meaningful action.
  - Discuss life changes proactively
  - Have a heartfelt conversation about the friendship's future
  - Be transparent in communication
- **STEP BACK:** Respond thoughtfully and allow space for others.
  - Listen and understand Louise's perspective
  - Give Louise the freedom to decide the friendship's course

- **STEP TOGETHER:** Support each other with respect.
  - Acknowledge the communication gap
  - Embrace vulnerability as a strength
  - Strengthen the bond through mutual understanding and forgiveness

Sylvia reflected and realized she must apologize and address the underlying issues. Moving from ME to WE involves understanding and addressing the impacts of humans' actions on others, and recognizing that every path, whether converging or diverging, is part of *Living in Choice*.

OUR PHYSIOLOGICAL RESPONSE HABIT: THE BODY SCAN

A *Body Scan* is more than just a moment of self-awareness; it's an intentional journey through your physical self. Starting from the crown of your head and descending to the tips of your toes, it encourages you to concentrate on each specific body part, and understand and acknowledge the sensations it hosts.

BENEFITS OF A BODY SCAN:

- **Bridge the Gap:** Strengthen the connection between your mind and body.
- **Spot the Tension:** Uncover hidden strains or stresses, sometimes in areas you wouldn't expect.
- **Alleviate Discomfort:** Recognize it so you can address and potentially release pain that might be amplifying certain emotions.

- **Enhance Mindfulness:** Be present in the moment and aware of your physical self.
- **Diminish Stress:** Find pockets of tension and consciously release them, which can lead to a more relaxed state.
- **Dismantle Negative Patterns:** Recognize and understand physical responses to help you navigate emotional thought distortions.

Research from multiple institutions, including the of California, Berkeley and the *Journal of Behavioral Medicine*, supports the efficacy of *Body Scans* in conjunction with practices like meditation and yoga, and highlights their roles in enhancing your self-awareness and well-being.

HOW TO DO A BODY SCAN

1. **START AT THE CROWN**: Begin your scan at the crown of your head, gradually focusing your attention downward toward your toes.

2. **NOTICE SENSATIONS**: Carefully observe sensations in each body part. Don't rush; spend a few moments on each area.

3. **ACKNOWLEDGE DISCOMFORT**: If you notice tension or discomfort, acknowledge it without judgment and imagine breathing space into it to release it.

4. **MOVE SEQUENTIALLY**: Continue moving your attention gradually down your body, part by part, until you reach your toes.

ADOPT CONSCIOUS HABITS OF THRIVING: THE SPIRIT

Diving deeper into the intricate layers of your emotions—after deciphering your subjective experience and understanding your physiological reactions—the third dimension comes into the spotlight: your behavioral response. Just like in the example with Sylvia and Louise, actions speak louder than words.

Behavioral response is the externalized echo of your emotions, and the spirit has to *want to* behave in a certain way, especially if the behavior is not a representation of that emotion. While your internal sensations and reactions remain cloistered within, your behavioral responses (your body) manifest outwardly and act as conduits of communication with the world around you. As you journey toward your purposeful inner vision of murmuration, the essence of STEPPING BACK becomes crucial. It's about *wanting to Live in Choice* and allowing others to *Live in Choice* regarding the messages you convey and the ripples you create. The spirit has to be motivated to make this choice.

Your mind, typically a silent observer, becomes particularly vocal at this juncture. Your present actions and reactions, intentional or not, become clear messages that broadcast your inner state from your body to those around you, whether in writing, in words, or in your observable behavior. As you STEP UP, the act of communication is realized. Yet STEPPING BACK—offering space, respect, and understanding—becomes pivotal for harmony. Sometimes, the most profound statement you can make is to allow others to hold their perceptions, even if they misconstrue your intentions or actions. This is the hallmark of an enlightened human being.

Consider this: Your silence, in response to a partner's message, might be a way of signaling disappointment. We often resort to such indirect methods of communication—whether through actions, inactions, body language, or tone of voice. It is another example of the *Jam Jar*. Active communication, however, is critical as you move from ME to WE. The starling knows that, and you must learn it, too. On-going communication is key when moving from ME to WE.

Communicating and articulating your feelings and thoughts through words or definitive actions is the answer. This blend of expressive avenues (thoughts to words and actions) that each person employs is termed their "communication style." Navigating this style can be an exercise in both STEPPING UP to express yourself and STEPPING BACK to honor another's boundaries and perceptions. Of course, you also may be communicating something in a passive manner. For instance, in the story told previously, Sylvia passively communicated to Louise that she, Sylvia, no longer had time for Louise. And Louise received the message and moved subconsciously out of the WE relationship.

OUR HABITUAL COMMUNICATION STYLES

The following communication styles, as outlined in the work of Dr. Robert A. Cooke's Human Synergistics, highlight how different behaviors and patterns impact team dynamics and personal interactions. Understanding these styles provides insight into how you can shift your communication for greater collective success.

Passive

When you adopt a passive communication style, your voice remains subdued, your sentiments unspoken. There is a retreat from articulating your genuine feelings, which often stems from deep-seated Beliefs or fears. This form of communication echoes the emotions of "flee" or "fawn," with the subconscious sounding a silent alarm to hint that survival could be under threat.

Aggressive

An aggressive communicative approach resonates with overpowering volume and intensity, and leaves little room for dialogue. This style, marked by demands, stems from rooted Beliefs and emotions that often stifle positive, collaborative interaction. The underlying emotional charge propels a "fight" response, which is driven by the subconscious perception that your very survival might be in jeopardy.

Passive-Aggressive

On the surface, passive-aggressive communication might seem subdued or neutral, but beneath it lies a tempest of restrained aggression. While there's an Awareness of personal needs and desires, they aren't conveyed transparently. Instead, cryptic cues hint at underlying turmoil. The subconscious is engaged in a delicate dance as it attempts to bridge the chasm between wanting to express and fearing alienation.

Constructive

The constructive style of communication is the epitome of genuine communication. This approach is both clear and compassionate. It exemplifies a harmony between intention and expression that ensures your words are both decisive and amiable.

If the style of communication is constructive, acceptance is most often assumed by the other person. Acceptance leads to better WE engagement and collaboration. This communication style, used by someone STEPPING UP, can ripple through the team members and enhance their respect and collective performance.

In the words of co-author Robin Graham, "It is about energy and nonverbal communication. The idea that one's energy precedes their words highlights the importance of nonverbal cues in leadership and teamwork." The famous African quote, "I am because we are," emphasizes the interconnectedness and collective identity in teams. Again, Graham says, "Our energy goes into the room quicker than we do." This highlights the impact of your energetic nonverbal communication and presence.

Recognizing the body's role in these communication styles is paramount to your progression on the ME pathway. Beyond the introspection of your thoughts and emotions, it's about connecting your physiological responses your physiological responses with actions that mirror your inner evolution. By weaving the body into this intricate tapestry of transformation, you ensure your quest for conscious creation embraces the triad of your existence: mind, body, and spirit.

While evolution implies a forward movement, it's also crucial to understand the immediate reactions that might sometimes pull you back. Remember that one such intrinsic response mechanism is the amygdala hijack. It holds you back from evolving.

Your Silent Navigator

Remember, your reactions to events aren't random; they're molded by patterns rooted deep within your subconscious. While this *silent navigator* often operates autonomously, you do have the power to chart its course.

> ### THE REST OF THE STORY
>
> *In a candid message to Louise, Sylvia shared her feelings:*
>
> *"I never intended to cause you pain. Realizing that you felt 'ghosted' deeply saddens me. My life has been marked by significant challenges—the early loss of my father, the heartbreaking loss of my son, and personal health battles, including cancer. In these times of loss, my instinct was to withdraw and immerse myself in work as a way of coping.*
>
> *This habit of retreating often left me feeling isolated and disconnected. From the outside, it might have seemed like I was intentionally neglecting our friendship, but it was really a reflection of my struggle to cope.*
>
> *I understand this may have created a perception of abandonment, and for that I am truly sorry. It was never about you; it was about how I handled my pain. My journey has been one of love, joy, and sorrow, and I'm now trying to forge a new path.*
>
> *I sincerely hope for self-forgiveness and your understanding. Wishing you all the best, Louise."*

In this chapter, you ventured into the depths of your internal global workplace—mind, body, and spirit. By understanding that your cells can be reprogrammed with the power of your conscious mind's intention, your body's courage, and your spirit's passion, you explored how habitual conscious actions shape your experiences and interactions. Recognizing the role of your spirit—the deep-seated *want to* that drives transformation—you learned to harmonize these elements through Awareness, Belief adaptation, and meaningful Connections. This alignment not only fosters personal growth but also paves the way for collective thriving, which embodies the essence of murmuration.

YOUR TURN: MOMENT OF REFLECTION

REFLECT ON ALIGNMENT:

1. **WHEN HAVE I FELT A TRUE SENSE OF HARMONY** within myself?

2. **WHAT PATTERNS EMERGE** in these moments?

3. **WHAT BELIEFS** are beneath those patterns?

JOURNAL YOUR INSIGHTS:

4. **AS MEMORIES OF ALIGNMENT SURFACE,** jot them down.

5. **REMEMBER THE STRENGTH YOU BROUGHT** to these moments and the gifts you received from these experiences.

MEDITATE FOR CLARITY:

6. **MEDITATION CAN OFFER A CLEARER LENS** to observe your inner world.

7. **FOCUS ON THOSE INGRAINED PATTERNS** that foster alignment and positive thoughts, which enhance your journey toward mind, body, and spirit coherence.

How-to Skills: see pages 313–316 for more information

Adaptability Quotient (AQ)®
Body Scan
Footlights of Consciousness
Jam Jar
Laying New Snow
Pause, Notice, and Choose
Servant Leadership
The xchange Approach

Global Thought Leaders: see pages 317–320 for more information

Ross Thornley
Jack Lowe, Jr.

CHAPTER 5

INTEGRATING MIND, BODY, AND SPIRIT

A complex system is far from equilibrium. Small islands of coherence in a sea of chaos have the capacity to shift the entire system to a higher order.

—Illya Prigognine

IN THE PREVIOUS CHAPTERS, YOU EXPLORED THE PROFOUND IMPACT OF THE INTERCONNECTEDNESS OF THE MIND, BODY, AND SPIRIT, which will now be referred to to as the *Integrated Mindset*. The journey inward to integrate these facets of ME is essential for fostering a coherent and balanced existence. By examining the dynamics between these elements, you uncover the potential for personal transformation and collective elevation. Consider the mind as your inner thoughts, feelings, and attitudes; body as the avenue to move the inner to the external with behaviors and actions; and the spirit as the connection beyond self which brings about an interweaving with others.

Understanding how these components interact allows you to harness your inner strength, adapt your Beliefs, and ultimately contribute to a harmonious and thriving community as you move from ME to WE to US. In Chapters 3 and 4, you have been on the inner journey of understanding ME. You have dissected ME into mind, body, and spirit, and have been led along by the belief that you—an individual ME—can *Live in choice*. There have been suggestions along the way that ME must be prepared and willing to address Beliefs and adapt to new perspectives. Chapters 5 and 6 provide you with the knowledge necessary to understand your Beliefs and shift your perspectives.

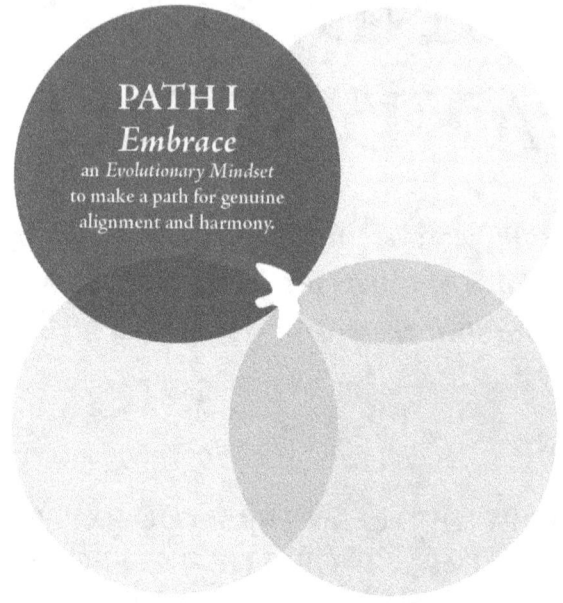

©2024 ABC's of Murmuration

PATH I

Embrace an Evolutionary Mindset

At the heart of the discussion of Beliefs and adapting to new perspectives is the concept of Integrated Mindset: a seamless blending of mind, body, and spirit that includes thoughts, feelings, emotions, logical analysis, and intuitive insight. It brings together all aspects of the individual, of ME, to enhance adaptability, creativity, decision-making, and problem-solving skills. Integrated Mindset is a balanced state that accesses both the logical and creative processing capacities of your mind, body, and spirit. When all are engaged, there is measurable **brain coherency**, which allows you to think clearly, be more effective, and see new perspectives.

What is a coherent feeling? A sense of coherence has been defined as a global orientation toward life that involves cognitive, behavioral, and motivational elements and is expressed in the belief that the world is comprehensible, manageable, and meaningful.

You (as a ME) have your own personal past experiences and perceptions that impact your decisions and actions in every aspect of your life. These merge and combine to create Beliefs about your sense of self and capabilities. When your personal perception is that "nothing I do will be good enough," that impacts your effectiveness across all interactions and activities. Awareness of your underlying belief of "not good enough" can help you focus and apply efforts to accomplish tasks more effectively. However, the energy it takes to repetitively overcome this limiting belief blocks you from having the freedom to use that energy in other creative ways. When the shift has been made to an Integrated Mindset then the conflict thought being fed by "not good enough" is relegated to a whisper, or not heard at all. This frees you up to broaden your perspective for decision making and lets you choose whether or not to act.

Reshaping entrenched Beliefs and adapting to new perspectives can awaken dormant creative potential. This transformation is not limited to personal growth; it enhances interpersonal relationships, professional achievements, and your ability to navigate the complexities of life. This is why it is critical for every ME to have an Integrated Mindset. This mindset allows a single ME to adapt and expand outward to form an integrated WE and, ultimately, a cohesive US.

When a congruent ME joins another as a WE, the group is aligned and moves together. The flow and exploration of ideas and agreement created by the WE provide the best action to take. One congruent ME merging with another congruent ME is what creates the WE success. In embracing this *Evolutionary Mindset*, you not only unlock your full potential as individuals, but you also synergize your efforts to achieve unprecedented collective success as WE and US. This shift of mindset on your part, plus the understanding of its power to shift Beliefs, is evolutionary for each individual.

As you move forward, you'll delve deeper into the practical steps that each ME can take to create this integration and contribute to the collective WE and US.

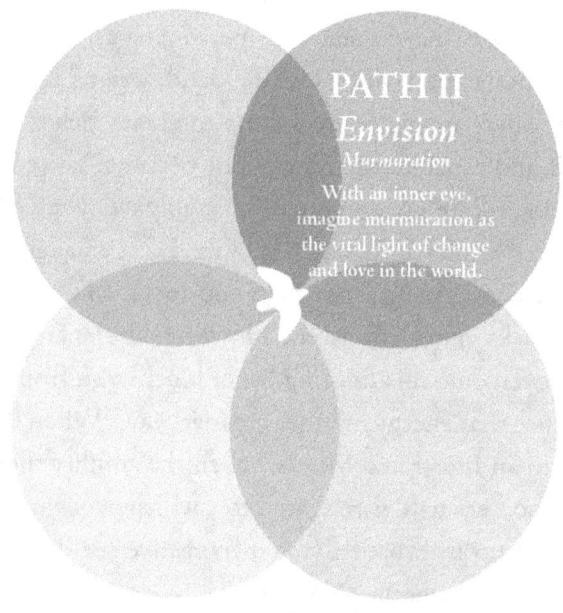

©2024 ABC's of Murmuration

PATH II

Envision Murmuration

Drawing inspiration from the natural phenomenon of starlings' murmuration, you find a profound metaphor for human community and organizational behavior. These birds represent a blending of mind, body, and spirit to demonstrate unity, adaptability, and collective wisdom; qualities essential in human systems. Through this book, you will explore how Awareness, Belief adaptation, and the art of Connectivity mirror these natural occurrences. The lessons drawn from these graceful avian displays provide valuable insights into enhancing human interactions, *Servant Leadership*, and community dynamics. Understanding the principles of murmuration in nature provides the model for the vision needed to create a more cohesive and adaptable human system, whether in teams, communities, or organizations, and it all starts with all starts with the individual ME. The foundation of unity is you. Having an Integrated Mindset, or an Integrated Mindset, or an alignment of mind, body, and spirit, expands your potential to be the best ME to engage with others by using an expansive approach.

©2024 ABC's of Murmuration

PATH III

Explore and Walk a New Way

Making conscious choices to navigate the journey of the starlings and *Walk a New Way* enables each ME to continue evolving. You can adopt these choices by using:

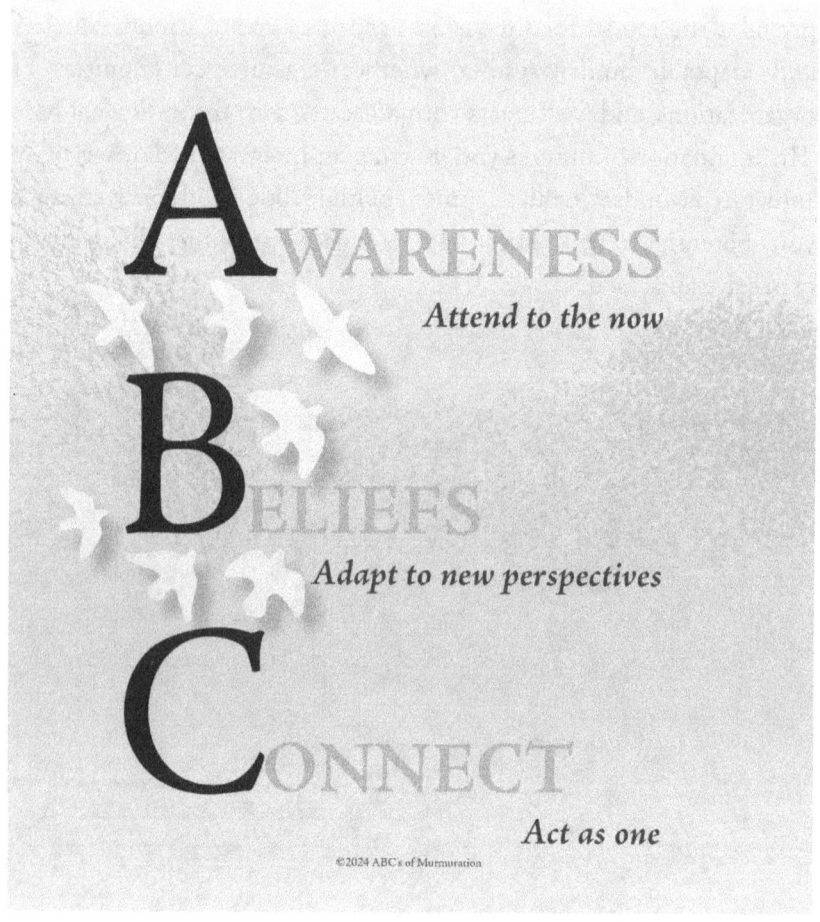

Next, look at how adopting an Integrated Mindset helps ME apply the *ABC's of Murmuration* across a variety of situations.

AWARENESS: ATTEND TO THE NOW

All change begins with the recognition or Awareness that there is a feeling, behavior, or experience that is uncomfortable or creates an issue. Once you are aware, then you can reflect on what you would rather experience and choose how to adapt to support that new option.

If you have a fear of being the focus of attention due to a previous humiliating experience, then you may be narrowly focused on not being "seen." This limits any capacity to express your thoughts or STEP UP. Basically, you are still humiliated, and it is hard for you to take the initiative and show up. If, however, you transform the previous experience into a new perspective (one that no longer humiliates you), you are able to STEP UP, speak up, or accept a new project. And, as a bonus, you are able to expand your horizons to see new ways of engaging with others, especially to STEP BACK to allow others to STEP UP. When you have the Awareness of what was holding you back from taking the initiative, then you can apply the Integrated Mindset approach that will be expanded upon in this chapter and the next one.

BELIEFS: ADAPT TO A NEW PERSPECTIVE

Your Beliefs and perceptions—many of which are formed in early childhood—dictate the narrative of your life. Based on your Beliefs, your mind perceives a stimulus as friend or foe and your body then responds accordingly. In this way, Beliefs link two key components of Integrated Mindset, the mind and the body. They are extremely powerful forces in your life.

The placebo effect—most well-known in drug research—is when a pill or solution believed to be an active drug creates the expected impact even though what was given was inert. The opposite is also true, a phenomenon called the nocebo effect. If you believe something will be harmful, it will be. These two well-documented effects illustrate how powerful belief can be in practice.

In *The Biology of Belief*, Dr. Bruce H. Lipton shared, "Our positive and negative Beliefs not only impact our health, but also every aspect of our life... Your Beliefs act like filters on a camera, changing how you see the world. And your biology adapts to those Beliefs."[31]

The following story is an example of how internal perceptions and Beliefs can create a physical reaction.

UNLOCKING NEW POSSIBILITIES THROUGH PERCEPTION

The subconscious mind forms connections that are often beneficial, but occasionally they can lead to adverse outcomes.

Graham's client, whom we'll call Sam for confidentiality, revealed that he had avoided bananas for more than a decade. Sam had relished bananas for most of his life, but one day, he suffered a severe bout of sickness that lasted for eight hours after consuming one. Following multiple similar episodes, he identified bananas as the common factor. Despite his efforts to avoid them, he occasionally ingested them unknowingly in shakes or salads, leading to repeated illness.

Using Graham's expertise with PSYCH-K® (for more information on this modality, see subsequent pages as well as the PSYCH-K® reference page at the back of the book), Graham and Sam worked on altering the stress associated with bananas and the related illness. During the process, Sam had an epiphany: His aversion to bananas started concurrently with his unwelcome divorce.

While the subconscious does an amazing job with operating the physical body, it can also perceive something as a threat, i.e. a spouse leaving, and then establish a possible protection behavior, i.e. getting ill. In this case, the situation included eating a banana. Sam had formed a subconscious Belief that being ill might prevent his spouse from leaving, a Belief he realized may have originated during a moment involving a banana. Consequently, eating bananas triggered his sickness. Even though the divorce proceeded and the illness didn't prevent it, his banana intolerance persisted.

After undergoing the PSYCH-K® process to reframe his perspective on bananas and, symbolically, his ex-spouse, Sam felt prepared to challenge his aversion. Just five minutes after completing the process, Sam faced a banana. For years, merely touching or smelling a banana would cause his lips to tingle, and tasting one would quickly lead to illness. Sam held the banana, smelled it, and peeled it, and remarked on his lack of adverse reaction. Bravely, he took a bite and experienced no ill effects.

This breakthrough happened years ago and since then, Sam has been able to enjoy bananas without fear. The PSYCH-K® process not only allowed him to enjoy bananas again but also demonstrated the powerful impact of reshaping your perceptions on your interactions with the world. Sam's shift in belief about himself, which occurred in his mind, created a change in how his body reacted. And together, those two changes freed up new space for his spirit to expand. He is well on his way to adopting an Integrated Mindset.

The majority of your perceptions about yourself were established prior to the age of 7. However, over the past few years, **neuroplasticity** research has revealed that your capacity to adapt is a constant throughout your life. It is exciting to realize that you are not a victim of your past experiences or decisions! You have the ability to make new choices and change your perspectives about yourself, a group you are Connected with, and the greater potential of everyone. By *Walking a New Way* and applying the foundation of Beliefs adaptation, ME can flow to WE and WE can flow to US so connection can occur.

CONNECT: ACT AS ONE

The starling murmuration is made up of individual birds, many ME's. They are aware of each other and aware that they are part of a whole. It can be easy to forget that your individual action can ripple out to impact others in your community, yet it does. This demonstrates the interconnection you have with each other even when you are not aware.

Imagine that a manager decided to share an internal document about project A with a trusted friend who didn't work for her company, knowing it would help that friend prepare for a critical meeting. It did. However, while the trusted friend was preparing for a different meeting, he asked a *different* manager for a similar internal document about project B, explaining that the first manager gave him a document referencing project A. The second manager felt pressure to comply, and provided the trusted friend with an internal document for project B. And then the scenario repeated a third time.

However this time, the "trusted friend" of the first manager asked a managing director for documents on project C and was denied. The managing director said, "No, I can't do that. It's an internal-only document for project C and not intended to be freely provided to an external person, friend or not." The concern is that this sets a risky precedent: If internal documents are shared externally when requested by a "trusted friend," it's possible that the "trusted friend" would do the same to help a friend of *theirs* who is entirely unconnected with the organization. Policy gets further eroded, internal information spreads, and trust is broken.

The first manager was thinking of helping her friend and did not consider the larger impact and ripple effect of providing the initial document about project A. The second manager felt pressured to follow what had been established as an acceptable practice by a colleague. It took the managing director's input to end the cycle.

What insight can you glean from this story? When the original decision was made from a limited viewpoint—with the main intention to be helpful—the broader impacts were not considered. When

Integrated Mindset is engaged, decisions are expanded beyond the immediate situation and players; all future impacts are considered. When you are relaxed and accessing an Integrated Mindset, you are able to process information with an analytical, detailed view; recall experiences from your past; access creative opportunities for the future; and see the holistic impact of a decision. You would ask yourself, "How does this decision impact other managers, clients, and the organization?" When you consider a decision within a broader viewpoint, you can clearly see if the decision is based on the limited perspective of one person, or if it actually is best for everyone.

©2024 ABC's of Murmuration

PATH IV

Engage in Conscious Habits of Thriving

Chapter 5: Integrating Mind, Body, and Spirit

Personal growth begins with introspection. It is critical to understand how your internal dialogue shapes personal development and your external relationships. By recognizing and transforming limiting Beliefs and the experiences they create, you will expand your Awareness, which opens you up to new perspectives and possibilities. This process is also essential for fostering more meaningful connections with others.

You have internal perceptions and Beliefs that impact your behaviors and actions. *Some common individual blocks include:*

- not being good enough
- not feeling safe
- fear of rejection or humiliation
- powerlessness
- lack of trust in self and/or others
- not wanting to succeed beyond what parents presented as an example
- the feeling of not belonging

Let's look at the impact of Beliefs on taking action with the *Conscious Habits of Thriving*:

STEP UP
Initiate the first action

STEP BACK
Allow others to STEP UP

STEP TOGETHER
Embrace mutual trust and respect

©2024 ABC's of Murmuration

STEP UP: INITIATE THE FIRST ACTION

It is challenging to navigate your external environment if your focus is on how others perceive you. Preoccupation with the opinions of others creates actions based on fear, and thus self-protection. This fear of being rejected limits your ability to share ideas, express disagreements, and trust others to support you.

By embracing an Integrated Mindset, each ME can become less fearful and more open to collaboration. Remember the murmuration: The initial starling, seen in your terms as a servant leader, STEPS UP and moves up for the benefit of the other six team members. They are functioning with Awareness of the present and the belief that they must use adaptation to protect the group.

Examples of Limiting Self-Perceptions or Beliefs that Impact STEP UP:	Possible replacement Beliefs to support STEP UP:
No matter what I do, it is never good enough.	I do my best and my best is good enough.
If people knew the "real" me, they wouldn't like me.	Being who I am invites people to accept and like me as I am.
I can't trust people to support me. All they really care about is themselves.	I trust that as I support others, they will trust and support me.

©2024 ABC's of Murmuration

STEP BACK: ALLOW OTHERS TO STEP UP

As servant leaders, there are times when you must recognize that others may in a better position to navigate a situation or engage individuals for impact. It is critical to explore your own Beliefs about taking the initiative inherent to *Servant Leadership*. Does leadership mean "making all the decisions"? You may initially respond, "Of course it doesn't," but consider what level of decisions you invite others to make. Are you making room for the people around you to lead and grow? STEPPING BACK and supporting others to STEP UP to initiate and take responsibility is one of the skills that defines a great servant leader.

Examples of Limiting Self-Perceptions or Beliefs that Impact STEP BACK:	Possible replacement Beliefs to support STEP BACK:
I can't trust others.	I can trust others to do their best.
I have to control this because then I have power and that is the only way to succeed.	Collaborating and working with others creates greater success than doing it all by myself.
I blame others (boss, coworkers, partner, etc.) for my problems.	I take responsibility for the outcomes that I impact.

©2024 ABC's of Murmuration

STEP TOGETHER: EMBRACE MUTUAL TRUST AND RESPECT

In order to STEP TOGETHER, you must feel that you belong. If you have a perception that you are disrespected, not accepted, and don't belong, then becoming Connected is impossible. If you believe you can achieve more by yourself and must shine above others, then the potential for cooperation and collaboration is lost.

There is a widely held belief that competition is the way to survive and thrive. However, that is not true, even in nature. Individuals who are most adaptable and work together have shown the highest sustainability. This, of course, includes the starlings. It's worth noting that the word "competition" was originally derived from two Latin root words that mean "to strive together." Humans have wandered far from that definition now, and adopted one that pits people against each other instead of encouraging collaboration.

As you explore ways to STEP TOGETHER and thrive as a collective, you can look instead to the traditional African concept of Ubuntu. It roughly means "humanity toward others" or "I am because we are." This philosophy emphasizes the interconnectedness of all individuals and their mutual responsibilities toward each other and toward their environment. Ubuntu represents the spirit of

STEPPING TOGETHER with harmony based on mutual trust and respect for each other.

Examples of Limiting Self-Perceptions or Beliefs that Impact STEP TOGETHER:	Possible replacement Beliefs to support STEP TOGETHER:
I can get more done and done better by myself.	The potential results are expanded when everyone works within their capacity.
Others disrespect me because they disagree with me.	Disagreements with me show respect of my ability to explore various options.
Unless I am seen as the leader, then I am a failure.	My strength as a leader is demonstrated when I STEP BACK so others can be recognized, which allows all of us to STEP TOGETHER.

©2024 ABC's of Murmuration

As you review the transition from limiting Beliefs to supportive Beliefs to STEP UP, STEP BACK, and STEP TOGETHER, you may wonder how it is possible to create and sustain these new Beliefs. We have found that PSYCH-K® is a solution.

A BRIEF INTRODUCTION TO PSYCH-K®

A methodology that is effective, efficient, and expansive is PSYCH-K®. This is a transformational method that encourages the internal congruency referred to as an Integrated Mindset regarding areas of conflict, resistance, and struggle. Often the results of using PSYCH-K® are expressed as finding an inner confidence, experiencing an openness and calmness, and accessing ease with others based in compassion. When you establish internal congruency, then navigating the external environment is smoother. More will be shared about the foundations of PSYCH-K® in Chapter 6.

The following story is an example of what occurs when limiting Beliefs are rewritten into supportive ones.

SELF-DOUBT SHIFTS TO TEAM TRUST

An international director, Francis (not her real name), had been placed in a new city with an established local team. She discovered that her own self-doubt was impacting her leadership and thus preventing her team from trusting her. She felt the team did not want her there; that they wanted the previous director who they knew and understood how to work with. During a private coaching session, she realized that her own self-doubt as a leader was impacting her ability to bring the team together under her leadership.

Through the private sessions, Francis was able to identify several areas limiting her. They included a past experience of rejection and failure, along with her own doubts about whether or not she was the best candidate for this position. Using an Integrated Mindset process of PSYCH-K®, she transformed her perception about herself, released the past experience, and gained self-confidence.

She discovered that when she was internally relaxed and confident, she stopped trying to do what she assumed was best for the team and instead explored with them what they saw as the best way to accomplish the group's goals. Some on the team leaped in and engaged immediately, while others were more cautious and watched if this shift would "last." Within a short time, they saw the collaboration and impact that the rest of the group was now experiencing and let go of their resistance so they could participate fully.

YOUR EVOLUTION WITH INTEGRATED MINDSET

This chapter has highlighted the profound capacity ME has for adaption of Beliefs, the ripple effect that ME choices have on the surrounding world, and the realization that you are the architect of your own reality. Each individual has varied levels of understanding of themselves, which means that multiple approaches to moving into an Integrated Mindset may be helpful.

Some of the simplest approaches to start are:

- **Ask for feedback** about how you are perceived in various situations. Remember, the *Jam Jar*. You are asking others to read and share the label they see on your jar of jam.

- **Allow the observer part of yourself** to determine if you are reacting instantly or taking the time to consider a conscious response. Practice becoming aware of and reading the label on your own *Jam Jar*.

- **Explore and expand your perspective.** Your approach to achieving a task may not be the only way. Be curious about how someone else might achieve the same end result but by a different approach. For example, putting a bookcase together can be done by reading the instructions, looking at the provided images for guidance, or pulling from past experience and knowledge to complete the task.

In addition, there are many assessments available to understand yourself and gain insights into your team. Assessments such as *Adaptability Quotient* from AQai®, DISC for behavioral styles, Values or Motivator insights, and others. These assessments assist in expanding your understanding and acceptance that other styles have value beyond what you bring. Gaining a greater appreciation for each other brings you into an Integrated Mindset.

As mentioned above, the methodology thought to be as most effective, efficient, and expansive is PSYCH-K®. For additional information about applying PSYCH-K® to establish supportive Beliefs and perspectives, visit the website ABCsofMurmuration.com.

This chapter is about how critical each ME is when joining into a group (WE). Here you will explore the impact of connection between ME and WE.

INDIVIDUAL CONTRIBUTION IN TEAMS AND COMMUNITIES

Overcoming personal barriers and shifting perspectives are both practices that are key to fostering cooperative and dynamic team environments. This extends to the practical application of an Integrated Mindset principles as you move between ME, WE, and US.

To further explore how the individual contribution impacts a collective murmuration, you can draw from quantum science. There is a proven concept of quantum *entanglement* within quantum science. Described simply, this is a researched phenomenon in which individual particles are impacted at the same time even when they are miles apart. The individual connection is beyond physical touch. When watching the starlings in a murmuration, there is no physical touch, yet thousands of birds move together by some unseen connection. In this book's terms, the ME Connects as a WE then moves seamlessly as the US. This is the spirit of interconnection.

Take the expanded perspective that everything is energy—including your thoughts—then everyone is interconnected with each other beyond what currently can be measured. Consider that your perception of a co-worker will impact how you interact with your co-worker, and their perception of you will impact how they interact with you.

If two guitars are next to each other and you pluck the A string on one, the vibration/frequency/energy will activate the A string on the other. If you put your finger on the first guitar's A string and stop it, within a short time the vibration/frequency/energy from the second guitar's A string will re-activate the A string on the first guitar. They impact each other.

With murmuration, each individual has a direct role in influencing the flow, harmony, and impact of the group because each individual is part of the whole. Just like a drop of water from the ocean is still part of the ocean. Erwin Schrödinger, a founder of quantum mechanics, stated, "The total number of minds in the universe is one." You are part of the whole of humanity, and as an individual you impact the whole. And thus you can facilitate better collaboration, innovation, and collective growth in various community contexts.

EXPLORING PRACTICAL APPLICATIONS: AN INTERVIEW WITH AN EXPERT THOUGHT LEADER

To illustrate the practical application of these concepts, here is an interview with an expert, who talks about how the success or health of a community is impacted by each individual.

> **INTERVIEW WITH DUCCIO LOCATI, D.O.**
> *Director of PSYCH-K® International and PSYCH-K® Instructor*
>
> Full interview available at ABCsofMurmuration.com

"In the corporate environment, we tend to think the individual is just a human being thinking about their job. They're not. If the individual has a conflict at home, the energy of this conflict will be brought into the job environment, which affects the performances of the individual (ME), the colleagues (WE), and the whole company, its products, customers, etc. (US). The company is like a living organism composed of many cells (the multiple ME). The organism is healthy if all the cells are healthy. So, the success of a company can be sustainable and exponential only if the individuals and the society are healthy."[32]

—Duccio Locati

Integrating these principles into your daily interactions and team dynamics can lead to a more cohesive and innovative community, where each individual's contribution is valued and amplified.

MOVING FROM A BROAD EXPLANATION TO A DEEPER ONE

As you approach the end of this chapter, you are just beginning to uncover the depth of understanding that individual transformation and collective rhythms offer. The insights and experiences shared here pave the way for a journey into a more profound understanding of how these concepts interplay. In the pages ahead, rich insights and practical approaches await, highlighting the significance of an Integrated Mindset and its impact on both personal and collective realms. This journey aims to guide you toward a more integrated self and a deeper connection with the world.

YOUR TURN: MOMENT OF REFLECTION

As you reflect on the content of this chapter, consider how the concepts of STEP UP, STEP BACK, and STEP TOGETHER apply to your own experiences and Beliefs. These reflective questions are designed to help you identify limiting Beliefs and replace them with expansive ones, which supports your growth and transformation as a servant leader.

Reflection Questions for STEP UP:

1. WHAT BELIEFS DO YOU HAVE that limit your capacity to STEP UP?

2. HOW COULD YOU CHANGE THEM so you can support yourself in STEPPING UP?

Reflection Questions for STEP BACK:

1. WHAT BELIEFS DO YOU HAVE that limit your capacity to STEP BACK?

2. HOW COULD YOU CHANGE THEM so you can support yourself in STEPPING BACK?

Reflection Questions for STEP TOGETHER:

1. WHAT BELIEFS DO YOU HAVE that limit your capacity to STEP TOGETHER?

2. HOW COULD YOU CHANGE THEM so you can support yourself in STEPPING TOGETHER?

How-to Skills: see pages 313–316 for more information

Jam Jar
Servant Leadership

Global Thought Leaders: see pages 317–320 for more information

Bruce H. Lipton
Duccio Locati

PSYCH-K®: see pages 321–322 for more information

CHAPTER 6

INTEGRATING THE POWER OF YOUR INNER ADAPTABILITY

It is time we heed the wisdom of the ancient indigenous people and channel our consciousness and spirit to tend the garden and not destroy it.

—Bruce H. Lipton, Ph.D.

AS YOU DEEPEN YOUR UNDERSTANDING OF THE FOUR-PATH JOURNEY, YOU RECOGNIZE THE POWERFUL INFLUENCE OF YOUR SUBCONSCIOUS BELIEFS AND HOW THEY SHAPE YOUR REALITY. In this chapter, you will expand on Walkway I: ME, and explore how adapting your Beliefs is essential for personal and collective evolution. Understanding the intricate dance between your thoughts and physical responses, and how to leverage the power of both, can help you create a harmonious and effective path forward. Embracing the principles of Integrated Mindset and neuroplasticity, you unlock the potential within you, which paves the way for personal growth and collective success. This journey from ME to WE to US is grounded in the belief that transforming your inner world can profoundly impact the larger community.

In Chapter 5, you had an overview of how Beliefs fit into the *ABC's of Murmuration*. This chapter aims to dive deeper into this topic to broaden your understanding of your innate potential. The authors have found that the method of PSYCH-K® is a game-changer to cultivate an Integrated Mindset by transforming Beliefs and adapting new perspectives. PSYCH-K® blends elements of psychology, neuroscience, kinesiology, and spirituality to facilitate profound changes in self-perception and worldview. This methodology also engages both the conscious and subconscious minds to develop new neural connections, thereby aligning your subconscious Beliefs with your conscious aspirations. This approach helps identify and modify ingrained Beliefs that may be limiting you, and alters your automatic reactions toward more intentional and empowering behaviors. By adjusting your Beliefs and perspectives, you create a more harmonious and fulfilling life for yourself and others, while you also contribute to the well-being and unity of the collective.

FROM BELIEF TO BEHAVIORAL CHANGE

Your Beliefs form the foundation of your thoughts and your habitual behaviors. By modifying these Beliefs, you can consequently alter your experiences, which ultimately leads to shifts in your perspectives and behavioral habits. Recognizing and intentionally emphasizing or de-emphasizing certain Beliefs can significantly influence your experiences and the communities you create by changing your behaviors with them. This understanding empowers you to smoothly transition from individual perspectives (ME) to collective Beliefs (WE) and eventually to unified actions (US).

By identifying your thought patterns and emotions, you become equipped to make conscious behavioral choices. Realizing you have the power to shift perspectives and rewire your mental frameworks allows you to manifest transformation in your world. Individually, remember that embracing an *Evolutionary Mindset* can spark profound changes in WE and in US as you move toward your vision of murmuration.

However, understanding isn't enough. To achieve tangible results, it's crucial that you integrate this newfound knowledge into your actions. Individuals and organizations invest heavily in training programs to replace outdated habits with innovative methodologies. Yet, as studies reveal, this investment often doesn't correlate with anticipated success. The traditional approach to training—even with strategies to enhance retention—are often inadequate for ensuring long-term habit change.[33] There must be an innovative change methodology for individuals so their limiting and fear-based Beliefs and habits can be shifted, which impacts ME engaging with WE and US. The authors use the PSYCH-K® method for effective change.

To draw an analogy, consider a diverse food buffet. You approach it with established preferences that are influenced by past experiences. However, trying something unfamiliar might introduce you to a new favorite dish. Similarly, you are invited to be open-minded and explore uncharted avenues for transformative change.

MASTERING THE DUO OF MINDSET AND SKILLSET

In your journey to transform yourself (and consequently your environment), you must first understand the pivot points of this transformation: mindset and skillset. As has been stated in previous chapters, the aim is to inspire a change within the individual (ME) to bring together mind, body, and spirit as a coherent Integrated Mindset. This, in turn, ripples outward to influence the collective (WE). This combination of mindset and skillset gives birth to an environment that nurtures growth and transformation for everyone involved (US). This environment can be as public as your workplace or as intimate as your home.

The magnitude of this change can be gauged by the heightened experience both with internal emotions and in external behaviors. How do you impact these outcomes? *Here are three possible approaches:*

Rethinking Repetitive Actions

The age-old saying, "Insanity is doing the same thing over and over again and expecting different results," remains true today. Sticking to repeated actions—out of mere comfort or paralyzing fear—will not herald a new era of outcomes. A change in direction is essential. To experience renewed results, you must revolutionize your thinking and reimagine your words and behaviors.

The Art of Working Smarter

Another popular mantra is, "Try and try until you succeed." While the sentiment is commendable, the application is often misguided. The perception that burning the midnight oil or stretching your limits will inherently result in superior results is a fallacy. Instead of pressing harder, it's imperative to be more effective, more curious, and smarter. Seek innovative and imaginative avenues to notch up sustainable success.

Mindset and Skillset

A prevalent perspective is that to uplift your results, you need to upscale your skills through extra training or by adopting new methodologies. But let's reflect on those times when you were well aware of *how to* do something and yet you faltered. Out of avoidance, procrastination, or just blatant oversight—often dubbed as self-sabotage. These aren't birthed from a lack of skillset. These are the offspring of your mindset, the *want to* of your actions. Your lack of *want to* about new and different approaches hampers your ability to change your habits and behaviors. Hence, while skillsets equip you, it's mindsets that truly empower you to utilize those skills to their utmost potential. However, it is also imperative that you *want to* or have the internal motivation to make changes to upgrade your results. Remember, motivation is about "trying to win" rather than "trying not to lose."

The following sections will explore the intricate dance between mindset and skillset, and will provide strategies to seamlessly integrate them for optimal impact.

UNLOCKING EFFECTIVE MINDSET AND SKILLS

According to Mahzarin R. Banaji, Max H. Bazerman, and Dolly Chugh, "We doubt that a well-intentioned just-try-harder approach will fundamentally improve the quality of executives' decision making…training must be broadened to include what is now known about how our minds work, and must expose managers directly to the unconscious mechanisms that underlie decision making."[34]

Combining mindset and skillset offers a unique perspective on the potential impact individuals can have. The quadrant below is the result of Graham's four-plus decades of consulting and coaching. She first presented the following information during an educational session at a business conference.

Here are the key terms and definitions for the chart below:

TERMINOLOGY FOR MINDSET AND SKILLSET

MINDSET:

- **Definition:** Your *want to* and inner attitude.

- **Components:** Thoughts about yourself and others, Beliefs in your capabilities, and confidence in applying the necessary skills.

SKILLSET:

- **Definition:** Your *how to*.
- **Components:** Skills related to technical situations, human interactions, or conceptual processes like problem-solving or collaboration.

REFERENCE CHART

VERTICAL AXIS:

- **Integrated Mindset:**

    Definition: An aligned combination of Beliefs, thoughts, feelings, and emotions.

    Outcome: Empowers you to be congruent with your words and behaviors.

- **Divided Mindset:**

    Definition: Inner conflict that stems from doubts and limiting perspectives.

    Outcome: Can cause turmoil during decision-making and action, often leading to self-sabotage and conflicting behaviors.

HORIZONTAL AXIS:

Definition: Represents skillset, varying from low to high based on your level of experience or expertise.

Outcome: Impacts capability of achieving results.

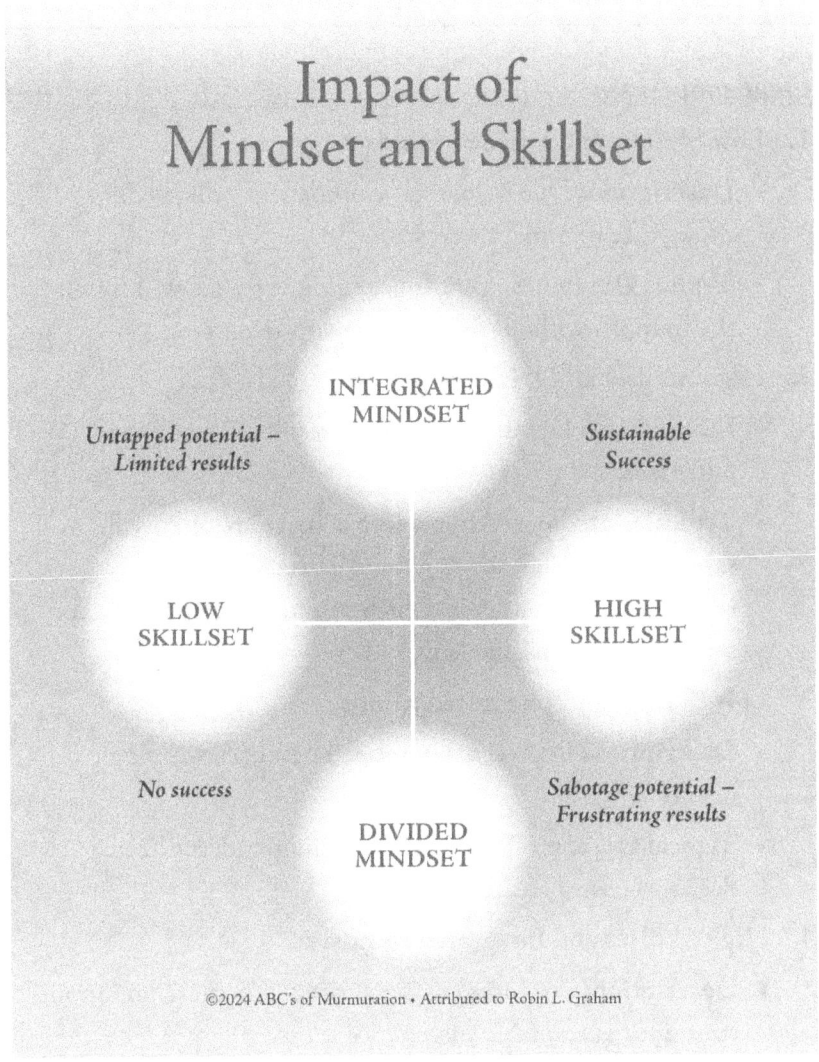

The concept for this graphic was developed by co-author Robin Graham.

Let's look at the impact of the four quadrant areas, which emphasize how critical mindset and skillset are to sustainable success:

INTERSECTION OF MINDSET AND SKILLSET

Quadrant Areas

1. **Low Skillset and Divided Mindset**
   - **Description:** Due to low self-confidence, individuals experience minimal success.
   - **Typical Outcomes:** Quitting, getting fired, going through the motions without progress, impact, or results.

2. **High Skillset and Divided Mindset**
   - **Description:** Low self-confidence results in frustrating outcomes.
   - **Typical Outcomes:** Attempts to achieve are often self-sabotaged, which leads to failure. This creates a cycle of resistance to trying again, which results in more failure and self-protection mechanisms.

3. **Low Skillset and Integrated Mindset**
   - **Description:** Represents untapped potential with limited results.
   - **Typical Outcomes:** Frustration, feeling underutilized, desire to have a greater impact.

4. **High Skillset and Integrated Mindset**
   - **Description:** Produces greater success and, more importantly, continued sustainable success.
   - **Typical Outcomes:** Engaged and using a leaderful approach with a willingness to learn, adapt, and collaborate with others.

MINDSET OVER SKILLSET: INSIGHTS FROM IBM RESEARCH

An IBM white paper titled *Making Change Happen* highlighted the significant challenges affecting project management outcomes. The study reveals that 58 percent of these challenges stem from mindset-related issues, and of those, 49 percent can be attributed to corporate culture, which is essentially a reflection of the collective group's mindset.[35]

Thus, the majority of the time, it is mindset that impacts success, not skillset alone.

This underscores the profound influence of mindset compared to skillset. Often, skillset is categorized as a "hard skill," whereas mindset falls under the "soft skill" umbrella. A frequently heard sentiment in the business realm is, "The soft stuff is often the hardest to change." The *ABC's of Murmuration* introduces you to new approaches that make changing the soft stuff surprisingly easy. The following exercise invites you to experience how you are hardwired to respond to something, yet the "soft skills" of Awareness give you an option to choose differently.

BEHAVIOR: HARDWIRED AND INSTINCTUAL REACTIONS

You might believe you're fully in tune with each of your behaviors, but let's explore that idea. *Try this exercise to get a feel for it:*

Exercise 1
From the top box to the bottom box, moving from left to right, state the **POSITION** of the word, **NOT** the word itself.

BOX SET #1

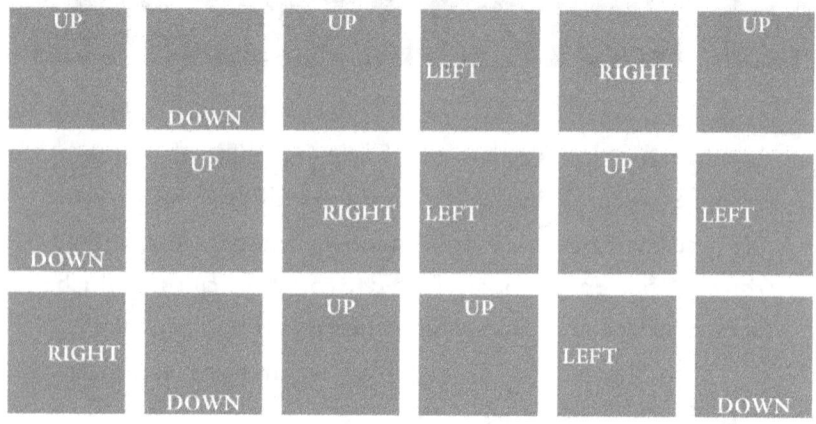

Adapted from
Source: University of Washington Faculty – July 2022[36]

Note the ease and speed with which you identified the words. Switching gears now...

Exercise 2

Again, from the top box to the bottom box, moving from left to right, state the **POSITION** of the word, **NOT** the word itself.

BOX SET #2

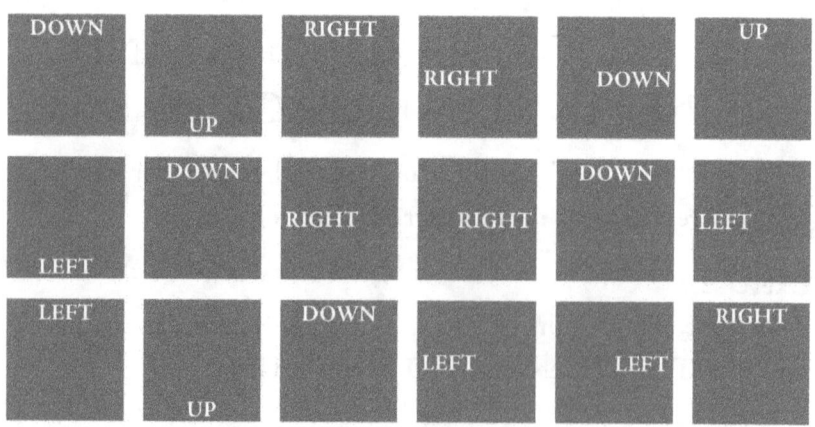

Adapted from
Source: University of Washington Faculty – July 2022

Was the second exercise equally smooth? Many individuals naturally pronounce the word first, then catch themselves, pausing before stating the correct position. Others might hesitate completely before revealing the position. The takeaway? Your mind is conditioned to act on automatic reflexes before your conscious thought processes can steer your intended reactions.

While PATHS I and II are always important, PATHS III and IV are especially relevant to the links between belief and behavior. Let's expand specifically on those paths and explore why they are critical to understanding the power you have within.

©2024 ABC's of Murmuration

PATH III
Explore and Walk a New Way

AWARENESS: ATTEND TO THE NOW

The first step is always Awareness, the cornerstone of making intentional choices, which means paying attention to this NOW moment. However, sometimes your innate reactions interfere and propel you in directions you hadn't consciously planned. The simple task of identifying a position rather than stating a word, as you attempted in the previous exercise, showcases the challenge of inhibiting your automatic reactions.

The ever-evolving field of neuroscience offers insights into these split-second decision-making processes. In David Rock's book, *Your Brain at Work*, he quotes research that, in the previous exercise, the human brain requires about three-tenths of a second to process both the word and its position in the previous exercise.[37] Then, you have a mere two-tenths of a second to choose your response. That is one-half of a second before action is taken! Did you follow your instinctual reaction and state the word, or did you override that instinct and consciously respond by stating the position? It's an intricate dance of reaction, decision, and response, played out in a mere split-second.

HOW EXPECTATIONS SHAPE OUR REACTIONS

Between stimulus and response there is a space.
In that space is our power to choose our response.
In our response lies the growth and our freedom.

—Viktor Frankl

What happens as you are opening your business mail and see a letter from your country's tax authority, such as the United States Internal Revenue Service (IRS)? Unless you are expecting a refund check, the instant reaction is typically one of slight panic, with a short intake of breath and a fluttering of nerves in the gut. There is a feeling of dread based on anticipation of bad news. After that reaction, you open the envelope and find out you had miscalculated your previous payment and the IRS has issued you a refund. Now your instant reaction switches to an exhale and release of the stress you were holding within. Your internal experience was 100 percent based on your perception and expectations rather than on any reality in the situation.

Furthermore, a separate study by "ScienceDaily" suggests that it might take up to seven seconds before you are consciously aware of your intentions.[38] To continue the above story, when you see the envelope and you have the instant reaction, that can trigger a cascade of additional reactions before you are even aware. Such as, you yell to your partner, "What did you do that the IRS is contacting us?" Or you spin the story into having to pay thousands of dollars in fines—money that you don't have—or you will be put in jail. All of this happens in a few seconds!

If you miss this split-second opportunity to override your instincts, you often succumb to automatic reaction. This can sometimes result in a puzzling scenario that leaves you wondering, "Why did I do that, even though I knew better?" This cycle of stimulus, thought, and response is a core aspect of your daily experiences.

With conscious Awareness, you can choose to activate to a new action and respond with corresponding words or behaviors. For example, if you are at a family reunion and a relative makes an argument that you believe is misguided, rather than interrupting to state an opinion, you can STEP BACK and listen to understand. Conscious Awareness makes this possible.

In the following image, there is a stimulus, yet which path is taken? An automatic habit and thought leading to a reaction? Or a proactive thought leading to an intentional response?

STIMULUS

HABIT
thought

PROACTIVE
thought

REACTION
with automatic words
and behaviors

RESPONSE
with intentional words
and behaviors

©2024 ABC's of Murmuration

Understanding Behavior Mechanics:
Stimulus + Thought Process = Reaction or Response Behavior

BELIEFS:
ADAPT TO NEW PERSPECTIVES

Transitioning from the foundational principles of Awareness, you now move toward understanding how Beliefs shape behaviors. It's crucial to recognize how deeply ingrained habits and automatic reactions can influence your actions and perceptions. Explore the domino effect of these habitual responses and how they impact your daily life.

Consider a familiar scenario: You're in a meeting, eager to share a burgeoning idea. But as you scan the room, the weight of impatience bears down. You notice subtle cues of frustration from colleagues eager to conclude the gathering. Your instincts kick in, urging you to withdraw. Thoughts spiral: "Perhaps it's best not to elongate the meeting. Will my idea even be considered valuable? Or will it face criticism?" Consequently, you withhold your idea, letting the meeting wrap up. The sting of regret soon follows when you discover someone else introduced the very idea you'd been holding onto, which was met with admiration and approval. The culprit? Your own self-imposed barriers and self-doubt.

In the next meeting, armed with Awareness of your prior inhibitions, you see an opportunity to speak up. It's a chance to push past that ingrained hesitation and actively choose to vocalize your ideas. As elucidated in *Presence* by Peter M. Senge, C. Otto Scharmer, Joseph Jaworski, and Betty Sue Flowers, your behaviors often echo long-standing habits. In their words: "Our actions are actually reenacted habits, and we invariably end up reinforcing pre-established mental models."[39] The deep-seated perspectives, Beliefs, and mindsets you harbor don't just passively linger in the background; they actively sculpt unintended reactions. In turn, this creates behavior and experiences that are not consciously intended.

THE POWER OF PERSPECTIVE AND EXPECTATION

Imagine a solitary, incomplete circle. Just a fragment on a page. Seems simple, right?

Now, watch the magic unfold when you combine multiple such fragments. What do you see?

A triangle? An arrow? Yet, if you look closer, there's neither a complete triangle nor a solid arrow. It's your brain's knack for pattern recognition that fills in the gaps. It sees what it expects to see based on past experiences and inherent assumptions.

PERCEPTION BLINDNESS AND PRIMING

Perception blindness is a term the authors are offering when what you see is different than what is actually there. Perception blindness includes *change blindness* and intentional blindness. You may see things that are not there (such as the triangle or arrow in the image above) or you may miss seeing something that others perceive. According to a study on change blindness by Melinda S. Jensen, Richard Yao, Whitney N. Street, and Daniel J. Simons, "Change blindness and intentional blindness are both failures of visual Awareness. Change blindness is the failure to notice an obvious change. Intentional blindness is the failure to notice the existence of an unexpected item."[40] There is a famous study in which observers of a video are told to count the number of times the ball is caught by the participants wearing the white shirts. While their attention is focused on where the ball going, a person dressed in a gorilla suit walks from one side of the circle to the other. When the observers were asked if they saw the gorilla, most said no. When watching the video again, they all laughed when they saw the gorilla.[41] Perception blindness shows up in your life in various ways, so consider areas where you may be seeing something that's not there or missing something that is there. This could pertain to a person, a situation, or a viewpoint.

Priming is experienced when you are exposed to certain external stimuli (words, images, sounds) and have a response that is outside of your Awareness.[42] A previous connection was made, and the exposure triggered an automatic response or reaction. Perhaps due to priming, the image used above may have activated a memory of playing the original PAC-MAN video game with friends.

The partial circle images encapsulate how your expectations can mold your perspective and prompt you to "see" things that may not truly exist. Drawing a parallel to the earlier meeting anecdote: there was a perceived lack of interest or time from the colleagues, which led to a withholding of the burgeoning idea. But was that perception grounded in reality, or was it a mirage crafted by self-imposed doubts?

Challenge yourself daily. Ask if what you're perceiving, especially in interactions or situations, is genuinely there. Could you be overlaying the scene with assumptions based on past experiences or deep-rooted expectations? Always be curious and open-minded, ensuring you aren't confined by the limitations of your own perspectives.

THE POWER OF THOUGHT ON THE BODY

Ralph Waldo Emerson once remarked, "The ancestor of every action is a thought." Taking that notion a step further, it can be said that at the foundation of every thought lies an inherent Belief or perspective. Living in the duality of mind and body, you can delve deeper into the interplay of thoughts, Beliefs, and perceptions on your physiological self, and consider their broader ripple effects on the world around you.

THE MILKSHAKE EXPERIMENT

A captivating study conducted jointly by Yale and Arizona State Universities revealed the potency of perception and priming.

Participants were given milkshakes on two separate occasions, each labeled differently: one as an indulgent shake boasting 620 calories, and the other as a health-conscious Sensi-Shake with just 140 calories.

Participants reported that the "620-calorie" shake was richer, more satisfying, and better-tasting, whereas the "140-calorie" shake was perceived as lighter and less satisfying, but healthier. Interestingly, the researchers monitored the participants' Ghrelin levels; a hormone linked to hunger and satiation. Ghrelin responses mimicked participants' perceptions: Levels acted as if participants had consumed a 620-calorie treat or a light, 140-calorie refreshment. Here's the twist: Both shakes were identical, each containing 380 calories! Evidently, the label—and the perceptions it created—automatically influenced the body's physiological response.[43]

Such findings prompt the question: How are external cues shaping your feelings, actions, and behaviors?

Let's try a simple exercise. Reflect on something you enjoy, such as eating chocolate, receiving a hug, or playing with a pet, and observe your internal response. Now, pivot your thoughts to something you aren't fond of, such as stinky fish, slimy food, or police lights in your rearview mirror, and once again tune into your internal experience. Did you sense a shift?

Taking it a step further, let's integrate a physical dimension with the Swallow Exercise:

1. Hold a thought of something you enjoy, then swallow. Observe your body's response.
2. Now, with a thought of something you aren't fond of in mind, try to swallow again. Notice any differences?

More often than not, you might find you swallow with ease when reflecting on enjoyable thoughts, whereas the opposite thought might make the action slightly more challenging. This showcases the profound influence thoughts wield over your physical body. Such reactions arise from your autonomic nervous system, a system that governs bodily functions like breathing and digestion that typically operate outside your conscious control.

Your thoughts and Beliefs can indeed bring about physiological changes in your body, as suggested by *epigenetics* research.[44] The next time you consider the power of your mind, remember it doesn't just shape your world, it also shapes you.

CONNECT: ACT AS ONE

As you move from understanding how your thoughts impact your physiological reactions to exploring the broader concept of collective growth, you can see that your individual responses and behaviors have profound implications at both cellular and societal levels. This journey from the micro to the macro highlights the interconnectedness of your actions and their ripple effects on the larger community.

Research presented by Dr. Bruce H. Lipton has shown that individual cells, in their primitive intelligence, gravitate toward what they perceive as sustenance and retract from what they interpret as toxins. Intriguingly, your human body, composed of an astounding 30 to 50 trillion cells, seem to follow a similar pattern on a macro level.[45]

When you reflected on something you enjoyed, your entire body—all those trillions of cells—leaned into the sentiment of enjoyment, which made physical actions like swallowing easy. Contrastingly, facing an aversive thought seemed to invoke a cellular-level response resembling fear or stress, which made the same simple, physical task a bit more challenging.

Digging deeper into this phenomenon, studies that investigate the interplay between emotions and your very genetic material uncover fascinating patterns. When subjects were immersed in fear, their DNA strands contracted. On the flip side, feelings of love and warmth caused DNA to loosen and relax. This resonates with insights shared by researcher and educator Gregg Braden, who has studied the influence of emotions on human DNA.[46]

Dr. Bruce H. Lipton offers a beautiful analogy of unity and collaboration. Individual cells, in their evolutionary wisdom, found strength and efficiency in specialization. These specialized cells then congregated to form organs. Organs, in their collective might, banded together to create the marvel that is the human body. This mirrors societal structures, in which individuals (ME) come together in harmonious collaboration (WE) to form communities and cultures (US). The health and vitality of this macro-organism hinges upon alignment between individual intentions and collective values.[47]

Ultimately, your journey boils down to the choices you make. It's about how you perceive the world and, subsequently, how you react to it.

Now dive into PATH IV and see how it helps you adapt your Beliefs for personal and collective evolution.

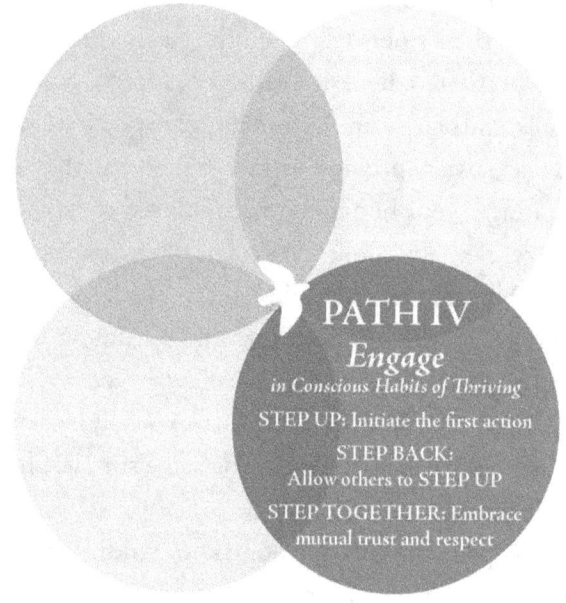

©2024 ABC's of Murmuration

PATH IV

Engage in Conscious Habits of Thriving

This book presents a golden opportunity: a chance to drive growth and unity through the conscious habits of STEP UP, STEP BACK, and STEP TOGETHER. Embrace these concepts and discover how they can lead you and those around you toward a richer, more interconnected existence.

> *Deep, transformational change*
> *requires that we literally rewire our brains,*
> *that we grow new neural connections.*[48]
>
> —Danah Zohar

DECIPHERING THE BRAIN AND THE MIND

Having examined the influence of thoughts on the body, now shift your focus onto the intriguing realm of the brain and the mind. It's common for people to use these terms interchangeably, but they signify distinct entities.

Picture the brain as the tangible hardware of a computer: it's physically present and can be touched and observed. Contrarily, the mind mirrors the intangible software: it can't be seen or touched but runs the show by fueling all operations of the computer. And a significant chunk of this "software" operates subconsciously, beyond your immediate conscious grasp.

Neuroscience is the study of how the nervous system develops, its structure, and what it does. Neuroscientists focus on the brain and its impact on behavior and cognitive functions. ***Here's a look at some awe-inspiring facts about your brain:***[49]

- It's an organ of marvel, weighing around 3 pounds.
- A significant part, about 80 percent, is water.
- It's quite the energy guzzler, consuming 20 percent of the oxygen you inhale and 20 percent of your total energy requirement.

- It brims with around 100 billion neurons and countless supportive glial cells.
- Each neuron can form connections, or synapses, with up to 40,000 other neurons. When you do the math, the magnitude of these connections far surpasses the number of stars in the cosmos!

Research in neuroscience has divided the brain into defined parts and functions. While there are many approaches to describing the physical brain, these are two great ones:

Triune Brain Framework

One popular and often referenced theory is the Triune Brain Concept presented by Paul D. MacLean in his 1990 book, *The Triune Brain in Evolution: Role in Paleocerebral Functions*, which describes three main areas of the brain:[50]

1. **Cerebral Cortex or Complex Functioning**
   - Primarily hosts the prefrontal lobe, or the "executive suite"
   - Grants you the unique human ability to consciously make decisions

2. **Limbic System or Midbrain**
   - Houses the amygdala, your emotional filter
   - Contains the hippocampus, crucial for forming long-term memories

3. **Primitive, Brain Stem, or Reptilian Brain**
   - The watchdog of your essential life functions like breathing, heartbeat, and digestion
   - Shared with many other species

Recent research has identified the brain as a ***whole system*** of ***interdependent*** and interconnected neural networks that allow for collaborating, responding, and adapting to current and future needs and situations.[51] This goes beyond the evolutionary sections described in the Triune Brain concept.

The Adaptive Brain Concept

Building on the Triune Brain Concept, the Adaptive Brain Concept, as discussed by Patrick R. Steffen, Dawson Hedges, and Rebecca Matheson in a National Library of Medicine article, expands from the developmental aspects of the three brain regions to how the brain functions during daily life.[52] There are three key concepts:

1. **Interdependent:** While brain areas have specific functions, they work together to interpret incoming information to determine the current situation or predict the future environment based on previous experiences and information about past internal and external environments. This prediction initiates the regulation of the heart rate, blood pressure, and other internal chemicals, as well as what is experienced as emotions and cognition (knowledge).

2. **Interconnected:** Thoughts are transmitted via neurotransmitters and neurochemicals in your brain. These neurochemicals—such as dopamine, oxytocin, and cortisol—produce emotions such as happiness, love, or stress, and create related physical body reactions.

3. **Plasticity:** Based on the internal and external environments, the adaptive brain creates changes in neural networks, whether of expansion or elimination, to integrate current learning or experiences.

Most often the brain that resides in your head is the only organ considered when referring to "the brain." But the same chemical messengers, called neuropeptides, found in the "head brain," are also present in the heart and gut.[53] Ever wondered why you feel "butterflies in your stomach" before a significant event?[54] This interplay explains the physiological, somatic, or bodily sensations linked to your emotions and perceptions. As the authors refer to Integrated Mindset, this includes alignment with head, heart, and gut neurons, as well any other neurons throughout the whole body.

The head brain contains the cerebral cortex, which is bisected into *left* and *right brain hemispheres*. These sides interpret and process information uniquely, and also collaborate for expanded processing:

LEFT BRAIN	RIGHT BRAIN
Words	Images
Parts	Whole
Analyze	Synthesize

As you can see, the processing functions are different, yet both are critical for daily functioning. And it's important that both hemispheres work together.

The **Whole-Brain State** is when the two hemispheres are in harmony and coherency with each other. This alignment sparks heightened creativity, enhanced problem-solving, sharper focus, and a marked reduction in stress levels. This can also be referred to this as the Integrated Mindset.

INSIGHTS FROM DR. JILL BOLTE TAYLOR'S STROKE EXPERIENCE

Explore the experiences and insights of Dr. Jill Bolte Taylor, a neuroanatomist who personally witnessed a stroke's effects on her brain.[55] You can learn more details about her journey as shared in her well-known TED Talk as well as her book, *My Stroke of Insight*. During her stroke, she recognized that her left-brain hemisphere for processing words and logic was no longer online. Her entire perception became one of connection with her right brain processing, which made it challenging to function in the daily environment. Her experience highlights the critical balance of both hemispheres. Above, we introduced the Whole-Brain State, which is the state of optimal functioning when both hemispheres are integrated rather than in conflict or, in Dr. Bolte Taylor's experience, not online.

ADDRESSING THE NEUROPLASTICITY OF THE EVER-ADAPTABLE BRAIN

In the vast world of biology, neuroscience is the realm dedicated to unraveling the mysteries of the brain and the nervous system. The complex web woven by billions of neurons within your nervous system, all of which are intricately connected not just among themselves but also to various other systems in the body.

Neuro-imaging provides an illuminating window into the realm of brain wave activities. The intriguing part? More often than not, these brain wave patterns remain consistent, termed as the "default mode." It's rare for these patterns to undergo a shift, unless prompted by rigorous, consistent brain training or a traumatic event. Enter neuroplasticity, a remarkable trait of your brain that allows it to continually evolve and adapt throughout your life based on your experiences.

Brain mapping, an advanced neuro-imaging technique, offers an even more fascinating insight. It has the ability to translate the energetic patterns of EEG brain waves into visual data, which allows you to see the brain's activity in various shades and perspectives.

Before

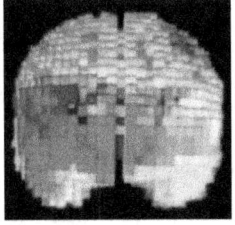

What you see above is Graham's brain image. This first image captures the brain's activity when she was presented with a word that symbolized an activity she knew she had been avoiding. This system pinpoints heightened activity on the brain's right side (as seen on the left side of the image) as a marker of avoidance. Indeed, the brain scan substantiated Graham's aversion to the activity in question.

Seeking to validate the ability to transform the avoidance, Graham requested a five-minute break to adopt a fresh perspective toward this activity to employ PSYCH-K® processes to mitigate the associated stress and view the task more favorably.

The follow-up scan done within 10 minutes, as seen in the subsequent image below, reveals a dramatic shift: a harmonious balance between the brain's hemispheres, indicative of a Whole-Brain State. The implications? Graham's perception of the once-dreaded activity had undergone a complete transformation. The entrenched neural pathways linked to aversion had been overhauled and replaced with new, more positive connections. She had activated an Integrated Mindset about the activity.

After

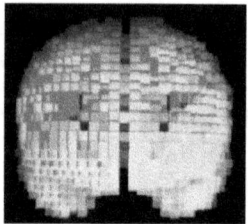

The true test, however, was in the real world. Upon returning home, Graham discovered that her earlier reluctance had evaporated, and was replaced by a newfound ease toward the activity. But she wondered, would a subsequent brain scan mirror this change in behavior? Would it display a predominant activity on the opposite side, symbolic of acceptance in the brain-mapping system?

One year later, Graham's quest for answers led back to the aforementioned equipment and technician. The same procedure was repeated, this time centered on the very activity that had previously been a source of avoidance. With a year's worth of engagement with the task as proof, the burning question was: had the brain's perception of the activity genuinely transformed?

One Year Later

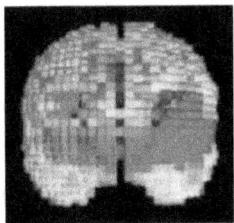

The answer, as visualized in the scan, provides profound insights into the brain's adaptability and the power of perspective. The follow-up scan starkly highlighted heightened activity on the left side of the brain (as shown on the right side of the image above), a clear marker of acceptance. It's worth noting that technological advancements had led to the software's enhancement over the past year. Given that it generated rapid, dynamic videos, the final image wasn't a direct inverse of the initial resistance portrayal. Yet the technician confirmed its significance, concurring that this new image reflected acceptance, which served as a stark contrast to the original stance of avoidance.

For Graham, this was more than just a scan; it was tangible evidence of a cognitive transformation. This wasn't merely an academic exercise but a lived experience. The shift in perception was evident not just on a digital monitor, but also in real-world actions and behaviors almost immediately after the original transformational session a year prior.

So, what does this mean for you?

Graham's journey offers compelling evidence of your innate ability to reshape your perceptions. It demonstrates that not only can you rewire your mind and transform your behaviors, but also that these shifts manifest in the very neural patterns of your brain. What's even more encouraging is the swiftness with which these changes can take root and, more importantly, their longevity. This isn't about fleeting alterations but enduring transformations.

Your brain, with its intricate web of neurons and inner connections, isn't set in stone. It's dynamic, adaptable, and waiting for you to take the reins. As showcased by the extensive research in this field, including contributions from Fannin and Williams, your potential for change is not just theoretical but is tangible, measurable, and attainable.[56]

Embrace this knowledge and realize that the power to transform your mindset—and by extension, your life—lies squarely in your hands. Your brain is ready for transformation. Are you and your mind ready to choose?

CONSCIOUS AND SUBCONSCIOUS MINDS: THE DRIVING FORCES BEHIND YOUR ACTIONS

While the head brain is tangible and definable by parts, the other critical component is the mind, which is identified as an energetic frequency that intertwines with yet remains distinct from the physical brain.

Your mind is a treasure trove that brims with thoughts, Beliefs, and emotions that shape every facet of your life. To visualize its vast expanse and multi-faceted nature, recall the image of an iceberg floating on water in Chapter 3. As you've learned, the tip peeking above the water's surface represents the conscious creative mind, which reflects thoughts and emotions you're actively aware of. Below the waterline, vast and deep, is the subconscious mind. This hidden giant is your autopilot, which steers from Beliefs and perceptions that lay the groundwork for your thoughts and actions.

Expert Dr. Lipton shares how autopilot takes control when you are focused on external tasks:

INTERVIEW WITH DR. BRUCE H. LIPTON
Cellular Biologist and Best-Selling Author

Full interview available at AbcsofMurmuration.com

"When the conscious mind is busy doing other tasks, the subconscious mind is the autopilot that will take over. This is because the subconscious has learned and habituated to life activities such as driving a car, riding a bicycle, or playing a musical instrument.

Throughout the day, we are internally thinking various thoughts or about activities, yet at the same time, we are engaged in an external behavior. This means that 95 percent of the day we are on subconscious autopilot programs, and 5 percent of the day we are being our consciously creative selves.

Most of the programs did not come from you. They are copied from other people's behaviors. When these programs are played out, you often are not aware of them because you are focused on something else when they get activated." [57]

—Dr. Lipton

Want to see changes in your actions and behaviors? Start by altering your foundational Beliefs and perceptions. After all, they're the root cause. But how does understanding this dynamic play into your larger goal of embarking on a new journey—of nurturing ME, strengthening WE, and harmoniously transitioning into US?

Changing your perceptions about yourself and others is not only possible but transformative. Instead of battling with self-doubt or dreading certain interpersonal interactions, you can choose to empower yourself. Decide what to believe about your abilities and determine how you want to engage with others.

Why is exploring your internal world critical? Because here is a staggering fact: The energy of your thoughts is infinitely more potent in influencing cell activity (and consequently behavior) than any external chemical, i.e. sugar, aspirin, or such. If behavior modification is your goal, your best bet is to address your thought processes, especially the foundational Beliefs and perceptions that set them in motion.

Let's look at an image that represents the cycle of how Beliefs create thoughts, which create behaviors, which yield results. The key is that the result has to support the originating belief, whether that belief is supportive or sabotaging. This is often referred to as the self-fulfilling prophecy.

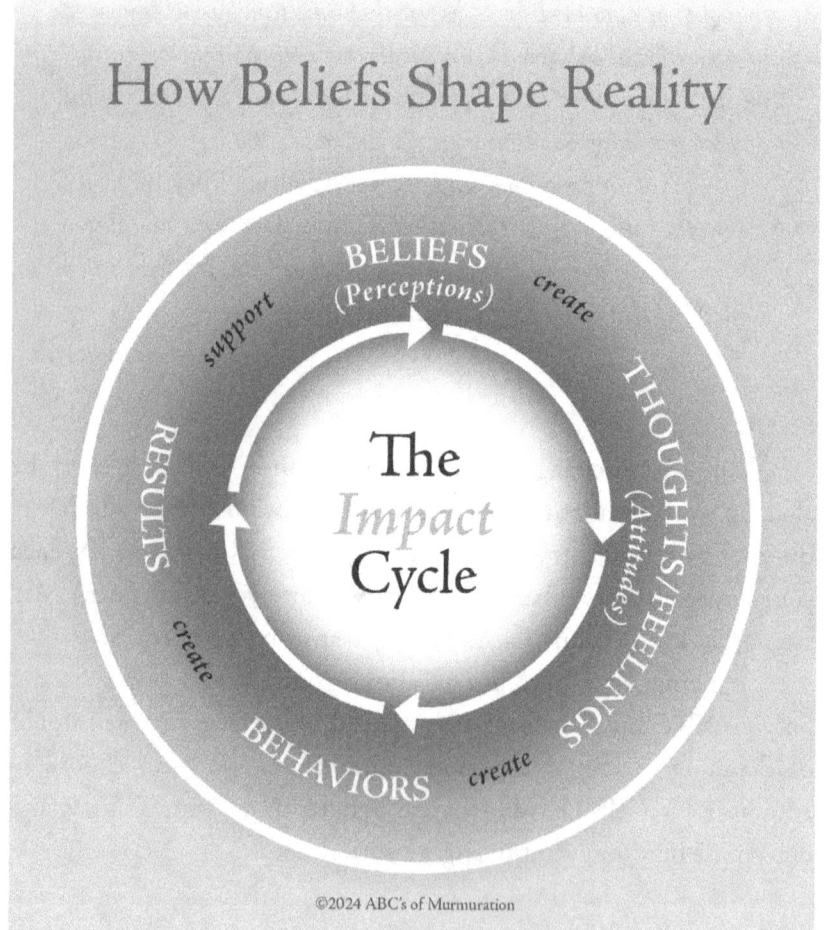

To shed light on the image, consider this scenario: You are invited to submit an article about your favorite topic. There is a deadline for the submission to be accepted. Your internal attitude is excitement. You begin the external behavior of writing out your ideas. Then, you get interrupted with a deadline for a work project and a family commitment you forgot about. Your writing stops and the submission deadline is missed. Once you realize you are past due, your self-talk becomes, "There it is again, I never finish anything!" Which is based in a subconscious belief that that, "I never finish anything." This may have been initiated as a child playing with toys and being told, "You never finish anything."

When you hear your self-talk and become aware of this pattern, it allows you to explore new options. Rather than staying in the trap of the self-fulfilling prophecy, you now have the choice to do something different. Often the first option is to look at how to change the behavior or the attitude to get a different outcome. But here lies the pitfall. Attempting superficial changes without addressing the root cause often demands constant reminders, which taxes your mental energy and resolve.

Remember the earlier experiment in which substituting the word with its position proved challenging? That's the same struggle you face when trying to alter your ingrained Beliefs or perceptions. Using sheer willpower is like the conscious mind's meager 5 percent trying to overpower the commanding 95 percent of the subconscious; a battle it's bound to lose before long.

To achieve genuine, enduring change in a relatively short span, the strategy is clear: Harmonize subconscious Beliefs with conscious goals and actions. It's about achieving a coherent perspective by fostering an Integrated Mindset, as presented previously. This isn't just about mental alignment; it's about reshaping your life's trajectory.

Through each chapter so far, your journey has taken you through the Four Paths to Transformation, in which you explored how critical you are as a ME. To evolve from ME to WE to US, you continue to embrace the steps necessary for personal and collective growth. Moving forward, you are invited to envision murmuration, and recognize your influence in engagement within a WE and impact with an US.

In order to reach murmuration, you will continue to explore and *Walk a New Way* as you deepen your understanding of the *ABC's* (*Awareness, Beliefs, Connect*). Remember, the actions to take are to STEP UP, STEP BACK, and STEP TOGETHER. Combined, these principles guide you on your path to becoming a unified force, and help you transform individual actions into collective harmony.

YOUR TURN: MOMENT OF REFLECTION

1. **REFLECT ON AWARENESS**: Each day, challenge your perceptions, particularly in interactions. Are you seeing the true situation, or are you influenced by past experiences or assumptions? Maintain curiosity and openness to avoid being trapped by your own limited viewpoints.

2. **EXAMINE BELIEFS**: Identify outdated Beliefs you're holding onto. What strategies can you implement to actively change these habits when you recognize them?

3. **EXPLORE MINDSET**: Where do you encounter frustration or feel conflicted? Consider alternative perspectives and seek others' viewpoints to broaden your understanding.

4. **DEVELOP SKILLSETS**: Identify areas in which you're willing to act but lack the necessary skills. Where can you acquire these skills?

5. **ENHANCE CONNECTION**: Learn about the interconnectedness of mind, body, and spirit. Explore resources like Dr. Lipton's *The Biology of Belief* book or watch interviews to deepen your understanding.

6. **INCORPORATE PSYCH-K®**: For those interested in practical tools to adjust subconscious Beliefs, consider exploring the PSYCH-K® method to facilitate personal transformation.

Global Thought Leaders: see pages 317–320 for more information

Bruce H. Lipton

PSYCH-K®: see pages 321–322 for more information

WALKWAY II: WE

An Invitation to Step Up, Step Back

CHAPTERS 7 - 8

CHAPTER 7

THE STRENGTH OF THE PACK

For the strength of the pack is the wolf,
and the strength of the wolf is the pack.

—Rudyard Kipling

HOW DOES THE INDIVIDUAL BRILLIANCE OF ME CONTRIBUTE TO THE COLLECTIVE SUCCESS OF WE? The journey from ME to WE emphasizes how individual strengths are amplified within a cohesive group. In this chapter, you will learn how unified vision and collaboration transform personal talents and assets into groundbreaking outcomes. You are invited to consider how the dynamic interplay between ME and WE fosters a resilient, harmonious collective that is ready to navigate the complexities of your interconnected world.

STRENGTH OF COLLECTIVE UNITY

The profound observation by Kipling you see at the beginning of this chapter captures the essence of your journey toward understanding the interconnectedness of individuality and collectivity. Just as the wolf draws strength from the pack, and the pack from each wolf, so too does the individual—ME—find strength and purpose within the collective—WE. This symbiotic relationship underpins the core of your exploration into the *ABC's of Murmuration*, which guides you to Connect and act as one.

As you explore this dynamic further, it's crucial to recognize that the path from ME to WE isn't a departure from individuality but a harmonious extension of it. Even Deepak Chopra's insight is that your mind, body, and spirit are not separate compartments. His observation that "Wholeness, which is what you are, cannot depart from itself, lose itself, or come back to itself," further illuminates this point.[58] The seamless integration of your individual essence—mind, body, and spirit—serves as the foundation for collective action and shared success.

Consider the transition from wolf to pack. It's like acknowledging a single wolf's presence even when it is clearly part of the pack. This phenomenon, called *superpositioning* in quantum physics, means that something can exist in multiple states at once. Imagine a coin that is both heads and tails until it is observed. This analogy extends to the understanding of consciousness, in which different states coexist, each serving unique roles. The individual self, ME, while maintaining its identity, becomes an integral part of WE. In this sense, ME is not lost in WE; rather, it is a continuous presence, a core that binds together a collective, a group of seven starlings, WE.

WE emerges not only as a team but as a dynamic embodiment of shared consciousness, in which each ME remains vital within the WE. Each individual starling moves from the inner intelligence that is created and managed by each ME to the WE collective intelligence that provides the capability to thrive in the larger environment. Together, they form the foundation of US, the murmuration.

WHAT ARE THE CONNECTED PATHS IN NATURE?

Nature's Connected paths converge like a river. The paths of the mind, body, and spirit flow as ME. The Connected paths of individuals converge as a team (WE), and the Connected paths of teams converge as an US. What is fascinating is that the principle of superpositioning insists they all exist at once!

Observe the murmuration (US) and ultimate success of starlings. It is a perfect representation of teams of WE, a singular entity borne from the collective strength of multiple teams of WE. The connections of nature are amazing! There are multiple connections in nature, such as monarch butterfly migration, bat colony intercommunication, shoals of fish (many of which move like a murmuration), prides of lions that divide duties amongst individuals, and fungal colonies and their communication.

In the face of danger or conflict, this unity, this WE, becomes a formidable force, far surpassing the capabilities of a lone ME, or a lone wolf. This isn't just a gathering; it's a phenomenon in which each starling's actions and Awareness ripple through the entire collective of WE to create a responsive, agile whole. The Awareness of one affects all, and casts a perception net far wider than individual interactions. Thus, each starling contributes to and is influenced by the collective consciousness, which allows the final US murmuration to respond as a critical system, perfectly poised to adapt to environmental challenges. In this dance of unity, ME seamlessly becomes WE, and together, they Connect.

The remarkable synchronization observed in starlings offers profound lessons for addressing the complex challenges of present-day life. By embracing the principles of collective consciousness mirrored in nature, you can forge a resilient and unified response to the escalating global crises that demand collective action and Awareness.

Collective consciousness Connects individual minds, thoughts, and hearts into a unified entity, which is essential for balance and harmony in both the world and in nature. As global crises continue to worsen, the Awareness of this collective consciousness has become increasingly vital. It enables each ME to be more aware of issues that may not affect you individually but are tearing humans apart across the globe. These issues may not be recognizable by ME at the present, but the collective wisdom amplifies the urgency.

Over generations, the need for this Awareness has grown, which reflects the urgency of the times. To shift from a singular perspective (ME) to a collective one (US), you must embrace new ways of thinking and acting—essentially, *Walking a New Way*. Fortunately, technology has provided a vehicle for collective wisdom for the Awareness, Beliefs, and Connect to be almost instantaneous.

This collective information is true not only for a crisis, but also for magnifying the success of ME to become the success of the collective. This balance between individual contributions and collective unity is beautifully illustrated in the journey of The Beatles, in which the ability to STEP BACK and let others shine became a crucial element of their success.

THE BEATLES: THE STRENGTH OF STEPPING BACK

The Beatles' success was not just a result of individual talent, but also of knowing when to STEP BACK and let each member shine. Throughout their careers, the band members demonstrated a deep understanding of when to lead and when to support another member. Many times there were multiple conflicts to resolve, but they made it through. This balance was crucial to their collective strength and groundbreaking achievements.

Paul McCartney often took the lead in crafting some of the band's most iconic songs, but he STEPPED BACK when another member's vision took center stage. George Harrison, who initially contributed fewer songs, gradually emerged as a powerful songwriter in his own right. His compositions, like "Here Comes the Sun" and "Something" added profound depth to The Beatles' later albums.

This dynamic of STEPPING BACK, even when contentious, allowed The Beatles to integrate their individual strengths into a unified whole. It wasn't about any one member dominating; it was about recognizing the right moments for each member to lead and when to let others take the spotlight. This approach not only strengthened their music but also solidified their bond as a band.

The Beatles' journey illustrates the power of collective unity; how STEPPING BACK at the right time can enhance the strength of the pack and allow each individual's brilliance to contribute to the success of the whole.

HARNESSING NATURE'S COLLECTIVE WISDOM: THE LOGIC OF FLOCKS

In the realm of starlings, the significance of the number seven emerges through their exceptional model of communication, coordination, and consensus. Professor Naomi Ehrich Leonard's research at Princeton on *Flock Logic* indicates that starlings tracking more than seven neighbors face increased complexity and energy demands, balancing responsiveness to social cues with efficiency essential for murmuration.[59] This insight from nature offers profound lessons for human team dynamics. As social animals, humans may also struggle if forced to collaborate with teams of seven or more people.

In 1956 a psychologist named George Miller published a paper about the significance of the number seven. The paper is titled, *The Magic Number Seven, Plus or Minus Two: Limits on our Capacity for Processing Information*.[60] Miller's research showed that short-term memory, or working memory, had a limit on the information it could hold at one time. He found that people could hold seven digits as they thought about things. Researchers have also found that a team size of seven seems to be the magic number. More than seven proves difficult to maintain the information. Teams of 10 or more have proven impossible to keep everyone informed.[61]

The collaborative project, "Flock Logic," which involved Choreographer Susan Marshall and Professor Ehrich Leonard, applies these avian behaviors to enhance human group interactions.[62] Supported by institutions like the U.S. Navy, Army, and National Science Foundation, their work on how groups move explores the efficiencies of connective movement, which is relevant to both animals and human teams.

In his article, "As Agile as a Flock of Birds," Joris Celis has this to say: "In a flock, it is not necessary for birds to systematically fly in the same direction, but it is important to fly at the same speed."[63] Each bird communicates with the seven birds closest to them. They do this continuously, constantly, and quickly.

As soon as one bird senses danger or a change in its environment, it immediately reacts by changing direction. The birds closest to it follow while avoiding collision. They follow the direction of the bird in the lead, and stay as close as possible to those in their immediate vicinity. One of the main reasons a flock frequently changes shape is because no bird loves to fly on the outside. That's where you are most likely to be attacked by predators. Inside the flock, it's cozy and safe and you can keep a low profile.

Collaboration and movement aren't the only activities central to WE. Drawing parallels between starling motivations and human needs—similar to Abraham Maslow's hierarchy of needs—reveals a universal quest for balance and belonging. Starlings, motivated by basic needs such as food and safety, reflect human drives for physiological needs, safety, belonging, esteem, and self-actualization. In the world of starlings, WE makes the seeking and procurement of these basics a shared burden for each individual ME: collective needs are tended in a collective way.

Among humans, however, there is a disconnect. While ME has transitioned into an interconnected world, it continues to act independently. While it is true that ME maintains its individual identity while in collaboration with WE, it's also true that—to contribute to and benefit from the collective WE—ME must also be willing to act in concert with others. To make choices and take actions that benefit the group, not just the individual. Changes need to take place in ME. ME must have Awareness of present situations, adopt new perceptions and Beliefs, and Connect with WE and US. Discovering your global interconnectedness isn't enough if you fail to align with it. Individual independence and selfish mindsets must evolve. ME must realize and coexist at the WE and US levels. Doing so would uncover a new dimension of collective wisdom, intelligence, and balance with nature.

NAVIGATING THE FOUR-PATH JOURNEY OF WE

To transition from ME to WE, understanding the Four-Path Journey is crucial. Here are the mileposts that will guide you on this journey of WE as you continue to Connect and act as one.

THE FOUR-PATH JOURNEY

EVOLVE *from* ME *to* WE *to* US

PATH I
Embrace
an *Evolutionary Mindset* to make a path for genuine alignment and harmony.

PATH II
Envision
Murmuration
With an inner eye, imagine murmuration as the vital light of change and love in the world.

PATH III
Explore
and Walk a New Way.
Actively navigate the *ABC's*:
AWARENESS:
Attend to the now
BELIEFS:
Adapt to new perspectives
CONNECT:
Act as one

PATH IV
Engage
in *Conscious Habits of Thriving*
STEP UP:
Initiate the first action
STEP BACK:
Allow others to STEP UP
STEP TOGETHER:
Embrace mutual trust and respect

©2024 ABC's of Murmuration

GROWTH BY SUPERPOSITIONING

Embracing an *Evolutionary Mindset* is about recognizing and leveraging the dynamic interplay between individual experiences and your collective growth. This approach is not just about adapting to changes, it is about actively engaging with changes to foster personal and communal development. By understanding and applying the concept of *superpositioning*, you can see how your individual states coexist and influence your collective experiences to provide a richer, more connected way of living.

BEING A SECURE BASE

Your humanity is defined not in solitude but through your connections with others. Embracing this truth as an *Evolutionary Mindset* is vital in the transition from ME to WE. It requires an acute Awareness of the profound impact relationships have on your personal growth. Throughout life, you will find strength in others who become your *secure bases*, just as you offer the same solid, reliable foundation to them. Think of close friendships maintained over the years. Think of the WE that was trusted and relied on. This concept of a secure base, deeply ingrained in human psychology, transcends cultural and generational boundaries. Initially understood in the context of a child's bond with their mother, the need for a secure base is equally crucial for adults.

Becoming a secure base for others begins with fostering a sense of safety and protection through responsive bonding. This responsiveness is not about reactive behavior but a conscious, supportive response to another's needs. It's about active listening, encouraging, challenging, and trusting, thereby building a robust bond of trust. By affirming your belief in another's potential, you not only empower them but also reinforce the dynamic of mutual support and resilience. This is one of the steps that allows ME to become an integral part of WE.

CHARACTERISTICS OF A SECURE BASE

- Demonstrates responsiveness to the needs of others
- Encourages seeing beyond conventional limits
- Assists others in achieving the extraordinary
- Furnishes energy to others for growth and development
- Enhances resilience in others through support
- Generates a collective energy greater than what could be achieved alone
- Recognizes the natural progression of separation and independence
- Creates a genuine space for emotional expression and processing
- Embraces gratitude as relationships evolve and grow

These characteristics define the essence of a secure base, which guide you to build strong, supportive connections that form the foundation of a resilient and cohesive WE. Remember, ME is an integral part of WE and is constantly growing through this *superpositioning* activity of being a secure base.

Let's look at ME within the characteristics of a Secure Base:

LESSONS OF A SECURE BASE FOR ME

- ME learns to be responsive to the needs of others
- ME determines how to encourage another beyond conventional limits
- ME participates in achieving the extraordinary
- ME gains energy from others to grow and develop
- ME becomes more resilient when helping others
- ME gains energy greater than what could have been achieved alone

- ME recognizes the natural progression of separation and independence
- ME creates a genuine space for emotional expression and processing
- ME embraces gratitude as relationships evolve and grow

Being a Secure Base

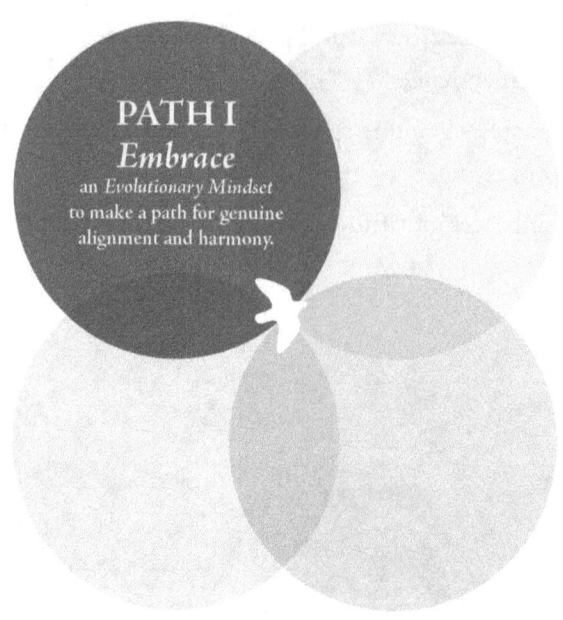

©2024 ABC's of Murmuration

PATH I

Embrace an Evolutionary Mindset

As was mentioned earlier, to successfully flow from ME to WE, adopting an *Evolutionary Mindset* is crucial. Here are some practical tips to allow for maximum harmony as you move from ME to WE:

1. **Do Mindset Checks Regularly:** In challenging situations, consciously shift from negative to positive. Take a deep breath, *Pause, Notice, and Choose* before reacting, Apply the *SCARS Model*:[64]

   - **STOP:** Focus on the positive. Think, "We get to do this together" instead of "I have to do this alone."

- **CALM:** Stay calm. When feeling anxious, angry, hungry, or tired, make a small change to prevent slipping into negativity with another. Ask yourself, "What can I learn here?"
- **ALLOW:** Recall those who have been a secure base for you. Reflect on what you admired in their actions and what you learned from them. Be that secure base for others.
- **REINVENT:** Change your thought patterns to offer a secure base to another, and remember to STEP BACK to provide them space to STEP UP when they are ready.
- **SHARE:** Share with others your practices to be a secure base for another.

2. **Influence Positivity:** Daily, choose three people to positively impact. Share encouraging messages or Beliefs in order to foster their confidence and optimism.
3. **Enroll in a Vision:** Encourage your team, your WE, to focus on a positive future. Collaborate to envision and believe in the success of this vision. Your enthusiasm will inspire others to participate actively.

By integrating these practices, you can nurture a collective mindset that supports growth, resilience, and harmonious collaboration.

ADDITIONAL TIPS FOR BONDING (WE)

Building sustainable teams requires a foundation rooted in compassion and the willingness to take risks. These tips help foster a nurturing and evolutionary environment that enhances team cohesion and mutual growth.

Effective bonding among team members involves ME remembering to do these things:

MINDFUL COMMUNICATION:

Focus on aligning words, tone, and body language to provide a positive and meaningful impact on another.

SEIZE THE MOMENT:

Value the power of spontaneous remarks, which can be as impactful as formal statements. Be responsive and not reactive. Make them count toward a collaborative WE.

CLEAR, POWERFUL MESSAGING:

Communicate ideas clearly and succinctly. STEP BACK and opt for a less-is-more approach, which often allows others to shine and contributes to effective team bonding.

These actions and tips enhance your natural ability to Connect with others in WE. Dr. Dan Siegel, a prominent author, notes that you are inherently equipped to understand the minds of others, a process facilitated by what he calls *mirror neurons*. This neurological feature enables you to empathize deeply and tune into the emotions of those around you. Siegel states that, "When we attune to others we allow our own internal state to shift, to come to resonate with the inner world of another. This resonance is at the heart of the important sense of 'feeling felt' that emerges in close relationships. Children need attunement to feel secure and to develop well, and throughout our lives we need attunement to feel close and connected. This connection is crucial not only for secure and healthy development, but also for maintaining close and meaningful relationships throughout our lives."[65] By focusing on someone else's distress and acting as their secure base, you can develop the ability to respond thoughtfully and constructively. This, in turn, prepares you to offer meaningful support, which enhances the collective ability to navigate complex emotional landscapes together.

Next, let's learn how to use murmuration as a mental template for shared success. One that ME can leverage in the journey toward WE.

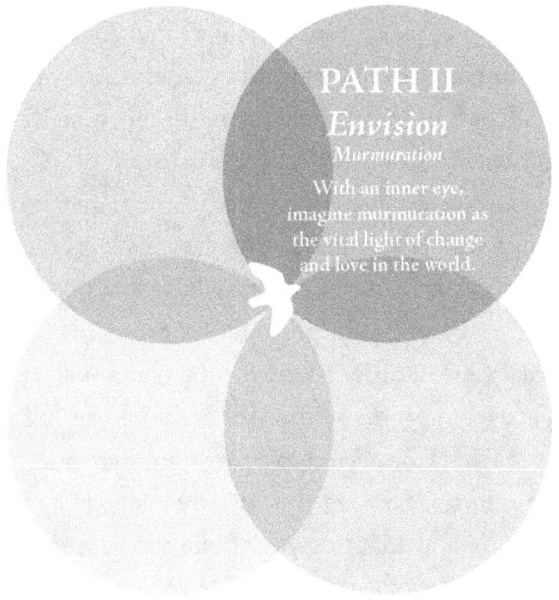

©2024 ABC's of Murmuration

PATH II

Envision Murmuration

When ME makes the necessary changes in mindset and communication that enable bonding, the stage is set for a transition to WE. Trust is built, and the emerging WE is primed to work in harmony. But what will this harmonized group do together? To find out, ME must **look out to look in.**

Begin by "looking out" to observe the synchronized flight of starlings as a powerful metaphor for successful collaboration. This external perspective helps you focus on achieving collective victories while you steer clear of the pitfalls of defensive or avoidance-based strategies such as fight or flight. By visualizing success in the form of murmuration, you can shift the team's focus from potential risks to the thrill of achievement, which can therefore cultivate excitement, determination, and joy.

Next, "looking in" to enhance the personal Awareness of ME in the present moment. This introspective process involves assessing and adjusting the Beliefs of ME to foster a mindset conducive to collective success. It's crucial to monitor the personal state of ME, and ensure that it aligns both internally (mind, body, spirit) and externally with the team's objectives. Remember, you are inside a *Jam Jar* in which your actions and words are visible to others, which shapes their perception of you. Consider aligning your personal behaviors to reflect positively on this external view in order to mirror the team's collective goals.

As ME actively engages with WE, embrace the full potential of teamwork by staying Connected to the vibrant dynamics the vision of murmuration offers. Choosing this vision means living intentionally, and being aware of and adapting your Beliefs to support the collective journey of WE as it evolves into the cohesive US of murmuration. Each ME has the amazing opportunity to fully embrace their role in this transformative process, and look for opportunities to actively STEP UP and enhance the collective strength and unity of the team.

With this understanding of how individual Awareness influences your collective dynamics, continue to explore how these concepts manifest in the broader context of your team's collective mind, which can be visualized again through the metaphor of the collective iceberg.

WHAT WE SEE: VISUALIZING THE ICEBERG

In Chapter 3, you explored ME as represented by an iceberg. You considered the subconscious and conscious mind of ME. Now, extend this analogy to understand the conscious WE. Just as you dissected the role of the subconscious and conscious mind of ME, you will now examine how these concepts function within a team setting. Picture a vast and majestic iceberg, but this time it symbolizes the collective minds of the team as a whole (WE).

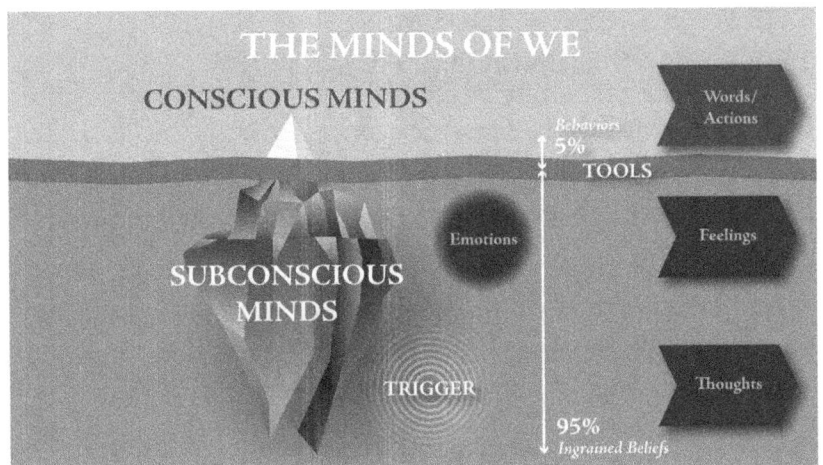

The Minds of WE: Iceberg Model
This graphic illustrates the conscious minds (5 percent) as the tip of the iceberg, while the collective subconscious minds (95 percent) lie beneath, and drive shared thoughts, feelings, and emotions that influence collective behaviors (words and actions).

THE WE CONSCIOUS MIND: THE PEAK ABOVE

The tip of the iceberg symbolizes the team's collective conscious mind. It reflects the now, the present moment. This is where current actions, words, and observable behaviors of the team are manifested. It's the realm in which the team actively makes choices and decisions, such as which project will bring excellence to this work and how you can make the biggest difference in your communities. For instance, if the team was working in a physician's office, the team could determine the best way to enhance the patient's experience if they were from Generation X, Y, or Z. The team could collectively decide that changes needed to be made with the office because it had provided health care to mostly baby boomers over the last 20 years. Collective wisdom here is the answer. This conscious process begins with each individual: with ME. The WE consciousness is the cumulative 5 percent of each ME. Therefore, doing this work with intentional collective wisdom is critical.

THE WE SUBCONSCIOUS MIND: THE EXPANSE BENEATH THE WATER

Beneath the surface, the immense submerged section of the iceberg mirrors the extensive collective subconscious of the team. As with ME, the collective subconscious of WE controls the remaining 95 percent. *It plays three critical roles for the team:*

Steward of Vital Functions: It manages essential bodily functions for each of the team members, which ensures the smooth operation of the team members' bodies.

Securer of Memories: It manages things that happened to the team, that everyone remembers together, and that shape the team's dynamics in the present.

Storer of Reactions: This aspect acts like system software, guiding the team's collective reactions based on stored experiences and memories that team members share. Think of an NFL team that recently lost the Super Bowl. Its primary goal is to maintain the safety and well-being of the individual and the team, but the team also has stored reactions to major events!

Further exploring the subconscious influences that shape team dynamics, it's important to recognize the control you possess through conscious decision-making. This insight leads to an important aspect of your journey: the capacity to choose deliberately.

WHAT WE WANT: TO LIVE IN CHOICE – THE POWER OF CHOICE FOR WE

In Chapter 3, you learned about the *Living in Choice* model, introduced by Dr. Gary Cone, which emphasized the importance of selecting your mental states deliberately at the individual (ME) level. Now, extend this vital model to your collective (WE), and examine how these personal decisions influence team dynamics and overall success. This transition from the individual ME to WE's team-wide application illustrates how each member's choices can either enhance or impede the collective efficacy and emotional environment of the team. ME is the central component of the WE providing either a responsive and creative team atmosphere, or an atmosphere that is unable to contribute effectively to the vision of murmuration.

Consider these behaviors and accompanying mindsets presented in the *Living in Choice* chart that illustrate a shift from a reactive state to a responsive, creative state, thereby enhancing the collective WE:

1. **You have Courage:** You commit to *Living in Choice* now, and embrace the present moment with bravery.
2. **You are Willing:** You show readiness to shift Beliefs and embrace growth.
3. **You are Neutral:** You trust others and are satisfied with your position in life.
4. **You have Acceptance:** You embrace your responsibility to *Live in Choice*, and manage your thoughts, feelings, emotions, and behaviors as an integral part of WE.
5. **You have Reason:** You utilize wisdom to foster healing and understanding.
6. **You have Love:** You offer forgiveness, and extend understanding and compassion.
7. **You have Joy:** You welcome feedback from others as opportunities for improvement (think about the label on your *Jam Jar*).
8. **You have Peace:** You align with the vision of murmuration and its requirements for Awareness of the now and adoption of responsive behaviors; you STEP UP and invite team members to join you.
9. **You are Enlightened:** You recognize and understand the current state of your reactive thinking, feeling, and emotions, and limit reactivity within your team.

By revisiting the principles of the *Living in Choice* model from a personal perspective of ME and extending it to your collective actions as WE, you underscore each team member's ability to be a central driving force in influencing the team's culture. Mastery of these principles enables members to effectively contribute to a harmonious and dynamic team environment in which the collective objectives are achieved through individual contributions of choice and Awareness.

EMCS® Living in CHOICE
Levels of Responsibility

EMOTION

COURAGE
Affirming, empowered, feasible, constructive, strong, active, positive, engaged, excited, imaginative, possible, feasible

WILLING
Intentional, optimistic, enthusiastic, prepared, courageous, adequate, creative, playful, active, invigorated, answerable, worthwhile, responsible

NEUTRAL
Trust, satisfied, interested, fascinated, welcomed, needed, essential, tuned in, appreciated

ANTAGONISM
Hides inadequacy, feels attacked, annoyed, combative, indignant, bothered, counter-active, burdened, opposing

PRIDE/INDIFFERENCE
Belligerent, demanding, scornful, pessimistic, immobilized, numb, unfeeling, stagnant, destructive, disconnected, rigid, detrimental

ANGER/RESENTMENT
Hides behind "You hurt me and that gives me the right to protect myself," confused, incensed, over-wrought, wounded, hysterical, wrathful, fuming, furious, abused, unappreciated, rejected, numb, offended, hurt & used

FEELING

ACCEPTANCE
Harmonious, forgiving, adaptable, worthy, open, amused, approachable, deserving, choosing to, owning

REASON
Wise, understanding, bold, proud, daring, protected, selfless, thoughtful, motivated, considerate, understanding

LOVE
Reverent, benign, revelatory, risking, trusting, caring, knowing, pleasurable, secure, respectful, giving, responsible

DESIRE/HOSTILITY
Blaming, "Someone else is responsible for me not getting what I want.", Frustrated, picked on, sarcastic, trapped, mean, deprived, withholding, vindictive

FEAR
Anxious, escape, "Something will be taken away from me," avoids, uncared for, trapped, disappointed, frightened, threatened, overlooked, unacceptable, unwelcome, defeated

GRIEF
Regretful, despondent, tragic, self-blaming, victim, depressed, unacceptable, morose, melancholy, defeated, deserted

THOUGHT

JOY
Serenity, whole, exuberant, fulfilled, energetic, complete, unencumbered

PEACE
Perfection, bliss, harmony, trust, thoughtfulness, nurturing, complete

ENLIGHTENMENT
Pure, sincere, ineffable, aware, respectful, appreciating, powerful

SHAME
"I won't survive," humiliation, cowardice, betrayed, disgraced, self-blaming, dishonored, bad (embarrassed), doubtful

SEPARATION/GUILT
Self-destructive, non-entity, "God does not love me, therefore, I am unlovable," lost, ruined, condemned, ineffectual, conquered

APATHY
Waiting to succumb, resigned, hopeless, takes no responsibility for cause, uncared for, insignificant, powerlessness, distrustful & suspicious

| PRO-ACTIVE | REFLEX/ | RE-ACTIVE |
| State of Mind | BELIEF | |

Copyright 2003 • Gary Cone Corp. Inc. • Living in Choice Levels of Responsibility is used in the Energy Matrix Clearing Systems

Now let's see how ME in transition to WE can actively navigate the *ABC's of Murmuration*.

©2024 ABC's of Murmuration

PATH III
Explore and Walk a New Way

Exploring new paths, shaped by fresh experiences, often introduces stress for both individuals and the team—the collective WE. It's crucial to recognize that stress can significantly hinder mental performance. And to navigate these new challenges effectively, it's vital to engage in active communication as outlined by the *ABC's of Murmuration*. This approach can be applied not just individually (ME), but also collectively (WE), which enhances your unified ability to adapt and thrive.

THE ABC'S OF WE (TEAM) MURMURATION

- **AWARENESS**
  Be present and attentive to the needs of both individual (ME) and team (WE). This Awareness ensures that team actions are aligned with shared goals.

- **BELIEFS**
  Encourage the adaptation of new perspectives to promote team growth and resilience.

- **CONNECT**
  Foster unity and cooperation within the team to achieve collective objectives.

WHY AWARENESS MATTERS TO TEAMS (WE)

Why is Awareness critical? It involves balancing *what you really want* with *what you settle for*. In other words, it helps the WE *Live by Choice* rather than defaulting to the shared subconscious. For ME, recall that this Awareness starts with continuously and deliberately focusing on your mind, body, and spirit. You must pay immediate attention to your triggers. Understanding your subconscious mind's vast capabilities empowers you to harness this enormous database of information and channel it to your conscious mind. As you learned in previous chapters, you must learn to consciously use this information instead of letting it drive you and direct your destiny. You want to avoid an amygdala hijack. Learning to harness the subconscious is not easy, but this focused Awareness enables you to make decisions based on conscious choices rather than the automatic defaults of your subconscious system. These choices take work and courage!

An example of this interplay of emotions happened recently in a team meeting with a client. One of the team members faced open criticism in the meeting. Instead of reacting defensively due to an amygdala hijack, the team member then *Paused* to process the feedback, *Noticed* that they could use the criticism as an improvement platform, and *Chose* to engage in a constructive dialogue with the team to find solutions.

This example effectively illustrates the principles of Awareness, *Walking a New Way*, and STEPPING BACK to create a collaborative environment. The team member made conscious choices instead of yielding to the subconscious mind, and in doing so fostered positive dynamics in team communication. Everyone wins!

Enhancing Awareness paves the way and clears the brush so that your mind, body, and spirit can consciously choose your next steps. Becoming aware of what you really want affects not only your personal growth but also influences how you are perceived within the collective—your WE. As previously discussed, Ross Thornley's *Jam Jar* metaphor illustrates how—unknowingly confined by your subconscious—you may be unaware of how transparently your actions and attitudes are viewed by others. Many times your behaviors, as clearly written on your jam jars, dictate your teammates' responses or reactions to situations.

Thornley also shares another valuable skill to assess adaptability: the *Four Worlds of Adaptability*. These worlds—Thriving, Collapsing, Survival, and Growth—represent different states of adaptability and are revealed to others through your behaviors, much like the labels on the outside of a *Jam Jar*. These labels give others a clear indication of where you stand in terms of your adaptability, which shapes their perceptions of you. Thornley emphasizes the importance of reading these labels—both in yourself and others—to gauge your adaptability and understand how well you can navigate changes and challenges.

The Four Worlds of Adaptability *provide a framework for understanding where you and others stand:*

1. **THRIVING**

   In this world, adaptability is at its peak. Individuals in the *Thriving* world demonstrate creativity, flexibility, and resilience. You can easily adjust to changes, make proactive decisions, and contribute positively to the group. When you're in this world, your behaviors signal confidence and openness to new possibilities, and you inspire those around you.

2. **COLLAPSING**

   The opposite of *Thriving*, this world reflects a state of overwhelm and rigidity. Individuals in the *Collapsing* world resist change and struggle to cope with unexpected challenges. Your behaviors signal fear, frustration, or defensiveness. The *Jam Jar* label in this state might read as *resistant to change*, and others will perceive this difficulty in adaptation.

3. **SURVIVAL**

   This world represents a state of simply getting by. Individuals here are reactive rather than proactive. While you manage to stay afloat during challenges, you are not fully adapting or thriving.

Your behavior may indicate a focus on short-term solutions, often driven by necessity rather than vision. This world signals that you are stuck in a reactive mode, and are attempting to avoid collapse but not yet moving toward growth.

4. GROWTH

In this world, you are evolving, actively learning, and improving your adaptability skills. You are not yet in a *Thriving* state, but you are making conscious efforts to move toward it. Your behavior shows a willingness to learn and adapt, and others see you as engaged and open to new ideas. The label on the *Jam Jar* might read as *on the path to change*, which signals hope and active progress.

By understanding these *Four Worlds of Adaptability*, you can better assess how adaptable you or your team members are in different situations. Thornley suggests observing others' behaviors and emotional states—the labels on their *Jam Jars*—to become more aware of your team's adaptability as a whole. This Awareness enables you to adjust your own behaviors and interactions accordingly, which ensures you're contributing to a collective environment that fosters growth and adaptability.

Ask yourself: Do team members generally exhibit behaviors associated with *Thriving, Collapsing, Survival,* or *Growth?* And, more importantly, what world do I tend to inhabit, and how can I move toward *Thriving?*

FOUR WORLDS OF ADAPTABILITY

1. THRIVING

- Do they appear to be flourishing? Are they engaging with smiles and laughter, which demonstrates enthusiasm and positivity in their interactions?
- *If so, they are highly adaptable, and embrace change with confidence and resilience. This thriving state suggests they can navigate challenges effectively and remain open to growth.*

2. **COLLAPSING**
   - Do you observe behaviors that suggest disruption or shutdown? Are they displaying signs of freeze, fight, flight, or fawn in response to stress?
   - *If so, they may be struggling with adaptability. These behaviors indicate they are overwhelmed by change and may need support to recover and regain balance.*

3. **SURVIVAL**
   - Does their behavior seem restrained, as if they are just getting by, like a car stuck in neutral? Do they seem reactive rather than proactive, maintaining the status quo without forward momentum?
   - *If so, they are in survival mode, managing to cope but not fully adaptable. They may need guidance to move from reactive responses toward a more proactive, growth-oriented mindset.*

4. **GROWTH**
   - Do you perceive expansion and improvement in areas that were previously stagnant? Are they making progress and learning from past challenges?
   - *If so, they are on a path of growth, actively improving their adaptability. This shows they are learning from challenges and working toward a thriving state with continued effort.*

By understanding and applying the *Four Worlds of Adaptability*, you can navigate the delicate balance between thriving and struggling within your teams. Awareness of these states—both in yourself and others—equips you with the insight needed to foster a more adaptable and resilient team environment. As you move forward, you must remember that the journey from ME to WE is not just about individual growth but also about the collective's ability to thrive together.

In the next chapter, you will explore the deeper dynamics of autonomy and *mutuality*, and understand how these principles shape your interactions within teams. You will dive into how the strength of individual contributions aligns with the shared goals of the collective to create a seamless flow from ME to WE, and ultimately, to US.

TEST YOUR INTUITION

Your intuitive mind Connects the personal ME with the collective WE, which opens a realm of limitless possibilities. By attuning to it, you can enhance your Awareness of team needs and dynamics. Consider these reflections, all of which engage the intuitive mind:

Contemplate Your Understanding of an Issue with a Team: Reflect on your understanding of the subconscious and conscious minds. What is something that happened in a team interaction that made you pause, based on a trigger (Subconscious)? What did you notice (Movement from subconscious to conscious)? What did you consciously choose to do (Conscious choice)?

Reflect on Behavioral Change: Recall a time when you consciously chose a new path as a team member (a ME part of WE). What was your behavior, and can you identify the exact moment when your Awareness shifted? What did it look and feel like?

The *Jam Jar* Metaphor: Try to see yourself from both inside and outside your own *Jam Jar* in the example from one of the two previous reflections. What was your label saying to others? Before your Awareness and conscious choice? After your conscious choice?

> **Examine Reaction vs. Response:** Consider a different situation in which you reacted rather than responding thoughtfully. Analyze your behavior from within the jam jar and then read the label. What underlying Beliefs might be influencing the words on the label?

WHY BELIEFS MATTER TO WE (TO TEAMS)

Why are your Beliefs critical to the WE? Your subconscious Beliefs drive all of your behavior unless you consciously choose to override them. Again, it's about balancing what each individual truly desires against what they typically settle for. Your Beliefs are ingrained in your subconscious from early in life—even before you were born—and are perceived as truths by your subconscious. These Beliefs shape your thoughts, feelings, and behaviors. Your Beliefs transform into habitual actions, which might be unacceptable, disrespectful, or hurtful, which affects not just you but others within the WE context.

Because of the vast capabilities of your subconscious, these habitual behaviors persist. The more frequently a belief or habit is triggered, the more challenging it becomes to alter the resultant behavior. However, remember that you are not bound by the default settings of your subconscious; you do have the power to change. Once you become aware of how your actions are received by others, or when you recognize how others perceive you—as if reading the label on your own *Jam Jar*—you can consciously decide to respond differently.

You are not doomed to react based on old habits. Being aware of behaviors that are reactive and potentially harmful allows you to choose a more constructive approach.

MY REACTIVE SUBCONSCIOUS STORY
By Kathy Hagler, Ph.D

During my 20-year tenure as a consultant for a particular company, a sudden change in leadership resulted in my dismissal. Initially, this left me feeling insignificant and powerless, emotions that spiraled into feelings of being unlovable and fearing for my survival—reflective of deep-seated apathy and guilt. Over the years, I had become deeply integrated into the company's culture, feeling like a part of its familial US. Our collective achievements had filled me with pride, which made the subsequent feelings of dishonor and disgrace even more painful.

As grief set in, it brought a profound sense of defeat and desolation, as if my professional life had abruptly ended. This grief evolved into fear and hostility, feelings exacerbated by a sense of displacement from a role I had cherished. Remaining employees wanted to keep in touch, but my responses were tainted by anger and resentment for being excluded from a circle where I once belonged. This led me to distance myself, a reaction I later recognized as antagonistic.

Years later, these colleagues accused me of ghosting them, challenging me to question the subconscious habits that had governed my actions. Had my deeply ingrained Beliefs, formed over years of camaraderie and now suddenly defunct, prompted me to instinctively sever ties and isolate myself?

Reflecting on what a more conscious approach might have looked like, I considered alternative responses that could have honored the deep connections formed over those two decades:

- **Enlightenment:** Acknowledging your shared growth and achievements
- **Peace:** Seeking closure in transitions rather than viewing them as endings
- **Joy:** Celebrating past collaborations despite the separation

Had I been equipped with a more profound Awareness and a mindset aligned with the principles of murmuration—Awareness, Belief, and Connect—perhaps my responses could have fostered continued relationships rather than estrangement. This introspective realization highlights the transformative potential of reevaluating your emotional responses through a more conscious and reflective lens to ask: What proactive choices could have sustained the WE that had thrived for so long?

What could have been a more conscious choice?

Reflecting on the principles of Awareness, Beliefs, and Connect, I now see how these could have reshaped my initial reactions:

- By recognizing the value of your past collaborations, I could have expressed gratitude rather than retreating.
- Opening dialogue about my departure could have facilitated a transition that honored mutual respect and appreciation.
- Maintaining connections could have transformed the pain of departure into a celebration of shared memories and ongoing relationships.

This reflective journey underscores the importance of understanding how deeply your subconscious Beliefs can affect your actions, and emphasizes the value of consciously navigating emotional landscapes to maintain and honor the collective WE.

WHY CONNECTION MATTERS TO WE (TO TEAMS)

When each individual (ME) Connects with another, that connective process involves tuning into the signals the other person emits about themselves, their emotions, and their needs, alongside the signals you emit about yourself. Being a responsive ME requires recognizing and interpreting these signals, which encompass both verbal and nonverbal messages. These signals provide insights into the authenticity of communications and can quickly convey messages of truthfulness or dishonesty. Essentially, signals can indicate if a person is engaging with, opposing, or distancing themselves from others. They can also reveal underlying motivations; what someone is thinking and feeling, and how their thoughts and feelings drive their behaviors.

While some signals are overt—like a hand gesture signaling "stop" or "go"—most are far more nuanced. For example, conscious signals like applause can denote congratulations, while subconscious ones like an eye twitch might reveal nervousness. We all constantly emit signals, mostly without conscious Awareness. In fact, it's virtually impossible not to communicate these signals when in the presence of another person.

In your next team meeting, take a few moments to observe the nonverbal cues of those around you. Pay attention to subtle signals such as posture, facial expressions, and tone of voice. Notice whether someone seems engaged, nervous, or disconnected based on these signals. Afterward, reflect on what you observed. Did any of the signals surprise you? How do these nonverbal cues shape the overall dynamics of the team? This Awareness of subtle signals can give you insight into how others are feeling, even when words may not fully convey their emotions. You can see them in their *Jam Jar*.

For a deeper Connection, try a paired feedback exercise. Engage in a five-minute conversation with a teammate about a project or task. After the conversation, share what signals you each perceived—both verbal and nonverbal. Discuss whether or not the signals matched the intended message, and if any cues were misinterpreted. This exercise can highlight the nuances of communication and help build greater understanding and alignment within the team.

Connection within a team goes beyond words; it's about tuning into the subtle cues that reveal what others are truly feeling and thinking. By becoming more attuned to these signals, you foster a deeper understanding of those around you and create an environment in which authentic communication can flourish. As you strengthen these connections, you move from individual efforts to collective harmony, and you can build a team that thrives on mutual Awareness, trust, and shared purpose.

©2024 ABC's of Murmuration

PATH IV

Engage in Conscious Habits of Thriving

Let's focus on the habits that contribute to building a resilient and adaptable team. Developing these habits requires conscious effort and a commitment to growth, both individually (ME) and as a group (WE). Here are some steps to guide this development.

CONSCIOUS HABITS (CAUSE) AND EXAMPLES OF BEHAVIOR (EFFECT)

Cause and effect, in many instances, are pretty obvious. When plants are consistently watered, they survive. If they are not watered, they die. Cause and effect. If the health and harmony of WE are consistently part of the Awareness of ME, it will thrive. If your behavior toward another is controlled by your subconscious and allowed to be reactive, the WE will soon disappear. Cause and effect. The effect first shows up in the behavior of ME and then in the continued thriving or demise of WE.

STEP UP: Initiate the first action
Example of Behavior: Shows initiative

STEP BACK: Allow others to STEP UP
Example of Behavior: Demonstrates love and acceptance (listens actively; allows personal space for another to initiate)

STEP TOGETHER: Embrace mutual trust and respect
Example of Behavior: Willingly and courageously communicates and resolves conflicts

To murmurate, both ME and WE must adopt all three starling habits that support conscious thriving: STEP UP, STEP BACK, and STEP TOGETHER. Here, "adopt" signifies embracing something new, beyond mere expansion of current knowledge. It means accepting these new behaviors mentally and then engaging in them as actively and as often as possible. Doing this requires effort at multiple levels. Integrating intentional habits demands mental openness and adaptability, rather than just tenacity and perseverance.

When faced with real or perceived threats to thriving, the instinctive response of your mind is often to resist change or avoid risk as a protective measure. However, the presence of a secure base within the team—one that is responsive and supportive—shifts the focus from pain, danger, fear, and loss to reward, opportunity, and benefit. The secure base allows you to intentionally practice the habit of STEPPING TOGETHER.

It's crucial to strike a balance in team interactions. Failing to inspire team members to explore and embrace challenges can lead to overprotection, which ultimately stifles their potential. Which is why you must all adopt the habit of STEPPING BACK to make room for others to STEP UP. Conversely, encouraging risk or change without providing the necessary safety, security, or compassion is difficult for the one being given space to STEP UP.

THE CONSCIOUS HABITS FOR WE

STEP UP: Initiate the first action
- First, inspire through modeling a responsive and creative behavior to others on the team
- Second, deliver a powerful message through courage and initiative
- Third, focus on the positive

STEP BACK: Allow others to STEP UP
- First, compassionately respond to another's initiative
- Second, influence by enthusiastically following them
- Third, actively help others improve their self-control

STEP TOGETHER: Embrace mutual trust and respect
- First, see the potential in the team

- Second, signal accessibility and compassion to others through words and actions
- Third, encourage collective risk-taking and growth

The wisdom and energy of WE starts with ME. Inside and around you are energy fields that many call your life force. Each of you has multiple fields that ebb and flow, and can merge with the energies of others. Imagine the fields of energy surrounding a WE! The combined wisdom and power that coalesces when each ME allows their energy field to merge with another ME. This chapter has encouraged you to open yourself to connection with a WE; to essentially prepare to share your energy field with others. In the next chapter, you will explore the relationship between the collective (WE) and the individual (ME) more in-depth so you can continue to ease into a *unified consciousness* with your team members.

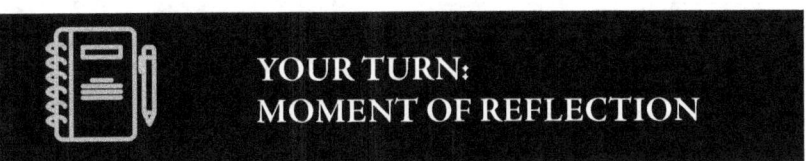

YOUR TURN: MOMENT OF REFLECTION

Reflect on your role within your own "flock"—be it your workplace, community group, or social circle. How do the dynamics of a starling murmuration mirror the interactions within your team? Use the insights from this chapter to evaluate how well your team communicates and collaborates, and consider the following:

1. **IDENTIFY YOUR NUMBER SEVEN:** Just as starlings effectively manage their interactions by limiting their focus to seven neighbors, identify seven key relationships in your team that most influence your work or behavior. How can improving these relationships enhance overall team dynamics?

2. **ROLE REFLECTION**: Consider your own role in team interactions. Are you more often STEPPING UP, STEPPING BACK, or STEPPING TOGETHER? How can you better balance these actions to support your team's goals?

3. **ASSESS TEAM SIGNALS**: Consider your *Jam Jar*. Think about the overt and subtle signals you and your teammates emit. Are these signals mostly positive, or do they sometimes create barriers to understanding and cooperation? How can you foster more positive communications?

4. **ENVISION THE ICEBERG**: Reflect on the "iceberg" of your team's collective mind. What is visible on the surface, and what might be hidden beneath? How does this hidden content influence the visible interactions and decisions?

5. **SET A GOAL FOR COLLECTIVE SUCCESS**: Based on your reflections, set a practical goal for yourself (for ME) that promotes a stronger, more cohesive team dynamic. Outline steps you can take to achieve this goal, inspired by the natural wisdom of a murmuration.

Take a moment to write down your thoughts and any specific actions you plan to take. Sharing these with a trusted teammate could be a powerful step toward transforming your collective environment.

How-to Skills: see pages 313–316 for more information

Four Worlds of Adaptability
Jam Jar
Living in Choice
SCARS Model

Global Thought Leaders: see pages 317–320 for more information

Gary Cone
Ross Thornley

CHAPTER 8

BEING ME AND WE: AUTONOMY AND MUTUALITY

A person is a person through other persons.
You can't be human in isolation.
You are human in relationships.

—**Archbishop Desmond Tutu** [66]

IMAGINE A RIVER MEANDERING BETWEEN THE BANKS. In it is a solitary droplet that is ME. As it travels it gains momentum, gathering more droplets, another ME, and begins to flow, bubbling along in a shared direction, embodying the collective WE. This confluence, where the singular ME merges into the WE, does not erase the essence of ME; rather, it honors each droplet, making it an essential part of the greater whole.

In nature, a single starling in a murmuration does not merely join the formation; it intentionally confluences with six others. This creates a dynamic and interconnected WE of seven, not a loss of identity but an expansion of being and achieving in a larger field of doing. In this dance, each starling, each ME, maintains its individuality while also becoming part of something larger, more exquisite, and profoundly interconnected. This harmonious blending—in which ME transitions and evolves into WE—is what is referred to as confluence, which allows the energy flow from ME to WE, the beginning of superpositioning. It's a dance as ancient as time, and underscores that each ME's true power expands in WE, which acknowledges that you are all part of a grander design. In the unity of confluence, you find strength, resilience, and an innate capacity to rise together.

In every institution, community, and gathering, the dance of murmuration calls forth, beckoning each ME to become a part of the river; the collective WE. Each ME enriches the WE and, in turn, each WE enlivens each ME, which illustrates a spiral of evolution and unity.

Thus, in the context of the *ABC's of Murmuration*, a fundamental truth is highlighted: ME flows into WE, and discovers in this confluence the energy of unity that defines and elevates human existence.

THE ESSENCE OF THE TEAM – THE WE

The strength of the team is each individual member. The strength of each member is the team.

—Phil Jackson[67]

In a team, or WE, the coming together of individuals influences and shapes the others. Each ME is uniquely shaped by their own subconscious and conscious mind, body, and spirit. The WE, especially in starlings, functions as one entity, with persistence, preparation, passion, and joint progress in their collective workspace.

By understanding that starlings have perfected the **art of iterative team formation**, you start to recognize the intricate link between their immediate, external environment and their internal reality. In 2020, scholar Cary Wolfe highlighted the importance of not viewing animals in isolation but considering the *situatedness* or position in their environment.[68] Starlings know that joining together to form a team of seven saves time and energy in unpredictable settings. A group of seven can discern the directional cues from the contrasting colors of each others' feathers, which guides them to STEP UP, STEP BACK, and STEP TOGETHER. This optimal team size facilitates their survival dance, and embodies their collective vision and purpose, and drives their intuitive and intentional actions toward their collective goal: US.

Each starling experiences superpositioning—existing in dual states—as an independent ME and simultaneously as part of WE, which then integrates into US. As you reflect on the interplay of nature's principles within team dynamics, consider the ease and comfort found in the company of a close friend. The individual identities remain intact, yet your paths merge seamlessly through shared conversations and actions. This fusion of experiences paves a new trail of collective growth and exploration. This imagery not only illustrates the process but also encourages you to examine how a team effectively operates as a cohesive unit.

Navigating survival in the natural environment often presents intricate challenges. Starlings, through their innate behaviors and collective actions, distinguish themselves in the wild by adopting routines that emphasize teamwork and community. They possess a natural ability to mirror the movements and actions of their neighbors, which is critical for their collective survival. Studies on starlings, even those raised in captivity, show that from a young age, they engage in communication with other birds in their flock, and quickly become part of a collective WE.

The survival strategy of starlings is rooted not in scarcity or fear, but in thriving together; a compelling drive that fosters their transformation into a cohesive WE. Unlike behaviors often observed in human groups, starlings exhibit no signs of limiting Beliefs, fixed mindsets, or aversion to challenges. They don't give up when faced with adversity. Instead, they leverage collective strength and intelligence to overcome obstacles. Their approach to survival is not about merely avoiding loss but actively pursuing success, with a clear vision of murmuration guiding their actions.

As you venture forth, your collective mindset shifts toward achieving murmuration. This phase of your journey emphasizes the importance of aligning your actions with a shared vision, and allowing emergent behaviors to guide you through the metaphorical forest toward the ultimate goal.

Next, you will be introduced to frameworks and strategies that fall under the Four Paths, all of which can be used to ease ME into WE. Beginning with PATH I, you will and see how adopting an *Evolutionary Mindset* can enable the formation of a productive and attuned WE.

©2024 ABC's of Murmuration

PATH I

Embrace an Evolutionary Mindset

Poet Max Ehrmann once said, "You are a child of the universe, no less than the trees and stars; you have a right to be here. And whether or not it is clear to you, no doubt the universe is unfolding as it should."[69] Scholar Cary Wolfe supports this philosophy, and describes resultant energy generated by these activities as the **Activity Field** of ME, or the **Energy of Doing**. This "doing" energy originates within the individual ME, and serves as the foundational energy of an individual, characterized by a dynamic and innovative flow, balanced symmetry, and gentle vibrations. It fosters sensitivity for the emotionally conscious mind of ME, discernment for the body to learn *how to*, and an inquisitive spirit to build a *want to*. Each are essential for personal growth, self-reflection, and actions.

However, since you are setting out on the journey of expanding from ME to WE, you should focus on the potential results of such an expansion to WE. The results are apparent in the **Relationship Field** (WE). People form WE to expand the field of energy and improve effectiveness. Relationship energy has the ability to multiply the sum of all individual energy contributions. Wolfe says that this field is the **Energy of Interaction**, which is generated in the WE. This energy exchange is communication. The information is experiential and empathetic. The measurable results of this field are verbal and nonverbal communication, and are discernible through the senses.

STRATEGIC DOING™ FRAMEWORK

In this spirit, you are introduced to the *Strategic Doing*™ framework, an action-oriented model that also fosters the development from ME to WE to US, which facilitates human murmuration. Created by Dr. Ed Morrison and his colleagues at Purdue University, this approach moves beyond traditional strategic planning. Instead of relying on rigid plans, *Strategic Doing*™ encourages real-time collaboration, in which groups identify shared assets, define mutual goals, and take immediate, iterative actions. The contributions of each team member's assets drive this exchange. Sharing assets facilitates a deeper appreciation of each person. Initiating open discussions about personal assets effectively assigns a "predefined label" to each person, which allows team members to recognize and value the unique attributes of everyone at the table. This STEPPING UP and STEPPING BACK creates leaderful interactions from the entire team and leads to remarkable outcomes. Each ME sees others as leaders and shifts from a one-leader mindset to shared leadership and responsibility.

This framework equips teams with other practical tools to navigate and adapt in real-time, which allows them to move fluidly within this dynamic "doing model." Similar to Wolfe's Energy of Interaction, which emphasizes the dynamic flow of energy during interactions, the *Strategic Doing*™ process facilitates this energy exchange through authentic communication and collaboration. ***The framework includes these key steps:***

- Research and identify a team project.
- Collaboratively discuss and identify each member's unique assets for this project.
- Identify possible ideas for addressing the issues the project presents.
- Prioritize ideas based on (1) potential impact and (2) feasibility. Which has the most significant effect, and which can be addressed now?
- Identify the *"Big Easy."* This is the strategy or solution that promises the most significant return with the least resistance.
- Create an action plan for the next 30 days and track progress.
- Communicate weekly.

The 30/30 meetings and reports involve committing collectively to be resilient by having each team member commit to spending about 30 minutes a week working on their part of the solutions and having a meeting every 30 days to create the next steps based on collective actions.

Strategic Doing™ enables groups, teams, and communities to Connect more effectively, especially in complex and dynamic environments. By focusing on "What we can do together?" this framework leverages each individual's strengths and resources to create collective momentum. By promoting action, *Strategic Doing*™ helps teams move forward quickly, make adjustments as needed, and achieve their shared purpose.

Throughout the rest of the book, you will learn how elements of the *Strategic Doing*™ framework contribute to the evolution from ME to WE to US, and you will gain insights into how these approaches can support personal and collective growth. Like starlings in murmuration, which seamlessly adapt to their environment as a collective, this framework provides a structured yet flexible way to align actions, strengthen team dynamics, and achieve collective success.

Furthermore, Patrick Lencioni's *The Five Behaviors*® serves as a comprehensive guide for understanding and applying the adaptive *Evolutionary Mindset* that is essential for transitioning from ME to WE. ***Like Strategic Doing*™, *Lencioni's model highlights key behaviors that are essential for collective collaboration and success:***

1. **Accountability**
2. **Commitment**
3. **Conflict**
4. **Results**
5. **Trust**

These behaviors and actions position each ME to align their own mind, body, and spirit in harmony, which prepares them to flow with others into a unified WE. You will first define what personal alignment looks like for ME around these five behaviors, and then show how the behavior provides the environment for the connection, the WE.

Accountability: Requires that each ME *wants to* own their responsibility and feel self-respect by consciously and honestly offering their assets to the team. It also provides tangible evidence to the potential WE that the ME is "playing to win."

Commitment: Always do what you tell yourself and the team by identifying those principles and actions that matter most, and never be at the mercy of those that matter least. As ME has a personal trust in self, that self-worth and follow-through shows to the other members of WE.

Conflict: Always use the *CLEAR Model* to resolve conflict. When resolving conflict within a team, the *CLEAR Model* serves as an essential skill to guide the process. This tool offers a structured approach to navigating difficult conversations and achieving mutual understanding. It also provides the other members with the confidence that this ME will be a trusted partner in WE.

- **CLARIFY** the issue using facts.
- **LISTEN** to the other person's perspective.
- **EXPRESS** your own perspective.
- **AGREE** on a mutual understanding.
- **RESOLVE** with a plan of action.

Results: Ask yourself: *Why* you *want to* do something (spirit), *what to* do to accomplish it (mind), and *how to* do it (body) to achieve the outcome you and the team agree to. Always, always check back (habit), using a scheduled practice of checking-in.

Trust: Trust can be defined as Honesty, Integrity, Promise-Keeping, and Loyalty. Honesty is important in both word and deed, and relates mostly to your behaviors (the body). Integrity is moral courage and relates more to your values (the spirit). Promise-Keeping is about avoiding bad-faith excuses that come from limiting beliefs (the mind). And Loyalty is about avoiding conflicts of interest (mind and spirit).

So how do you foster these five key behaviors within a team? Before you do anything else, you must establish a supportive environment in which every ME can freely contribute to the team their strength in these five behaviors, their assets, and their skills. This safe, inclusive setting allows each ME to reflect and appreciate the actions and attitudes of their peers, thus forming a cohesive WE. Only then can you progress to exploring Lencioni's behaviors and dive into the *Strategic Doing*™ framework. Now look at some of the tools and processes that will support each of Lencioni's five key behaviors.

TEAM BEHAVIOR #1: ACCOUNTABILITY

Perception Change: Understanding Other's Perceptions

The *Jam Jar* tool, which has been used throughout this book, provides a way to think about who you are to others. Through this tool, you can visualize how their perception of you impacts the ways they interact with you. And your perception of others influences the ways you interact with them. However, a first step is to understand that you are inside the jar and they are outside the jar. On the outside of the jar is a label describing your behavior that they can read and use to form a perception of you. This situation presents many unknowns. Accountability involves having a mindset of motivation, of *wanting to* be open to sharing your personal assets with the other team members.

If you are in the *Jam Jar* and are feeling like you don't want to participate in the WE, the team, it will show in your behavior, and the other team members can read the label on your jar that probably says, "I do not want to be here; let's get this over with." Similarly, you might read the label on their jar that says, "Then why should I participate if you are not going to?" Accountability requires conscious *want to* and follow through, and the requisite behavioral signs from your face and body.

This is where the skill *Zooming In* and *Zooming Out* becomes helpful. *Zooming In* allows you to focus on the specific details of your behavior, your emotions, and the signals you're sending. *Zooming Out* enables you to take a STEP BACK and see the bigger picture, understanding how your individual actions affect the entire team. See the label you are portraying to others. By utilizing this skill, you can assess both your immediate reactions and their broader impact, which helps you consciously decide, "What do I want instead?" This perspective shift empowers you to make more intentional decisions and contribute meaningfully to the team dynamic.

Team Skills: Sharing Assets

Familiarity with the team's assets is key to productive collaboration. To facilitate appreciation and accountability for each team member and their contributions, initiate open discussions about personal strengths. Allow team members to clarify their own assets and be recognized and valued for their unique attributes. These attributes then become the "predefined label" on each person's *Jam Jar*. Once these assets are declared by the team member and brought into the present moment, they become the standard for that team member's accountability. To further foster a cohesive team environment, each team member must do their best to adapt their perceptions based on these newly shared insights into the Beliefs and behaviors of each ME.

Motivation: Embracing a Leaderful Approach

Strategic Doing™ is about each team member being accountable for using their proclaimed assets to achieve the team goals. Their motivation is largely rewarded by the collective effort and unity that come from a **leaderful mindset**. By embracing a leaderful approach with all team members, you can shift from an authority-based mindset to shared leadership where STEPPING UP is key. In a leaderful team, each team member is accountable for team results.

TEAM BEHAVIOR #2: COMMITMENT

Perception Change: Lay New Snow by Zooming In and Out

The concept of *Laying New Snow* involves adjusting your actions and communication to ensure alignment with your intentions, making it clear to others what you stand for. (Having your behavior match what you choose, not what your subconscious drives you to do.) In other words, your conscious behavior and words must match. In a team context, this process requires a personal commitment and

STEPPING BACK to consider others' perspectives, likened to *Zooming In* on your own behaviors and *Zooming Out* to anticipate how others might interpret them. The goal is to pave new pathways of understanding and interaction—both for yourself and your team members.

Team Skills: Driving Innovation With Divergent Thinking

Commitment in a team setting is enhanced through the use of divergent thinking, in which open-mindedness and creativity allow for the exploration of novel solutions. This approach encourages each team member to bring their unique insights and strengths to the table to create a rich tapestry of possibilities.

In *Strategic Doing*™ commitment is deepened by the collective brainstorming of ideas and prioritizing them using the *"Big Easy"* rule—a process that identifies strategies that offer the greatest impact with the least resistance. By asking, "What can WE do that will have the biggest impact while being the easiest to accomplish?" teams surface, agree to, and pursue ideas that are both impactful and feasible.

This process fosters a shared sense of purpose and strengthens team commitment. As members collaboratively identify and prioritize solutions, their collective engagement grows, cementing their commitment to innovative actions that benefit the entire team.

Motivation: Embracing Change and Being Leaderful

The motivation to commit to the team mirrors the intricate dance of murmuration, in which each individual's contribution is vital to the group's ability to navigate and adapt. This resilience is built on a foundation of adopting new perspectives and a shared leadership approach, where every member feels empowered to lead, suggest, and support initiatives—that is becoming leaderful. As a leader or team member, find ways to ensure every individual ME in the WE you are creating feels comfortable voicing their views and offering their ideas. This, in turn, will cement their commitment to the group by bolstering their loyalty.

TEAM BEHAVIOR #3: CONFLICT

Perception Change: Engaging an Integrated Mindset

To quickly review, Integrated Mindset is a balanced state that accesses both the logical and creative processing capacities of the mind, body, and spirit. This approach equips individuals with the capability to navigate threats and collaborate effectively within a team. It provides the tools for a starling to react to a hawk when threatened, and to respond to neighbors as a collective WE. An example of this might be a conflict in a family setting. The teenage daughter is anxious to sprout her "driver's license" wings and take the family car to a party in a large city 50 miles away, at night, alone. The parents react with strong emotions to the threat they perceive for her. Their *Footlights of Consciousness* cause them to feel the pull of the subconscious to react verbally and vigorously to their daughter's request. They Pause and Notice that it is natural for their subconscious to respond immediately to danger. What they want instead is to maintain their good relationship with their daughter *and* respond to her with alternative, safer suggestions.

An Integrated Mindset also enables one to discern between immediate challenges and longer-term obstacles, and avoid reactionary responses driven by the amygdala. Their immediate reaction of fear and danger was driven by the amygdala. After *Pausing* and *Noticing* the potential to longer-term relationship damage, and also exhibiting behavior they would not want her to model, they suggested that since they have friends of their own in the city, she could drive the whole family over to the city. The parents could drop her off, go visit their friends, and pick her up at a reasonable time. They discussed the possibilities and jointly came up with the plan.

Team Skills: Implementing Multiple Moments of Pause

Critical when conflicts arise, this technique involves taking deliberate breaks to process and respond rather than react in the heat of the moment. Any of the following practices can help individuals respond to conflict in a way that is more productive than destructive:

- **PAUSE:** Courageously, choose to take a moment of calm and breathe.
- **NOTICE:** Picture yourself "putting the car in neutral," to pause and gain perspective on the situation and your subconscious reactions. Or think of yourself as a *Torchbearer in a Cave*, embracing the uncertainty but trusting the light you carry—your wisdom and Awareness—to guide you. In this state, you can choose a conscious response rather than relying on automatic reactions shaped by past habits.
- **CHOOSE:** Embrace vulnerability and decide to either STEP UP or STEP BACK to foster active listening and clear communication.

Team Skills: Active Listening and Straight Talk

Essential in resolving conflicts, these skills ensure that every team member feels heard and understood. Active listening involves fully concentrating on the speaker, understanding their message, providing feedback, and deferring judgment. Straight talk, on the other hand, is about communicating openly and honestly, ensuring transparency and fostering trust among team members.

Motivation: Fostering Adaptability and Autonomy

Adapting with a STEP BACK Approach: Reflecting the dynamic interplay seen in nature's murmurations, this strategy emphasizes the importance of releasing preconceived notions and embracing the moment with openness and flexibility. By STEPPING BACK, individuals can reassess their approach, granting autonomy to others and fostering a collective resilience that is vital for navigating conflicts successfully.

Caveat: It's crucial to acknowledge the potential health consequences of harboring negative Beliefs and engaging in toxic relationships. For example, you may blame sickness for an annoying headache and having trouble sleeping. According to the Mayo Clinic, stress not dealt with leads to many health problems, such as high blood pressure, heart disease, stroke, obesity, and diabetes.[70] The common effects of stress on your mood are anxiety, anger, sadness, memory problems, and feeling overwhelmed. In addition, this underscores the importance of adaptability and being attuned to your emotional and environmental contexts to prevent conflict from undermining the well-being of your mind, body, and spirit.

TEAM BEHAVIOR #4: RESULTS

Perception Change: Establishing a Secure Base

What people believe shapes what they achieve. When team members are confident that they have a secure base within the group, their actions reflect this security, which leads to positive outcomes. This concept draws a parallel with starlings, which rely on the support of their immediate neighbors to navigate and thrive. Similarly, by setting up clear cues and protocols, a team can establish a secure base, which enhances trust and reliability among its members. This secure base is not just about physical safety but also about psychological safety, which allows team members to take risks, innovate, and achieve collectively, which yields exponentially better results.

Team Skills: Strategic Implementation

- **Cultivating Collaboration:** Successful teams implement *Strategic Doing*™ by cultivating key skills that drive results. These include:

  - **Collaborative Problem-Solving:** Leveraging diverse perspectives to identify and tackle challenges efficiently
  - **Adaptive Action:** Responding swiftly to change and making decisions that keep the team progressing
  - **Clear Communication:** Ensuring that goals, roles, and expectations are understood by all members
  - **Responsibility Sharing:** Distributing tasks and responsibilities in a way that leverages each member's strengths and fosters collective ownership of outcomes

Motivation: Aspiring to Collective Excellence

STEPPING TOGETHER means "playing to win" and it involves more than just striving for individual success; it's about aligning individual assets and actions toward a common goal. This collective approach ensures that the team not only achieves its objectives, but does so in a way that is adaptive, cohesive, and mirrors the seamless coordination found in nature. As a leader or team member, cultivate mindsets that encourage individuals to aspire to collective excellence so the entire group can deliver extraordinary results.

TEAM BEHAVIOR #5: TRUST

Perception Change: Learning to Release the Past

Letting go of past experiences is essential for fostering trust with others. Much like starlings—which inherently trust their flock through established, ingrained habits—team members must learn to develop trust by becoming adaptable. This process involves creating a foundation in which individuals feel secure and supported, which enables the team to function as a cohesive unit. By prioritizing the release of past biases, fears, and expectations, and focusing on Awareness, Beliefs, and Connect (the *ABC's of Murmuration*), teams build a strong foundation of trust. In the past example, imagine that the parents of the teenage daughter had lost a son due to a drunk driver on the highway at night. Their past experience created a habit of reaction to danger that was understandable but needed to be released in order to create the ability to consciously choose in the future.

Team Skills: Strategic Communication for Trust Building

The *30/30 communication strategy*, an integral part of *Strategic Doing*™, is a structured approach designed to foster open, consistent, and forward-thinking dialogue within the team. Every 30 days, team members come together to discuss what they have accomplished in the past 30 days and set goals for the next 30 days. This regular cadence ensures that the team remains aligned, can quickly adapt to new challenges, and maintains momentum toward achieving their goals.

Teams that adopt the 30/30 approach learn to trust each other deeply through this process of consistent communications. They also gain a predictable and reliable means of interaction to push both individual and collective thought processes toward the realm of possibilities.

Motivation: Embodying Collective Trust

A mindset that empowers team members to STEP BACK and allow others to STEP UP fosters collective trust. This motivational stance is about expressing and embodying trust within the team. Saying "I trust you" is more than a verbal affirmation; it's a commitment to shared goals, mutual respect, and the belief in each other's abilities and potential. This approach encourages team members to rely on one another.

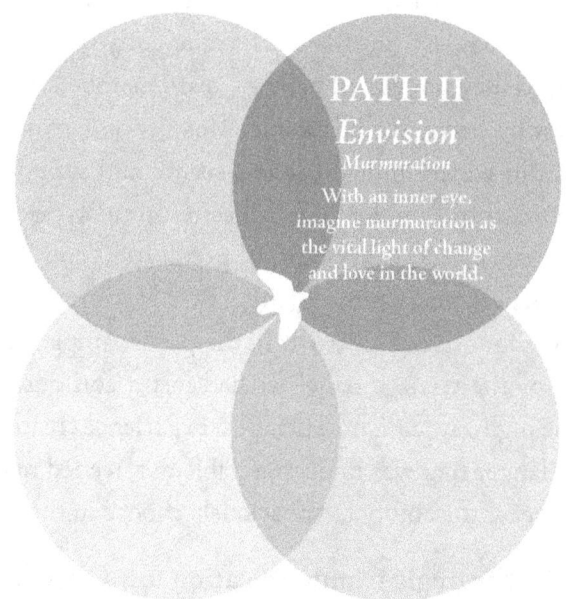

©2024 ABC's of Murmuration

PATH II

Envision Murmuration

Strategic Doing™ offers a robust framework for tackling multifaceted challenges. This includes a fundamental question that frames the collective inquiry, *What could we do together?* Imagining the possibilities and envisioning teams moving together as a murmuration, you position yourself to draw inspiration from the starlings.

> *Imagine if we could unite like a flock, shielding ourselves and each other from predators, adverse weather, and scarcity, achieving our highest potential despite environmental adversities.*
>
> —Robin Graham

Strategic Doing™ mirrors the preparation processes of starlings as they gear up for murmuration. This framework illuminates how, faced with environmental uncertainties, the collective mindset—the WE—can overcome significant challenges. These challenges primarily stem from the inability to fully acknowledge and confront subconscious fears and biases, which are deeply ingrained and often go unnoticed.

The journey toward consciousness as a WE involves confronting these hidden fears of the past and negative thoughts that sabotage their best intentions. Many individuals remain in denial to the illuminating moments that bring your deeper fears into the light of Awareness. The avoidance of these revelations, driven by fear, leads to a collective stagnation. The team gets undeniably stuck! This subconscious dynamic constrains the team, which limits their ability to consider alternative strategies or solutions. It underscores the importance of moving from a subconscious to a conscious mode of operation.

The essence of choosing a vision of murmuration lies in simplicity. It calls for a collective shift toward a consciousness in which each team member actively participates in transforming their individual fears into strengths. This transformation is central to the team's survival and success. As a WE, you must learn to move beyond reacting to your environment and start actively shaping your responses.

WHAT SHOULD WE DO?

Living in Choice, according to Dr. Gary Cone

Let's once again revisit Dr. Gary Cone's *Living in Choice* model, which emphasizes the significant impact that choice has on both personal and professional levels. There is power in your choice to consciously shape your reality.

As you'll recall from previous chapters, central to Dr. Cone's model are two distinct states of mind: the expansive, growth-oriented responsive state, and the constrictive, limiting reactive state. These states are not just for individual team members, but also for the collective mind of the team. Choosing between responsiveness and reactivity shapes your Beliefs, thoughts, feelings, and, ultimately, your actions. Your decisions play a pivotal role in team dynamics.

Choosing responsiveness unlocks potential for growth, innovation, and effective problem-solving. It fosters a mindset of flexibility and openness, which are crucial for navigating the complexities of team dynamics. Conversely, a reactive state can obstruct progress and escalate conflicts. Rooted in unchecked Beliefs and fears, reactivity curtails your capabilities and disrupts team cohesion.

The *Living in Choice* model emphasizes personal accountability as key in selecting your mindset. A team's commitment to be responsive rather than reactive enriches the team's ability to tackle challenges. By integrating Dr. Cone's insights, you're reminded of the transformative effect of conscious choice on your interactions and outcomes.

WHAT WILL WE DO?

Adopting the *Living in Choice* model means ME commits to a proactive, responsive mindset, which enhances your synergy with WE. This commitment translates into specific responsibilities:

EMCS® Living in CHOICE
Levels of Responsibility

COURAGE
Affirming, empowered, feasible, constructive, strong, active, positive, engaged, excited, imaginative, possible, feasible

WILLING
Intentional, optimistic, enthusiastic, prepared, courageous, adequate, creative, playful, active, invigorated, answerable, worthwhile, responsible

NEUTRAL
Trust, satisfied, interested, fascinated, welcomed, needed, essential, tuned in, appreciated

ANTAGONISM
Hides inadequacy, feels attacked, annoyed, combative, indignant, bothered, counter-active, burdened, opposing

PRIDE/INDIFFERENCE
Belligerent, demanding, scornful, pessimistic, immobilized, numb, unfeeling, stagnant, destructive, disconnected, rigid, detrimental

ANGER/RESENTMENT
Hides behind "You hurt me and that gives me the right to protect myself," confused, incensed, over-wrought, wounded, hysterical, wrathful, fuming, furious, abused, unappreciated, rejected, numb, offended, hurt & used

EMOTION

ACCEPTANCE
Harmonious, forgiving, adaptable, worthy, open, amused, approachable, deserving, choosing to, owning

REASON
Wise, understanding, bold, proud, daring, protected, selfless, thoughtful, motivated, considerate, understanding

LOVE
Reverent, benign, revelatory, risking, trusting, caring, knowing, pleasurable, secure, respectful, giving, responsible

DESIRE/HOSTILITY
Blaming, "Someone else is responsible for me not getting what I want.", Frustrated, picked on, sarcastic, trapped, mean, deprived, withholding, vindictive

FEAR
Anxious, escape, "Something will be taken away from me," avoids, uncared for, trapped, disappointed, frightened, threatened, overlooked, unacceptable, unwelcome, defeated

GRIEF
Regretful, despondent, tragic, self-blaming, victim, depressed, unacceptable, morose, melancholy, defeated, deserted

FEELING

JOY
Serenity, whole, exuberant, fulfilled, energetic, complete, unencumbered

PEACE
Perfection, bliss, harmony, trust, thoughtfulness, nurturing, complete

ENLIGHTENMENT
Pure, sincere, ineffable, aware, respectful, appreciating, powerful

SHAME
"I won't survive," humiliation, cowardice, betrayed, disgraced, self-blaming, dishonored, bad (embarrassed), doubtful

SEPARATION/GUILT
Self-destructive, non-entity, "God does not love me, therefore, I am unlovable," lost, ruined, condemned, ineffectual, conquered

APATHY
Waiting to succumb, resigned, hopeless, takes no responsibility for cause, uncared for, insignificant, powerlessness, distrustful & suspicious

THOUGHT

PRO-ACTIVE	**REFLEX/**	**RE-ACTIVE**
State of Mind	**BELIEF**	

Copyright 2003 • Gary Cone Corp. Inc. • Living in Choice Levels of Responsibility is used in the Energy Matrix Clearing Systems

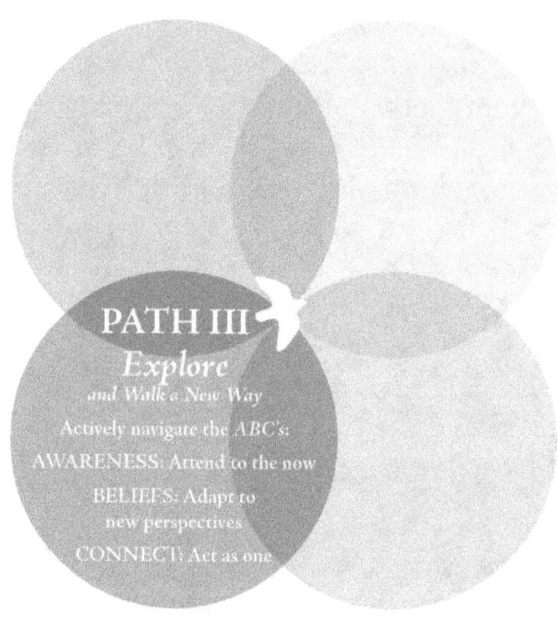

©2024 ABC's of Murmuration

PATH III

Explore and Walk a New Way

Walking a New Way invites each individual (ME) to harness their unique assets for the collective good, which marks the transition from ME to WE. It emphasizes the importance of recognizing and utilizing individual assets and merging them to create a collective path forward. By sharing assets, this encourages diverse thinking and open exploration of possibilities, which creates a judgment-free environment. This approach is foundational in building trust and ensuring all team members have an equitable opportunity to contribute, which lays the groundwork for effective collaboration.

See what it looks like to navigate the *ABC's of Murmuration* as a team.

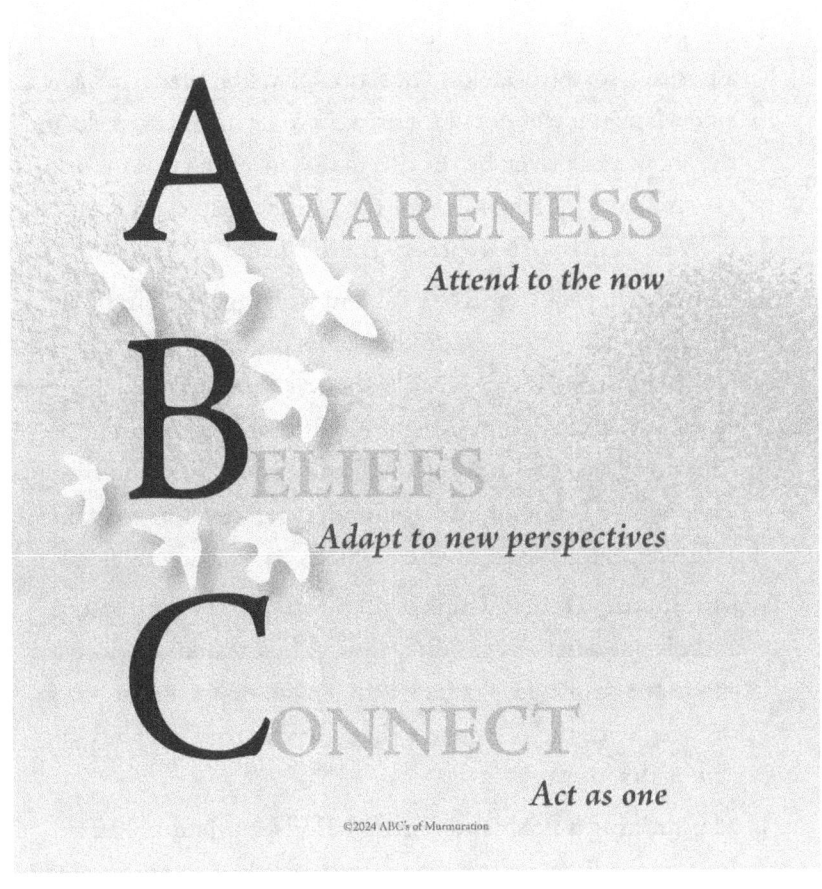

AWARENESS: ATTEND TO THE NOW

Are You Engaged in the Present Moment?

AWARENESS AND STRATEGIC DOING™

In the context of murmuration, Awareness emphasizes the importance of being present and fully engaged with the current moment. Applying practices from the *Strategic Doing*™ framework, this focus on the "now" is critical for dynamic and effective teamwork.

Key practices from Strategic Doing™ that support this focus include:

- **Developing a Framing Question:** Highlight the necessity of a positive, forward-looking question or vision that establishes a new landscape of possibilities, akin to laying fresh tracks in the snow, and driven by the diverse assets of the team. Use this question as a guiding force for the team to help every member of WE maintain Awareness of shared goals.

- **Committing to Adaptive Problem Solving:** Each individual commits their key assets to the team's problem-solving efforts, which ensures the group can respond effectively to challenges as they arise. The commitment of key assets to a current situation creates within each ME the opportunity and the *want to* STEP UP and use their talents in the now to make a difference for the team. It becomes very empowering.

- **Eliminating Deficit Thinking:** By recognizing the potential and diverse assets within the team, deficit thinking—viewing situations from a lens of lack rather than opportunity—is replaced with the Awareness that they are part of identifying new paths forward.

- **Maintaining a Problem-centric Mindset:** Maintain an Awareness of current challenges to keep the team grounded in the present. This approach leads to the proactive identification of successive solutions, which advances the team forward.

- **Engaging with Heart:** Each team member brings to the table their Awareness of the problem and their unique assets that can help address it. Their motivation or *want to* support the effort and succeed ensures that each individual is deeply invested in addressing the challenges at hand.

This approach to *Walking a New Way* underscores the power of collective action and the significance of staying present. By leveraging individual assets for the common good and maintaining a focused, engaged mindset, teams can navigate new paths with creativity, resilience, and a shared sense of purpose.

BELIEFS: ADAPT TO NEW PERSPECTIVES

Have you shifted your limiting perspectives to positive feelings of potential?

The transformation of Beliefs and the adoption of new perspectives in response to evolving challenges are both essential for fostering a mindset of learning and growth within the WE. Adaptability is at the heart of *Strategic Doing*™ as it encourages you to see yourself as interconnected parts of a larger whole. *Engaging in Strategic Doing's iterative learning practices involves leveraging these strategic mindsets:*

- **Motivation to Overcome Complex Challenges:** Like the adaptive strategies of starlings, embracing complex challenges requires moving beyond a deficit mindset to adopt a solution-oriented approach. This positive outlook transforms challenges into opportunities for growth and demands a strong desire for change within each individual (ME) and the team (WE).

- **Acquiring Knowledge for Shifting Perspectives:** The *Strategic Doing*™ process offers key practices that supports the shifting of limiting Beliefs. One such practice, *Doing the Doable*, emphasizes focusing on achievable goals and committing small victories to the team's larger success. This feeds the desire within each ME to adopt a new perspective and tackle challenges with fresh energy. Staying Present encourages individuals to let go of past limiting Beliefs and focus on current challenges with clarity. Lastly, Responding Instead of Reacting promotes *Pause, Notice, and Choose*, which allows for intentional decisions over impulsive reactions. These practices together help individuals contribute more meaningfully to collective goals.

- **Addressing and Mitigating Toxic Behaviors:** To stop behaviors that may be toxic to others, it is necessary that ME address limiting Beliefs that undermine team cohesion. For example, if ME has a habit of giving to others with the hidden expectation of getting what they want in return, even if that fact is hidden from another ME, the resulting relationships will suffer. Both parties will feel tricked and dissatisfied. Recognizing and modifying these behaviors is essential for the collective well-being and success of the team (WE).

By committing to conscious shifts in belief and perspective, each team member plays a crucial role in steering the team toward enhanced collaboration and sustained growth. This journey of transforming Beliefs not only enriches the individual but also strengthens the fabric of the entire team.

CONNECT: ACT AS ONE
Have you committed to collectively asking— What will we do?

First, each individual (ME) must commit to aligning mind, body, and spirit. Second, each ME must commit to fostering a deep sense of unity with WE. *The practices of Strategic Doing™ nurture a holistic connection and emphasize the synergy present with unified action:*

- **Leveraging Collective Intelligence:** When teams harness their collective intelligence, they enable agile responses to opportunities. This agility is achieved through a dynamic balance of focusing on immediate tasks (*Zooming In*) and maintaining Awareness of the broader context (*Zooming Out*), thus enhancing the team's adaptability.

- **Building Trust and Collaboration for Cohesive Decisions:** Establishing a foundation of trust is essential for effective collaboration. This involves not just the readiness to adapt to changing circumstances but also the willingness to shift perspectives as needed.

- **Cultivating Fun, Joy, and Engagement in Team Activities:** The process of planning and execution should be imbued with elements of fun and joy, which reflects the spontaneous harmony seen in a starling murmuration.

The reciprocal relationship between individual contributions and collective outcomes is a cornerstone of *Strategic Doing*™. This approach mirrors the natural world, in which the individual movements of starlings, each responding to its neighbors, result in the mesmerizing and cohesive patterns of a murmuration.

©2024 ABC's of Murmuration

PATH IV

Engage in Conscious Habits of Thriving

Chapter 8: Being Me and We: Autonomy and Mutuality

Within the collective ecosystem of WE, diverse skills and perspectives are not just respected; they're the cornerstone of the shared journey. *Strategic Doing*™ suggests identifying a **Pathfinder Project**, a collaborative endeavor that aligns team actions toward a common outcome. This process can be likened to the intuitive formations of starlings, which demonstrate collective movement toward a shared goal. For example, starlings might work together to find a warm place to roost. Similarly, a Pathfinder Project uses guideposts to keep everyone aligned and moving forward. Drawing on the wisdom of murmuration, individuals are encouraged to STEP UP, STEP BACK, and STEP TOGETHER, embodying collaboration and adaptability.

STEP UP
Initiate the first action

STEP BACK
Allow others to STEP UP

STEP TOGETHER
Embrace mutual trust and respect

©2024 ABC's of Murmuration

STEP UP: Initiate the first action

Why? To bring clarity and direction for the benefit of WE

What To Do? Approach initiation with confidence, yet without asserting dominance

How To Do It?

- Embrace broad, innovative thinking to pave new paths
- Promote transparency and open communication
- Create an atmosphere for others to contribute and lead

STEP BACK: Allow others to STEP UP

Why? To honor and value the contributions of others

What To Do? Recognize that STEPPING BACK is a proactive step toward fostering a cohesive WE

How To Do It?

- Cultivate growth by letting others know you are making space for their voices
- Allow autonomy to flourish, occasionally through use of strategic silence

STEP TOGETHER: Embrace mutual trust and respect

Why? To build a dynamic, energized, and committed community

What To Do? Encourage a culture of inquiry that propels WE forward

How To Do It?

- Support each member's unique contributions to the team's success
- Foster action-oriented collaboration
- Utilize group challenges as opportunities for learning and growth

By embracing these practices, you can expertly navigate your path and mirror the adaptability and cohesiveness of starling in murmuration. This guide is not just a method but a journey towards thriving together as a collective, embodying the principles of *Strategic Doing*™ with the grace of nature's guidance.

As you conclude Walkway II, the Walkway of WE, you've enhanced the understanding of the dynamics of WE, integrating strategic tools and behavioral insights essential for robust team collaboration and creating collective wisdom. This chapter has prepared you with actionable strategies and frameworks that emphasize the importance of every team member in cultivating a harmonious and effective work environment.

Moving forward, your journey will extend these concepts from WE to US in the subsequent Walkway of US. Chapter 9 will explore how to expand these collaborative principles to encompass broader organizational and community contexts. You will learn how individual strengths, when unified, can propel entire groups toward innovation and collective success. This next phase will focus on practical applications to transform individual efforts into cohesive group achievements to embody the spirit of murmuration on a larger scale.

YOUR TURN: MOMENT OF REFLECTION

As you conclude this chapter, engage with the critical behaviors for team effectiveness by reflecting on their applications and planning specific actions:

1. **ACCOUNTABILITY – PERCEPTION INSIGHTS**: Reflect on a recent team scenario where accountability was lacking. How could the introduction of the *Jam Jar* tool have influenced the outcome? Identify one action you can take to enhance accountability within your team using this tool.

2. **COMMITMENT – SKILL BUILDING**: Consider a current project your team is working on. What specific skills from the *Laying New Snow* approach can you develop to strengthen your commitment to the project's success?

3. **CONFLICT – STRATEGY APPLICATION**: Think of a recent conflict within your team. Using the *Pause, Notice, and Choose* technique, outline a strategy for more effectively resolving similar conflicts in the future.

4. **MOTIVATION THROUGH STARLING INSPIRATION**: How can the example of a starling murmuration inspire you to foster a more cohesive and resilient team environment? Identify one practice you can adopt—such as the STEP UP, STEP BACK, STEP TOGETHER method—to mirror the adaptive strategies of starlings.

5. PERCEPTION CHANGE – APPLYING INSIGHTS: Choose the behavior of Trust. Reflect on how changing your perception around trust could improve your team dynamics. Plan a small, actionable step you can take to begin this change using the "CLEAR Communication" framework. An example of this would be to remember the "CLEAR" protocol and always start conversations with "C"—Clarify the issues using facts. Always starting with this small, actionable step will cultivate the habit of stating the facts first, without the reactive behavior that occurs when the first step is to express your feelings stored in the subconscious mind.

How-to Skills: see pages 313–316 for more information
The Five Behaviors™ model
Footlights of Consciousness
Jam Jar
Laying New Snow
Living in Choice
Strategic Doing™
Zooming In / Zooming Out

Global Thought Leaders: see pages 317–320 for more information
Gary Cone

WALKWAY III: US

An Invitation to
STEP UP, STEP BACK, STEP TOGETHER

CHAPTERS 9-10

CHAPTER 9

BIRDS OF A FEATHER FLOCK TOGETHER

Individually, we are one drop.
Together, we are an ocean.

—Author Ryunosuke Satoro[71]

LIFE'S TRUE SYMPHONY UNFOLDS WHEN THE HARMONY OF ME (THE MIND, BODY, AND SPIRIT) JOIN WITH ANOTHER ME TO FORM A TEAM (WE). These teams must then form *cross-team collaboration* to move onto the conscious Walkway of US. US is a group, network, or community that works in concert to mirror the pure beauty of the universe. Imagine grass swaying in the breeze or a murmuration of starlings; ephemeral yet eternal, each participating individual a single note in the grand score of existence.

These natural marvels offer profound insights into the universe's mysteries, and elevate your understanding of collective consciousness. The collective consciousness moves from ME to WE to US, with ME always in a superposition with WE and US. In other words, ME coexists in each of the states of being, just like an individual starling. And each team of WE also coexists in US.

THE ESSENCE OF US

Look again at the wonderful world of murmuration. Cary Wolfe suggests that to truly understand animals, including ourselves, you cannot separate them from their environmental context.[72] In a murmuration, consider how a group of starlings don't just exist within an environment, they become one with it; their dance a testament to this unity. They are part of an expansive field of wonder, survival, and beauty. Each starling (ME) intricately Connects to the collective (WE), influencing and being influenced by their shared space, their field of energy. This dynamic interaction causes the constant evolution of the environment and that of each ME. This dynamic energy has the potential of evolving to US.

The COVID-19 pandemic slowed the pace enough that many could truly appreciate the intricate patterns of nature. The traffic slowed, the noise dampened, the sky was cleaner. This global pause allowed each ME to observe the lessons offered by murmuration, and emphasized the value of STEPPING TOGETHER as a WE. As you STEP TOGETHER, remember that this process is the individual ME transitioning into a broader existence, intertwined with numerous others and with the environment as your ally. COVID-19 also provided the stillness and quietness for teams of WE to come together. This manifested by using technology. Teams began to willingly use various synchronous platforms to Connect regularly. Because this could be done without extensive expense and travel, teams began to collaborate less reluctantly and more often. They started to *Walk a New Way*. The pandemic changed the nature of movement from ME to WE and the cross-collaboration of teams. In some ways, US has more potential than ever to be harmonious.

In understanding this transition from ME to WE to US, you see the environment's pivotal role in your evolution. The external world's complexities and pressures are integral to the collective experience. As you continue the journey through this book, you will explore the universal result of successful cross-collaborative teams that have aligned with the environment and are now US. The field of possibilities is endless. Recognizing the importance of ME, WE, and US interactions with the environment and its inhabitants provides valuable insights into the choices you make when navigating your paths with others.

PREPARING TO MURMURATE: BECOMING US

When organizations use the murmuration parameters as a template, they are better equipped to achieve their vision and mission. They do this by being Aware of the now, shifting their Beliefs and perspectives, and Connecting with their communities of clients, business partners, and resource providers. By understanding their role within the larger environmental field and the rapidly evolving global workspace, they are more adaptable. *Walking a New Way* enables organizations to know *what to* do, *how to* do it, and *want to* show up and shine in their markets.

You have read about many of these principles and skills throughout the book—but now you will see how they specifically tie into creating alignment and collaboration within organizations, helping each ME and WE contribute to a thriving collective.

1. An Attraction Zone: STEP UP to initiate

To create momentum, teams must **STEP UP** and cultivate an atmosphere of belonging and innovation. ***This means:***

- Modeling how to link and leverage assets to create new opportunities.
- Converting high-priority opportunities into envisioned results.
- Using knowledge-sharing as a driver of innovation, encouraging each ME to take the initiative and learn what it means to be "leaderful."
- Encouraging initiative-taking across the team, so each member contributes to achieving the team's vision.

2. Angular Alignment: STEP BACK to allow your neighbors to STEP UP

It is equally important to **STEP BACK** at times and support the growth of others. *This involves:*

- Creating a shared sense of belonging by fostering a culture of attentive and curious followership
- Being a secure base for others as they STEP UP, which allows each ME to contribute their expertise
- Facilitating the transfer of knowledge between teams for more effective communication and collaboration

3. A Repulsion Zone: STEP TOGETHER and fly in your own lane

STEP TOGETHER represents the synchronized movement of the team, where individuals take responsibility for their own role while collaborating seamlessly. *This can be done by:*

- Sharing responsibility for success, with each member taking accountability for their lane
- Eliminating information silos and promoting a culture of openness
- Ensuring a sense of belonging extends to every individual within the larger team, uniting efforts toward collective success

Finally, it's important to be mindful of common obstacles that can sabotage cross-team collaboration:

PEOPLE and Trust: A lack of trust between team members can hinder collaboration. To address this, create opportunities for trust-building and resolve trust issues as they arise.

PLACE and Physical Barriers: Physical separation or unclear collaboration spaces can create challenges. Agree on designated places and times for teams to meet in order to ensure smoother teamwork.

PROCESS and No Action Plan: Without a clear process or action plan, teams may lack direction. Establish civility rules and detailed action plans to keep everyone aligned and accountable.

EXPLORING THE COLLECTIVE PATHS OF NATURE

The journey of transformation from ME to WE and ultimately to US is seen in the chart below. Each step, whether embarked upon individually or collectively, marks a transition toward greater wisdom and a deeper connection with the ever-changing environment. As ME merges into WE, the collective Awareness of the present moment becomes crucial to navigating the challenges and opportunities that lie ahead. When multiple teams of WE transition into US, your Beliefs expand and evolve to accommodate the accumulated wisdom and adapt to the shifting sands of your surroundings.

This realization underscores the importance of US in maintaining the equilibrium of the collective. WE, STEPPING UP to initiate in the US; WE, STEPPING BACK to support others in the US; and WE, STEPPING TOGETHER with others to embrace respect and trust as a unified entity of US. Each of these actions helps maintain the balance for all participants.

In this dance of ME, WE, and US, you will find not just a path to growth and protection but also a deeper communion with the essence of life itself. As you've moved through these chapters, progressing from understanding the individual journey to embracing the collective voyage and realizing the oneness of US, you've learned how to harmonize with the external world. You are now empowered to craft a legacy of ultimate success through partnership and mutual understanding.

TRANSITIONING FROM CONCEPTS TO APPLICATION

Murmuration requires the presence of three entities. Each entity of ME, WE, and US has its own Walkway to master. Within each of these Walkways, there is a Four-Path Journey along with directions to guide the way for the ME, WE, and US.

Charting the Map of the ABC's of Murmuration

THE WALKWAYS	WALKWAY I WALKWAY II WALKWAY III				
THE FOUR-PATH JOURNEY	EMBRACE	ENVISION	EXPLORE	ENGAGE	EMERGE
	Evolutionary Mindset	Vision of Murmuration	Walk a New Way	Conscious Habits of Thriving	OUTCOME

This chart represents the Four-Path Journey of the ABC's of Murmuration: *Embrace, Envision, Explore,* and *Engage,* each associated with specific actions that lead to personal and collective growth. The Walkways, ME, WE, and US, guide the process from individual evolution to a collective vision, and foster new ways of collaboration and thriving.

NAVIGATING THE FOUR-PATH JOURNEY OF US

Why Embark on the US Journey?

At this point in your journey, you are invited to envision murmuration not just as starlings in flight but as a manifestation of human collective intelligence—whether in stories collectively shared on a stage, dancers around a campfire, or the intricate life of bees within a hive. Here, information flows seamlessly within a rule-based system, from the individual (ME) to the collective (WE) and encompassing the whole (US), in an effortless exchange of knowledge. This constant flow of information illustrates how collective wisdom emerges, and provides a framework for understanding your interconnectedness.

Remember, the common element within each stage of murmuration is ME. It is YOU. You are wired to be able to position yourself as a ME, as a neighbor or WE, and finally as an US, and you become embedded in the collective wisdom of the group.

So, what does ME gain by evolving into US? According to global thought leaders Jon Berghoff of *xchange* and Ross Thornley from AQai®, human murmuration, or US, provides countless gains. ME thrives by being part of the collective intelligence and capacity of US, adapting the mind, body, and spirit in the process. As ME, you must understand that your ears only hear and your eyes only see what your brain is conditioned to look for. Initially, ME operates with Awareness centered on the self, shaped by past experiences and subconscious filters. However, by shifting perspectives, ME can observe "what is" without relying on those past filters and judgments.

Both *xchange* and AQai® emphasize that the future is already here—it simply hasn't been evenly distributed yet. But it will be, and those who follow the *ABC's of Murmuration*—ME, WE, and US—are uniquely positioned to embrace it.

Let's take a look at how The Beatles reflected this type of adaptability while still maintaining their unique personalities. Remember, The Beatles created the possibility of becoming the distributor of a new music phenomenon by transcending their individual limitations and achieving a level of greatness that has left a lasting legacy in the world of music.

THE BEATLES: FLOCKING TOGETHER THROUGH SYNERGY

The Beatles—despite their individual differences in personality, creative vision, and musical style—consistently demonstrated the power of collective action and unity. Much like the mesmerizing murmuration of starlings, in which each bird contributes to the intricate and harmonious movement of the whole, The Beatles' true power arose when they worked as a group. They came together to create music that resonated across the globe. Their ability to set aside individual desires for the greater good of the group allowed them to produce timeless albums that continue to influence music and culture worldwide.

Throughout their career, The Beatles faced numerous challenges that tested their cohesion as a band. Yet they always found a way to harness their collective energy, and blended their unique talents to produce something far greater than the sum of their individual parts. Whether it was the groundbreaking *Sgt. Pepper's Lonely Hearts Club Band* or the introspective *Abbey Road*, The Beatles' albums are a testament to the strength of unity and the creative potential unlocked when a group works together with a shared purpose.

The synergy of The Beatles was not just about creating music but also about navigating the complex dynamics within the band. Each member had moments when he needed to STEP BACK and allow others to take the lead, and trust in the collective process. This mutual respect and understanding of their individual and collective strengths enabled them to evolve as a group, and create music that continues to inspire and resonate with audiences today.

In essence, The Beatles exemplified the concept of "flocking together" as they moved through their career. Their collective action, much like a murmuration, was a dance of unity in which each member played a crucial role in the group's success. This powerful synergy allowed them to transcend their individual limitations and achieve a level of greatness that has left a lasting legacy in the world of music.

The Beatles made their collaboration look easy and effortless (for the most part), but intense work was happening behind the scenes. This is because achieving synergy with others and accessing the collective wisdom of US doesn't happen without some effort. Now you will explore the steps teams must take to make this possible.

©2024 ABC's of Murmuration

PATH I

Embrace an Evolutionary Mindset

For teams (WE) to progress toward unity and collective action, a foundational transformation within each individual (ME) and their respective teams is essential. This transformation involves each ME learning to be adaptable and emulating the behaviors of their teammates (neighbors) within their seven-member group. These social processes empower each ME to operate interdependently, and enhance the collective efficacy of WE. **To make this possible, effective teams must:**

1. Embrace and enhance their evolutionary collective intelligence anytime the world shifts

2. Face the challenge of immediate Awareness by harnessing adaptable intelligence to *Zoom In* and *Zoom Out* to improve tacit knowledge transfer

3. Create a sense of trust by practicing STEP UP, STEP BACK, and STEP TOGETHER; fostering belonging; and supporting *Leaderful Behavior*

But even before teams can focus on these three key actions, they must first find ways to learn from each other. This journey of adaptation by adopting new perspectives to Connect with other teams is crucial and must be undertaken freely. Rumi's words, "Move within, but don't move the way fear makes you move," remind you of the importance of advancing as WE with a mindset rooted in growth and exploration, rather than fear.[73]

To dismantle fear, it must be acknowledged and addressed in the light of day—through open communication and deliberate actions. The fear response is a biological amygdala hijack that nearly puts you into a state of blindness. It overtakes parts of your conscious thought processes. And, not only is it about trusting adaptability, it's also about getting to a state of peace during that chaos to allow for creativity, and to assure you do not damage relationships. ME must learn from others (WE) without fear.

Learning from others is a significant gain for ME and involves paying attention to opportunities to build trust between teams. Remember ***The Three P's (People, Practices, Place)*** for teams. People must strive for trust at all times. Places and times to convene must be agreed upon. And finally, Practices and **rules of civility** are shared and agreed upon. This helps remove fear from the workplace.

By fully leveraging their assets and addressing team dynamics through effective communication and feedback, teams maintain Awareness of their external environment, adapt Beliefs as needed, and stay Connected. These adaptable teams are also capable of merging with other seven-member units as they progress toward the ultimate goal of murmuration.

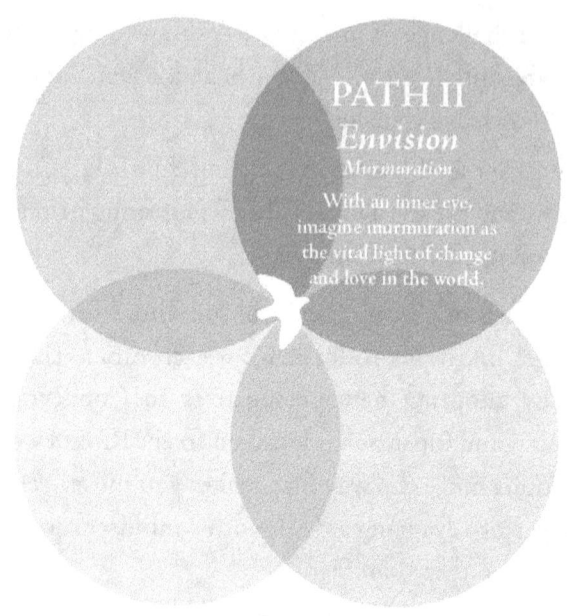

©2024 ABC's of Murmuration

PATH II
Envision Murmuration

Murmuration involves a deliberate process of adaptability in which teams collectively refine their Beliefs, thoughts, and behaviors to align their perspectives toward achieving a shared dream. This journey of adaptability is intertwined with trailblazing; a bold and radical advancement toward the envisioned state of thriving together. Adaptability includes **grit**, mental functioning, mindset, resilience, and unlearning.

One powerful tool that helps organizations assess and enhance their adaptability is the *AQai® Assessment*. This assessment measures the *Adaptability Quotient* of each individual (ME) within an organization, and provides valuable insights into their capacity to navigate and embrace change. By evaluating factors such as emotional intelligence, learning agility, resilience, and environmental awareness, the assessment offers a comprehensive view of how prepared both individuals and teams are for the challenges of a rapidly evolving world.

The *AQai® Assessment* doesn't just highlight areas for improvement; it provides strategic direction for organizations looking to cultivate a culture of adaptability.[74] In today's fast-paced environment where change is constant, having data-driven insights allows organizations to make informed decisions about training, development, and strategic initiatives. The true power of this process lies in the actionable data it provides, which enables teams to identify strengths, address weaknesses, and collectively enhance their ability to adapt and thrive.

The *AQai®* model provides a framework for individuals to understand their abilities, character, environment, and motivation. ***It provides individuals and organizations the tools to:***

- Assess the situational context (*What's it really like here?*) and understand its implications for the team, clients, and community
- Set a vision, mission, and goals to guide both immediate and long-term actions
- Anticipate change
- Adopt and STEP UP to new and emerging opportunities

For teams (WE), this path to murmuration is paved with trust, mutual respect, and a tangible demonstration of belief in one another's capabilities through action. It's about fostering an environment in which each member feels valued and heard, where the collective vision becomes a beacon guiding all decisions and actions.

Effective decision-making processes that balance robustness with decisiveness are critical on this journey. Such processes ensure not just the making of sound decisions but also a unified commitment to executing these decisions, propelling the team forward. Achieving the vision of murmuration requires more than just alignment; it demands action, perseverance, and a shared commitment to turning the vision into reality.

Through this collective endeavor, multiple teams of WE or US navigate the complexities of collaboration and change. By continually adapting and trailblazing, teams unlock the potential to thrive as humans, embracing the transformative power of unity and shared purpose.

THREE SKILLS FOR PRACTICING TEAM ADAPTABILITY

1. What To Do

According to adaptability expert Thornley, the key to true adaptability lies in your ability to *Lay New Snow*. He explains that just as skiers carve ruts and tracks by repeatedly following the same path, you, too, fall into habitual patterns of thought and action. While these familiar routes offer comfort and predictability, they limit your ability to innovate. To truly adapt, you must be willing to step outside of those well-worn paths and create fresh ones, embracing new mental flexibility and openness to novel solutions and approaches.

In *Laying New Snow*, the *Strategic Doing*™ framework can help guide this process by asking your team key questions like, "*What could we do? What should we do? What can we do? And ultimately, what will we do?*" This process promotes collective exploration and decision-making, which enables teams to chart new, more effective paths forward. How might you venture out of your familiar patterns and *Lay New Snow* in your own journey?

2. How To Do It

Thornley also explains the *how to* for developing team adaptability. He suggests that the team picture themselves being in a dark chasm of caves with only a Torchbearer illuminating what is within their immediate sphere of influence. It is not until the team walks to the edge of this light that new rooms—new opportunities—can be revealed. And even then, the team can't view it in totality because they only have the ability to see where the torchlight extends.

In this way, each team member holds a torch that represents their individual vision. As they move forward and explore the edges of their known environment, they reveal new possibilities. Together they must decide: Should we turn left or right? Should we go up or down? This ongoing exploration is key to fostering adaptability and discovering new pathways forward. What "edges" of your environment or understanding could you explore further to reveal new opportunities?

3. Want To Do It

It takes motivation to be adaptable, to have *grit*, practice mental flexibility, maintain a positive mindset, be resilient, and be willing to unlearn something you struggled hard to learn the first time. Think of a time when you were determined to accomplish something meaningful. Which of these characteristics played a key role in helping you move forward?

Achieving a vision of murmuration is about a sustained effort of adaptability. Aligning people's mindsets and inspiring them to act. It requires not just theoretical commitment but practical, everyday actions that embody the group's purpose and vision.

As teams embark on this journey, they will navigate through the complexities of collaboration and change. This process transforms groups of individuals (WE) into a cohesive unit (US) that not only shares a vision but actively works toward realizing it, which embodies the true spirit of murmuration.

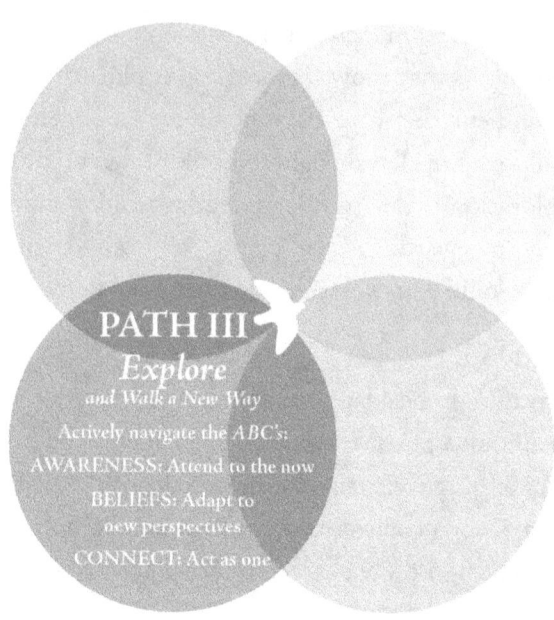

©2024 ABC's of Murmuration

PATH III
Explore and Walk a New Way

Momentum toward murmuration is fueled by a deeply ingrained drive: the instinctive pursuit of thriving, as seen in starlings. Central to this drive is the principle of "playing to win"—a concept introduced earlier that reflects the true motivation, the *want to* that drives starlings to achieve their collective success. In the context of human teams, this principle emphasizes the importance of having a clear purpose and commitment to propel individuals and teams toward a shared goal. This drive highlights the need for adaptability, in which embracing new directions and leveraging shared experiences and goals become essential.

However, one of the most overlooked dimensions for teams is the deliberate cultivation of habits that foster engagement and harmony, especially in a constantly changing, disruptive world. This dimension involves not just adapting but actively shaping the future by embracing principles like "playing to win" with both personal and collective focus, ensuring long-term growth and success.

The world and very existence are evolving at a pace that feels like warp speed compared to times past. Society often rewards knowledge—knowing facts (*what to*), know-how, and skills (*how to*) with praise, jobs, and degrees. Many times, you save time by bypassing the *want to* and ignoring the spirit. Are you motivated by "things" or your heart's desire? Can humans remain the dominant species intellectually and the ethically, compassionate, responsible being to ourselves and others and fully use our mind, body, and spirit?

Knowledge explains *what to* do and *why*. Skill is the *how to* do. But desire is the motivation, the *want to* do. To make something a lasting habit in your life, three elements must be present. However, desire is the fuel that propels ME to take proactive steps in life. Without it, the best knowledge and skills remain inert.

The *AQai® Adaptablility Quotient* Model also provides a template for individuals and team members to better understand their motivations. When applied within the context of a group (US), this understanding fosters a collective mindset of oneness, which paves the way for greater harmony and organizational effectiveness.

As both starlings and humans explore these paths, it's the collective spirit, the teams of WE, that craft the journey forward to US. This adaptation, this willingness to explore uncharted territories, is underpinned by the core principles of murmuration:

As you have seen, this triad of principles—Awareness, Beliefs, and Connect—serves as the compass that guides teams through the complexities of change and adaptation. It's through this dynamic process of exploring by walking new paths that teams, like starlings, achieve the synchronicity and unity that define the ultimate success of US. By embracing these principles, you ensure your momentum is not just maintained but accelerated, pushing you toward the realization of a collective vision.

IMPROVE CROSS-TEAM COLLABORATION WITH THE ABC'S

To achieve this collective vision, teams need practical methods for aligning their efforts and enhancing collaboration. The *ABC's* framework—Awareness, Beliefs, and Connect—provides the necessary structure for teams to navigate the complexities of working together.

AWARENESS
- Harness intelligence by *Zooming In* and *Out*
- Strengthen conscious leaderful capabilities
- Focus daily on the shared vision of murmuration

BELIEFS
- Empower each team member to STEP UP and STEP BACK
- Instill a sense of ownership
- Continually assess Beliefs and align to achieve the vision

CONNECT
- Invest in collaborative tools and technology
- Create a single source of truth for all teams and team members
- Encourage knowledge sharing and collaborative learning

PATH IV

Engage in Conscious Habits of Thriving

In nature, murmuration occurs when individual starlings synchronize their movements to create something much larger than themselves. In human teams, thriving collectively requires developing conscious habits that foster unity, adaptability, and shared purpose. These habits ensure that each individual (ME), team (WE), and the collective (US) can move together seamlessly, much like a murmuration of birds.

Just as starlings practice three core rules of flight, you can apply a similar set of principles to enhance your collaboration: STEP UP, STEP BACK, and STEP TOGETHER. These conscious actions allow individuals and teams to work together harmoniously while respecting each member's space and role in the collective journey.

MODELS OF COLLECTIVE INTELLIGENCE

In human teams, you can leverage powerful frameworks to guide you in aligning ME, WE, and US toward collective success:

- *Strategic Doing*™ teaches you how to effectively come together, much like the starlings gathering before flight. This model emphasizes that your collective success stems from combining your strengths and adapting together—one ME with another ME, and one WE with another WE.
- *AQai® Adaptability Quotient* framework, as discussed earlier, equips individuals and teams to navigate the complexities of change with adaptable intelligence. Just as starlings instinctively adjust to new flight patterns, this assessment helps determine whether or not individuals and teams are prepared to function as a unified US.

Together, these strategies deepen your understanding of effective teamwork and draw beautiful parallels between the natural world and human collaboration. Just like the starlings, when a team moves together in harmony, all become stronger and more resilient.

To understand how collective intelligence works in practice, look at how starlings first created teams of seven—highly skilled in flying together—before they were able to murmurate on a larger scale. *They followed three simple rules:*

1. **Attraction Zone:** STEP UP to initiate action
2. **Angular Alignment:** STEP BACK to allow your neighbors to STEP UP
3. **Repulsion Zone:** STEP TOGETHER by flying in your own lane, owning your space

By following these three principles, groups of seven starlings can fly together safely and harmoniously, forming a large, coordinated murmuration that protects them from predators and keeps them in sync with their environment. Human teams, too, can benefit from these principles as they collaborate across departments, organizations, or communities.

YOUR TURN: MOMENT OF REFLECTION

Reflect on your role within the wider community or your professional environment as you consider the transitions from ME to WE to US. How can the principles of unity, adaptability, and shared purpose, as discussed in this chapter, enhance the collective efficacy of a group or organization? Use the insights from Chapter 9 to evaluate and improve how your group collaborates toward a common vision:

1. **EVALUATE COLLECTIVE ALIGNMENT**: Look at how well your group's actions and goals are aligned with the shared vision. Are there inconsistencies between intentions and behaviors? Identify ways to strengthen this alignment to better support collective objectives.

2. **DYNAMIC ROLE ENGAGEMENT**: Assess your own contributions, first to the team, and second to the larger group. Are you more frequently initiating, supporting, or bringing others together? Consider how you might adjust your approach to better balance these roles and enhance group harmony, using STEP UP, STEP BACK, and STEP TOGETHER.

3. **STRENGTHEN SHARED PURPOSE**: Discuss with your group the underlying purpose that drives your collective efforts. Is everyone on the same page? Plan a session to revisit and possibly redefine this purpose to ensure it resonates with and motivates all members.

4. **FOSTER ADAPTABILITY**: Identify areas where increased flexibility could lead to better outcomes. What steps can be taken to make your teams and your group more responsive to changes without losing sight of your shared goals?

5. **COMMIT TO COLLECTIVE SUCCESS**: Set a concrete goal that reflects the collective ambition of your team or organization. Outline specific actions you and your group can take to achieve this goal by drawing on the cooperative spirit of murmuration.

Take a moment to write down your reflections and the steps you plan to take. Sharing these goals and actions with your team can help transform individual efforts into a powerful, unified pursuit of success.

How-to Skills: see pages 313–316 for more information

Adaptability Quotient (AQ)®
Laying New Snow
Leaderful Behavior
Zooming In / Zooming Out

Global Thought Leaders: see pages 317–320 for more information

Jon Berghoff
Ross Thornley

CHAPTER 10

THE JOY OF FLYING

*When once you have tasted flight,
you will forever walk the earth
with your eyes turned skyward.
For there you have been,
and there you will always long to return.*[75]

—Leonardo da Vinci

©2024 ABC's of Murmuration

PATH I

Embrace an Evolutionary Mindset

How do you embrace an *Evolutionary Mindset* to align ME, WE, and US around genuine harmony? By starting with ME! Embarking on a journey to murmurate, to fly, to flourish and persist, ME gathers with other individuals to form teams of seven, and evolves into a unified entity among thousands. This collective then gracefully interacts with its ever-changing environment, much like partners in a dance. The spectacle of murmuration, with each ME playing its part, embodies a seamless harmony among many individuals, whether they are starlings, neighbors in a community, or employees in an organization.

Leonardo da Vinci captured this desire to return to unity, saying, "For there you have been, and there you will always want to return."[76] This journey of ME, becoming part of a greater whole, captures the excitement and essence of moving together with purpose.

Immediately before any murmuration happens, a gathering must take place. Many times, this piece of the magic is left to chance. *A poem of gathering, paraphrased from Rumi:*

> "............
> In this gathering
> there is no high, no low,
> no smart, no ignorant
> no special assembly
> no grand discourse
> no proper schooling required
> There is no master,
> no disciple."[77]

Jon Berghoff of *xchange*, another one of this book's global thought leaders, emphasizes the importance of gathering to create collective intelligence and capacity. In their work, *xchange* models a healthy way to bring people together by preparing them to move forward in unison much like starlings in flight. They scale up members' curiosity with a subtle methodology and a set of finely drawn connectivity opportunities. Their methodology leverages the potential of groups by creating collective capacity and intelligence. The most important thing they create, however, is belonging; a sense of being part of a secure base.

The xchange Approach is simple yet powerful. It exemplifies techniques that address the mind, body, and spirit. They focus on the neuroscience of unlocking human potential, which enables people to gather, create, and grow successfully together. Their operating system revolves around how to initiate, design, and facilitate gatherings, intentionally guiding the flow of ME to WE to US.

The xchange Approach is a "what's left in" approach, not a "what's left out" approach. They scale up curiosity by starting with conversation around *Appreciative Inquiry* questions, which are drawn from the work of David Cooperrider, PhD. These questions establish a framework of searching for the best of what is and what could be. The answers to these questions, in an organizational setting, lead to systemic and organizational change. These questions are posed by a "guide on the side," and not a "sage on the stage." This design phase guides organizations and groups to Decide, Design, and Discover.

At the heart of *The xchange Approach* is the Transformation Triangle, also known as the 3C Framework, which parallels your focus on ME, WE, and US. ***The three components of this framework are:***

Intellectual Capital (ME): This focuses on equipping individuals (ME) with the knowledge and skills to think and act differently in a rapidly changing world. *xchange* refers to this as the content—what each individual needs to know and do to adapt to accelerated changes.

Similarly, in previous chapters, you explored how ME evolves to become an integral part of WE and US, and learned new ways to think and collaborate.

Social Capital (WE): This focuses on connections to foster a sense of togetherness within groups (WE). Like the starlings that learn to STEP UP, STEP BACK, and STEP TOGETHER, this component is about building relationships within the team, developing networks to face challenges, and pursuing shared aspirations.

Communal Capital (US): This is where *xchange* focuses on building community by fostering safety and belonging, much like the concept of US. This capital is what transforms individuals and teams into a unified collective that moves forward together to create a sense of purpose and security.

Just as starlings navigate an ever-changing environment, humans face the constant evolution of technology and societal shifts. The challenge is to remain adaptable and choose consciously how you interact with these changes. You must embody an *Evolutionary Mindset* that embraces flexibility and choice. This mindset demands an Awareness of *what to* do, the motivation (*want to*) to belong and thrive, and the knowledge (*how to*) of engaging in responsive rather than reactive behavior.

A recent event at a movie theater offers a profound lesson on the value of an *Evolutionary Mindset* and the contrast between reactive and proactive behavior. On a chilly, rainy Sunday, Theatre 5 brimmed with eager moviegoers of every age. As patrons, armed with popcorn and sodas, entered a pitch-dark theater, anticipation gave way to confusion. Youngsters with lights on their phones navigated the stairs in search of seats, while older attendees lingered below, unnerved by the blanket of darkness that enveloped the space.

Even after people were seated, the film did not begin. Eventually the delay stretched to 20 minutes, the air filled only with the sounds of forthcoming attractions, and the staff had yet to address the growing discomfort of darkness. When a young employee eventually appeared and shed some light on the issue—an outdated projector had malfunctioned—it was a stark reminder of how unforeseen challenges can disrupt your best-laid plans. Twenty minutes turned into an hour. This incident put the environment in control, and highlighted a missed opportunity for adaptive action by the theater.

If the theater staff had embraced an *Evolutionary Mindset*, upon first recognizing the malfunction, they could have immediately explained the situation to the audience and provided estimated timelines for resolution. Perhaps they could have offered free concessions or vouchers for future shows as a gesture of goodwill, which could have transformed a moment of potential dissatisfaction into one of enhanced customer loyalty. Such proactive measures—rooted in flexibility and a readiness to face challenges head-on—exemplify the power of an *Evolutionary Mindset* in fostering positive outcomes.

The theater incident underscores the essential need for this mindset; one that embraces change, choice, and the agility to respond proactively to unforeseen challenges. It illustrates that by adopting a proactive approach as an US—STEPPING UP, similar to the seamless, adaptive response of starlings to their environment—you empower yourself and your community to navigate disruptions with confidence and creativity.

By adopting an *Evolutionary Mindset*, you initiate a shift from merely reacting to unpleasant circumstances to choosing to actively shape your responses to them, perhaps turning them into immense possibilities! This mindset is critical for adapting and thriving, not just in moments of crisis but in your daily interactions and decisions.

To thrive as an US, you must begin with ME, and embrace an *Evolutionary Mindset* that is essential for adapting and thriving in the ever-changing world. Through this mindset, you transform challenges into opportunities for growth, collaboration, and collective success.

©2024 ABC's of Murmuration

PATH II

Envision Murmuration

Now let's examine the complex interplay between the individual (ME) and the collective (US). ME is portrayed as the keeper and disseminator of information, while US represents a broader, more permeable collective through which information flows and evolves. This ongoing exchange not only pulls insights from the environment but also cycles knowledge back to ME and across various teams of WE. This exchange fosters a vibrant dialogue with the world at large. This exploration centers on the vibrant exchange between ME and WE and US, and underlines the essence of a shared vision of thriving. This is where the concept of murmuration transforms into a collective query: "What would it look like if we could ___?"

This relationship between ME and WE and US, grounded in trust and in mutual information exchange, exemplifies a form of quantum entanglement. It's a state in which the unique nature of US, the mutuality of WE, and the adaptability of ME, converge in the continuous dance of existence to reveal a reciprocal and intertwined reality. The spiral, often cited as a symbol of time and consciousness, illustrates this entanglement, and echoes Carl Gustav Jung's insight that the journey toward self-actualization follows not a linear path but a spiraling one. This spiral dynamic, propelled by your interactions with past and future, invites you to advance by embracing transformative symbols from your subconscious and moving them into the consciousness of the present.

A murmuration doesn't just happen within an environment; it intricately folds into that environment to become materially entwined with it in a dynamic dance of co-creation. Each starling—and by extension each ME—is both a recipient and a transmitter of information that plays a role in shaping and being shaped by their surroundings, and also another ME that is engaged in their own unique interactions with the environment.

The view of xchange is that in order to *want to* murmurate, ME must do the inner work first. A huge part of this inner work is Awareness, or being consciously present. A colleague said recently in a meeting, "I really have to go out of my way to be present because whether it's the digital things that ding and ping and vie for my attention, or the fact that it happens so much, my mind wanders. What's going on in the background, combined with the stresses of being a dad or an entrepreneur, then compounded by today's chaos and conflict and disruption, makes being present challenging." Awareness to the present and being willing to shift your Beliefs and Connect with others is challenging. This, however, is the entry ticket for moving to US.

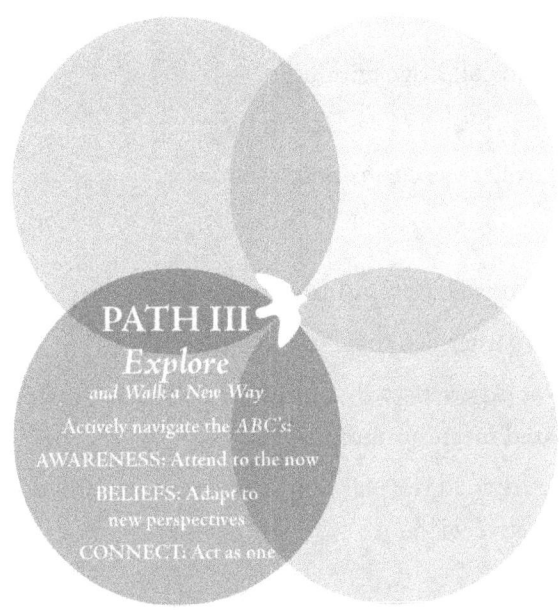

©2024 ABC's of Murmuration

PATH III
Explore and Walk a New Way

This stage marks a pivotal shift away from rigid beliefs that control behavior. You are moving toward practices that foster empowered and responsive decision-making. You are beginning to consciously navigate using Awareness of the now, your ability to shift your Beliefs, and Connect with others.

Explore how nature guides you through these steps:

For ME
- Participate fully, and be fully present with others
- Manage your attention and energy; know when triggers are possible
- Minimize distractions from other sources

For WE
- Maintain collective humility
- Prioritize health of each team member
- Spark collective curiosity in others

For US
- Create constellations of conversations
- Design gatherings that Connect people
- Suggest experiences that facilitate collective growth as well as shared meaning and purpose
- Realize that all the planning, conversations, and doing lead to collective wisdom

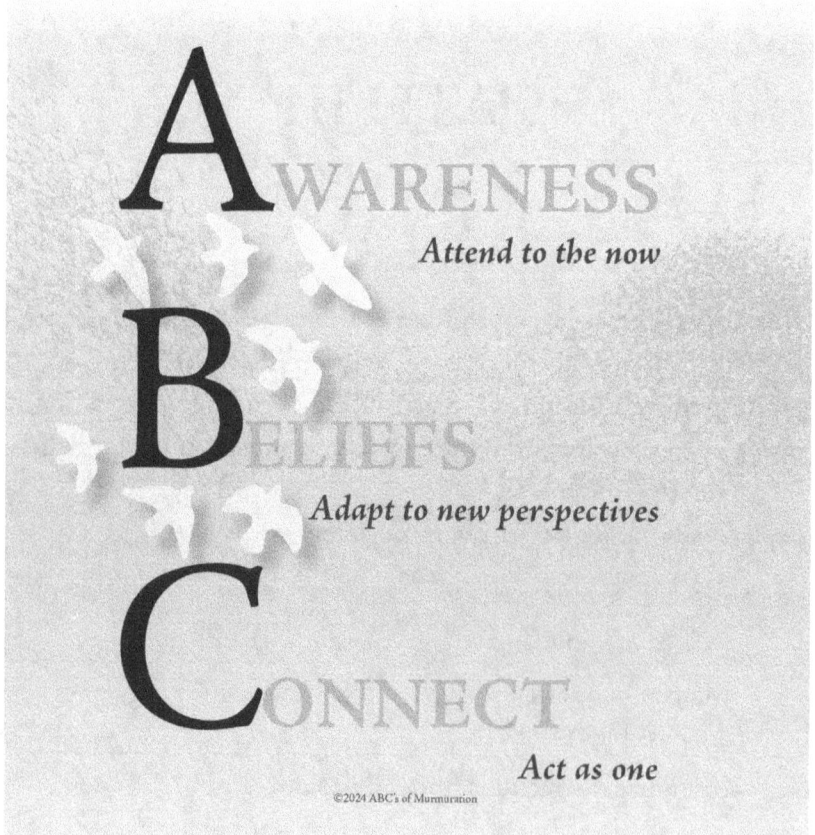

This phase is about moving beyond outdated, restrictive processes with empowering principles that enable ME, WE, and US to navigate new paths innovatively and cohesively. Through the *Theory of Mind* (thinking you know what others think) and the *ABC's of Murmuration* (Awareness, Beliefs, Connect), adapt your course in harmony with the internal dynamics of your mind, body, and spirit, and always pay attention to the external realities of your environment.

©2024 ABC's of Murmuration

PATH IV

Engage in Conscious Habits of Thriving

How do you take steps to initiate action, allow others to STEP UP, and embrace mutual trust and respect? In this final stage, you will explore the essence of creating your path through the adoption of conscious habits that foster thriving. These habits are pivotal in the transformation from individual action to collective synergy.

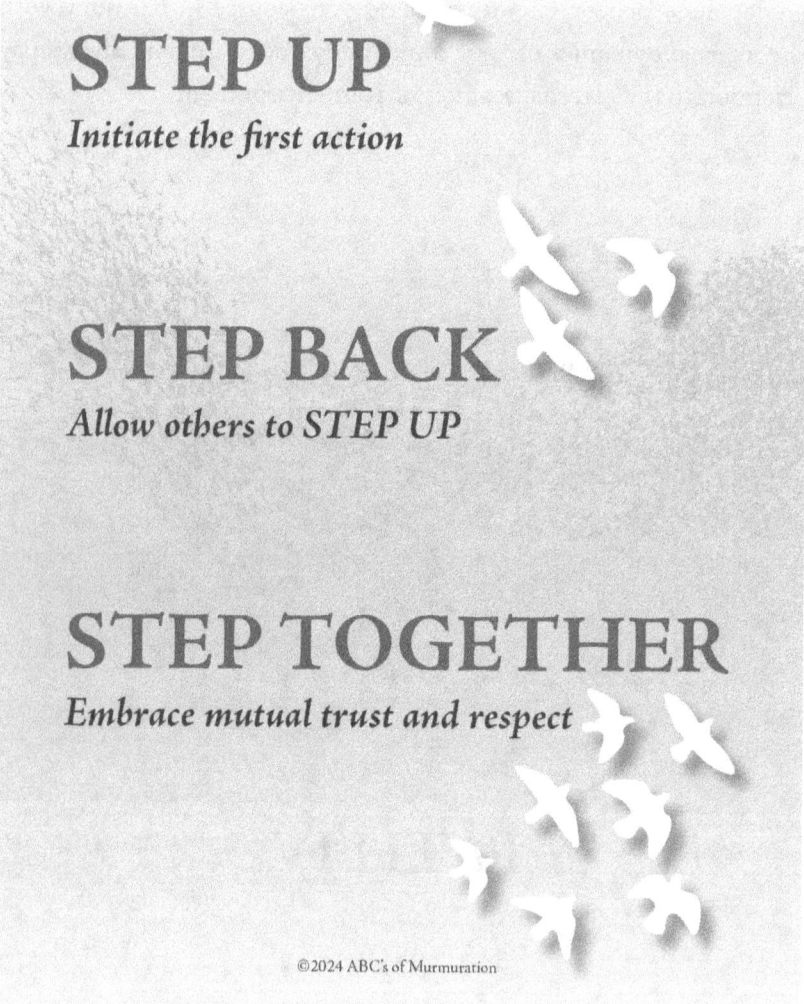

The conscious application of these habits ensures a dynamic and adaptable path-making process. Each habit serves as a stepping-stone toward the realization of your collective vision, and embodies the principles of Awareness, Belief adaptation, and Connecting that have guided you thus far.

By adopting these habits, you not only make your path but also redefine the journey of murmuration. Doing so is a testament to the power of collective intent and the transformative impact of unity in action. These habits are not merely strategies, they are the very foundation of your thriving as a collective, and encapsulate the journey from ME to WE, and ultimately, to US.

HABITS FOR COLLECTIVE THRIVING

STEP UP: Initiate the first action: Taking the initiative is the cornerstone of *Leaderful Behavior* and contribution within a group. It's about recognizing when to bring your unique strengths to the forefront and drive the collective toward your shared objectives.

STEP BACK: Allow others to STEP UP: Equally important is knowing when to create space for others to shine. This habit encourages a culture of inclusivity and respect, where every member of a group feels valued and empowered to contribute.

STEP TOGETHER: Embrace mutual trust and respect: The culmination of these habits leads to a cohesive unit that embodies mutual trust and respect. It's about moving in unison, where the success of the collective is elevated above individual accomplishments. Each member has a flying lane and specific assets they contribute.

DEFINING THRIVING: CONSCIOUS HABITS OF THRIVING FOR HUMANS

Align with the Starlings

STEP UP: Initiate the first action
- Initiate basic mindfulness
  - Focus on the present
  - Can I see, hear, feel the truth?

- Equanimity: Am I able to deal with the push and pull of life; can I be calm in this situation?
+ Do I have an active Belief in the potential of gathering?
+ Do I feel alive with the possibilities here?

STEP BACK: Allow others to STEP UP
+ Am I deeply convinced that taking care of WE takes care of US? And that US takes care of ME?
+ Is my ego and sense of personal identity secure?
+ Do I feel joy when I offer respect, serve others, and am open and humble?

STEP TOGETHER: Embrace mutual trust and respect
+ Thriving is when the complete system is in harmony. Humanity is in abundance.
+ Thriving is having the collective intelligence to gather and murmurate anywhere, anytime, when the world shifts.
+ Thriving is possible when each ME learns to STEP UP, STEP BACK, and STEP TOGETHER.

EMBRACING COLLECTIVE TRANSFORMATION

As you weave these habits into your collective journey, reflect on their broader impact. These are not just isolated practices but interconnected steps that enhance collective commitment and drive you toward shared goals. Transitioning from individual efforts to collective synchrony requires patience, empathy, and deep trust. Embracing these habits may present new challenges that test your resolve, but it is during these times that your collective resilience and strength become most evident.

Adopting these habits signifies a fundamental shift in how you engage with your collective narrative. It represents a commitment to a shared vision of thriving that transcends individual ambitions, with each step bringing you closer to your ultimate goal of collective success.

With this understanding, actively move forward, guided by these transformative habits and open to the endless possibilities that await as you continue to forge your collective path.

ADOPTING CONSCIOUS HABITS FOR THRIVING

Dr. Kathy Hagler once took a journey to Washington, D.C., to meet a colleague's acquaintance who was leading a significant project. The meeting unfolded into an enlightening discussion about fostering a thriving team culture. Here's the essence of that encounter, stylized as a script:

Jonathan: Welcome to my D.C. office, my second home!

Charlie: Jon, it's great to catch up. We think we've got some insights that could help with the team culture issues you've been facing. Kathy has quite the experience with such matters.

Kathy: Pleasure to meet you, Jonathan. Charlie has filled me in on some of the challenges. Your work sounds fascinating, and I'm here to see how we might navigate these waters together.

Jonathan: We've got some of the brightest minds from across the globe here. Their work is revolutionary, but harmonizing as a unit is where we're stuck.

Kathy: Can you give us an instance that highlights this lack of "click"?

Jonathan: Just the other day, during lunch, Mark voiced his usual grievances about not getting due credit, which led to a heated exchange with a colleague who couldn't stand the negativity anymore and left.

Kathy: Have you heard of the *Jam Jar* concept? It's a metaphor for how we see ourselves versus how others see us, based on our behaviors. Mark, for example, is in his *Jam Jar*, feeling undervalued, while others read his "label" from the outside, and see a brilliant mind overshadowed by constant complaints.

Jonathan: That's precisely it. Mark's brilliance is clouded by his demeanor, which makes collaboration challenging.

Kathy: The *Jam Jar* suggests humans can infer others' thoughts and feelings based on behaviors. By understanding and adjusting these *Jam Jar* labels, we can improve interpersonal dynamics and team synergy.

Jonathan: So, if I'm getting this right, by recognizing and shifting these labels, we could enhance how we work together?

Kathy: Exactly. Let's take Mark as an example. Imagine if a trusted colleague could help him see how his *Jam Jar* label is influencing others' perceptions and how changing his approach could lead to better recognition and collaboration.

Jonathan: This *Jam Jar* idea might be the key. I'm ready to take the lead, to show our team the power of understanding and changing our personal "weather." Let's make this happen, and unlock the full potential of our collective brilliance.

The discussion progressed to strategies for implementing the *Jam Jar* concept within the team in order to break down barriers and foster a culture of appreciation and collective success. This concept changed the trajectory of Jonathan's team, and positioned them to echo the principles of murmuration—where understanding and adapting individual actions leads to a stronger, more cohesive group dynamic.

THE WONDERS OF HUMAN MURMURATION AND THRIVING

To truly understand and harness the power of human murmuration and thriving, you must first cultivate a deep Awareness of the present moment and your role within the collective. Just as starlings synchronize their movements with those around them, you, too, must be attuned to the now by fostering connections that provide mutual support and safety. This foundation of Connection enables you to grow as an individual and as part of a thriving community. The first step in this journey is Awareness and attending to the now, where you explore how to be fully present and engaged in the world around you.

AWARENESS: ATTEND TO THE NOW

In the intricate act of murmuration, each individual becomes a secure base for others and offers protection and comfort in the present moment. This reciprocal support within communities and organizations encourages individuals to explore, take risks, and embrace challenges. To nurture this Connection, let's revisit *The Three C's Framework*, a model for fostering collective intelligence. This framework includes three components: Intellectual Capital (the knowledge or content individuals bring), Social Capital (the connections and relationships built within teams), and Communal Capital (a sense of belonging and security within the broader community). These elements work together to strengthen collaboration and unity.

The Three C's Framework is not only a tool for individual development but also a pathway to thriving as a group. By embracing Intellectual Capital, each person (ME) develops the knowledge needed to solve complex problems. As ME Connects with others through Social Capital, the attention shifts to deeper participation and conversations, which reinforces bonds of trust and belonging. Finally, through Communal Capital, you build a sense of safety and collective purpose, which expands your community and creates the foundation for lasting collaboration.

As Berghoff at xchange puts it, "The Three C's Framework should be on all of our walls!" It serves as a roadmap for creating secure, meaningful relationships within teams and communities. By understanding and leveraging these three forms of capital, you lay the groundwork for thriving together and adapting to challenges.

In recognizing your responsibility to foster these bonds, you strengthen the collective fabric of your communities and organizations. This profound understanding of your interconnectedness helps you build a foundation for thriving both individually and collectively.

BELIEFS: ADAPT TO NEW PERSPECTIVES

As individuals within an organization or community come together, united by a shared purpose and vision, a powerful opportunity arises for thriving and adapting new perspectives. This unity, inspired by the vision of murmuration, propels the collective toward greater success. To foster this alignment, three transformative perspectives are vital for every member of a community or organization: the *Art of Servant Leadership*, the *Art of Holding Space*, and the *Art of Belonging*.

Art of Servant Leadership

The journey toward supporting colleagues and neighbors involves STEPPING UP in a manner that's both proactive and sincere. It's about answering the call to action with clarity and directness.

QUALITIES OF SERVANT LEADERS

10 Pillars of Servant Leadership

1. PURPOSE-DRIVEN
Inspires leaderful growth of others toward compelling mission

2. PROACTIVE LISTENING
Heartfelt, open communication

3. COMPASSION
Understands and responds to others perspectives

4. RESTORATIVE ACTIONS
Promotes healing behaviors

5. SELF-AWARENESS
Knows and shares strengths and limitations

6. LEADERFUL MINDSET
Encourages without command and control

7. VISIONARY
Adopts possibility awareness and actions

8. ANTICIPATORY ADAPTABILITY
Foresees challenges and opportunities

9. RESPONSIBLE MANAGEMENT
Promotes sustainability through teams

10. COMMUNITY BUILDER
Prioritizes culture of belonging

©2024 ABC's of Murmuration

By embracing these perspectives, individuals contribute to a culture in which every member feels valued, understood, and integral to the collective's success. This shift in Beliefs toward *Servant Leadership* enhances not just individual but organizational wellbeing and efficacy.

Art of Holding Space For Each Other

Creating a harmonious WE involves learning to acknowledge and honor each individual's space and boundaries. In a supportive culture, every person (ME) is granted the autonomy to develop, reflect, and make meaningful contributions. It's crucial for each member to be mindful of their actions and considerate enough to allow others the room they need to grow and flourish.

Offering space to others involves more than just physical distance; it's about emotional availability and respect. Being present for someone means actively listening and empathetically responding to their needs and expressions, not merely projecting your own assumptions or solutions onto them. This often means setting aside your personal reactions or biases to fully honor and respect the individual's journey and space.

By practicing this level of respect and empathy, you not only support the individual growth of each member but also reinforce the collective strength and unity of the entire group.

Art of Belonging: Trust Unearned

People reach out to each other in various ways: through spoken or written words, body language, and other subtle cues. So do starlings, and in doing so, they create a shared sense of belonging. When part of their group signals to lead or follow, starlings understand this instantly and react without hesitation. This immediate sense of belonging is often interrupted in humans by the instinctual drive for self-protection, which causes a delay in response to these signals. However, if a bond of trust exists, akin to the trust among starlings in their group, it is much easier for humans to relax into a state that benefits both ME and US.

"Trust unearned," a vital aspect of this art, is akin to grace—freely given, not earned. It's a gift offered without expectation that fosters growth, better outcomes, and a culture of trust that can ripple through communities and organizations.

Cultivating the *Art of Belonging*—alongside practicing the *Art of Servant Leadership* and the *Art of Holding Space*—requires continuous practice and commitment. These dynamic skills are integral to fostering a unified mission and steering yourself and your community toward the collective vision of murmuration.

CONNECT: ACT AS ONE

Do not feel lonely, the entire universe is inside you.
Stop acting so small.
You are the universe in ecstatic motion.
Set your life on fire.
Seek those who fan your flames.

—Rumi [78]

In embodying Rumi's call to recognize the universe within and to act with the magnitude that this realization instills, you find the essence of connection. This connection transcends mere collaboration; it's about recognizing the shared flames and fanning them into a collective blaze of action and purpose. Acting as one isn't just about aligning your efforts; it's about amplifying the impact of your unified actions to achieve outcomes far beyond what you could accomplish alone. It means actively seeking out and nurturing those connections that elevate your collective mission, driving you toward the vision of murmuration in which each individual, in the ecstatic motion, contributes to a harmonious and thriving community.

ADVANCED, YET SUBTLE, LESSONS IN MURMURATION:

Recognize and STEP UP in attraction zones:

Moving toward your neighbor or coworker, you embrace proactivity. An *attraction zone* is where a starling responds to the call and STEPS UP to unite as a WE. Trust and reliability are the bedrock of such zones. For a culture steeped in trust to exist, knowing and supporting each other's actions and words is crucial.

STEP BACK to respect "no fly zones":

In an effort to maintain harmony, starlings heed the boundaries of others, a lesson in respecting personal and professional limits. This respect allows each individual (ME) the freedom to develop, think independently, and contribute effectively. It demands personal accountability, commitment to one's duties, and the wisdom to not hinder another's development. Treating each other with kindness and embracing diverse viewpoints are both vital. Disregarding others' no-fly zones disrupts the cohesion of WE.

> **Share the sky by aligning your vision and STEP TOGETHER:**

Understanding the importance of unified movement, starlings exemplify the essence of alignment. Sharing the sky means sharing successes and setbacks alike. Cultivating a culture rooted in fairness, empathy, and communal spirit is key to treating everyone with impartiality and equity. Sometimes, it necessitates forsaking personal preferences for the collective's progression. The dynamic interchange between ME and WE thrives on a seamless, ongoing exchange. A disruption in this flow indicates a need for ME to adjust their Beliefs and practices to uphold the principles of murmuration.

Here's to mastering the art of this eternal pull toward unity.

COLLECTIVE DYNAMICS AS THEY RELATE TO US

Insights from organizational development expert Dr. Robert Cooke offer a profound understanding that humans, within their cultures, must adhere to guidelines that echo the behaviors of starlings.

- **Collective Effectiveness and Growth:** Dr. Cooke emphasizes the importance of nurturing Beliefs that foster constructive behaviors, unity, and the common good, which resonates with the essence of US. For a culture to be genuinely constructive, it is imperative to embrace the collective spirit actively, and support Beliefs that bolster group dynamics and enhance overall organizational efficacy.

- **Overcoming Toxic Beliefs:** Identifying and reforming toxic Beliefs that obstruct the harmony and advancement of the collective is critical. By STEPPING BACK from focusing solely on individual (ME) and smaller-group dynamics (WE) to embrace a broader, unified perspective (US), you can mitigate the adverse effects of these detrimental Beliefs.

Dr. Cooke's insights into how toxic Beliefs affect group cohesion are invaluable for navigating toward a harmonious state of US.

- **Shared Beliefs and Goals:** Dr. Cooke also stresses the significance of shared Beliefs and the act of STEPPING TOGETHER toward a common goal for collective success. His focus on the collective's power and effectiveness over the individual mirrors the dynamics of murmuration in which each individual's actions are integral to the group's triumph.

These principles, drawn from Dr. Cooke's observations, underscore the parallels between human organizational dynamics and the natural world's instinctive patterns of cooperation and unity.

Reflect on the lessons of collective action and unity by going back to a powerful example from the world of music that embodies these principles. The Beatles' journey offers a profound illustration of how individual talents can merge into a harmonious collective to create something timeless and impactful.

THE BEATLES' FINAL PERFORMANCE: A SYMBOL OF COLLECTIVE UNITY

The Beatles' last performance together took place in 1969 on the rooftop of the Apple building. It was a symbolic end to a decade of unprecedented musical innovation and collective success. This final act of unity not only marked the culmination of their journey from ME to WE to US, but also underscored their lasting impact on music and culture.

As they stood together on that rooftop, each member brought their own unique strengths to the performance, but it was their unity that created something truly remarkable. John Lennon's raw energy, Paul McCartney's melodic leadership, George Harrison's introspective guitar work, and Ringo Starr's steady rhythm came together in perfect harmony. This final act of unity wasn't just the culmination of their journey; it was a testament to the power of collaboration and collective wisdom.

The Beatles' path through these stages showcases a remarkable evolution from individual talents to a legendary collective that forever altered the landscape of modern music. Their ability to blend their distinct voices into a cohesive whole not only defined their success but also left an indelible mark on music and culture. The Beatles' journey from ME to WE to US is a powerful reminder that when individuals come together with a shared vision, they can create something far greater than they ever could alone.

As you conclude your exploration within the US Walkway, this chapter has prepared you with insights and strategies for collective success that parallel natural murmuration in which individual actions synchronize to create a cohesive whole. Chapter 11 will extend these concepts, and offer practical applications and strategies to enrich both personal and communal aspects of your life. Move forward with a commitment to apply your understanding effectively and enhance your interactions in both natural and digital realms.

YOUR TURN: MOMENT OF REFLECTION

As you complete this chapter, take a moment to reflect on your journey from ME to WE to US. How have the principles of unity, adaptability, and shared purpose influenced your understanding of collective success? Consider these guiding questions to deepen your reflection:

1. **PERSONAL GROWTH**: How has embracing an *Evolutionary Mindset*, inspired by nature's lessons, changed your approach to challenges and opportunities? What steps can you take to continue evolving and adapting?

2. **TEAM DYNAMICS**: In what ways can you contribute to a collective vision of murmuration within your team or organization? How can you encourage others to STEP UP, STEP BACK, and STEP TOGETHER?

3. **COMMUNITY IMPACT**: Reflect on the broader impact of your actions within your community. How can you foster a culture of mutual trust and respect to ensure that each member feels valued and empowered, much like the starlings in their synchronized flight?

4. **FUTURE ASPIRATIONS**: What are your next steps in forging a collective path toward success? How can you apply the insights and habits from this chapter to create a thriving and cohesive environment, and draw on nature's example of harmonious collaboration?

Write down your thoughts and plans. Share them with your team to align your collective efforts and work toward your shared goals. Remember, each step you take as an individual contributes to the strength and success of the whole. Nature prepares you to fly together by demonstrating the power of collective effort and unity. Let these lessons guide you as you move forward.

How-to Skills: see pages 313–316 for more information

Appreciative Inquiry
Art of Belonging
Holding Space
Jam Jar
Leaderful Behavior
Servant Leadership
The Three C's Framework
The xchange Approach

Global Thought Leaders: see pages 317–320 for more information
Jon Berghoff
Dr. Robert Cooke

MURMURATION

*ME and WE and US
Emerge Into a Convergent Whole Field*

CHAPTER 11

CHAPTER 11

REALIZING OUR COLLECTIVE LEGACY

Unity is strength…when there is teamwork and collaboration, wonderful things can be achieved.

—Mattie Stepanek[79]

AS WE CONCLUDE OUR JOURNEY THROUGH THE *ABC'S OF MURMURATION*, WE REFLECT ON THE TRANSFORMATIVE WALKWAYS FROM ME TO WE TO US, AND REALIZE OUR COLLECTIVE LEGACY. Throughout this book, you've explored the crucial link between personal growth and collaborative engagement within your communities and workplaces. Now, integrate these individual and collective advancements into a unified vision of transformation. This final chapter will synthesize your discoveries, and show you how personal changes—from the singular brilliance of ME to the supportive strength of WE, and finally to the collective wisdom and spirit of US—lead to a legacy of profound change and unity.

*Imagine all the people / Sharing all the world /
You may say I'm a dreamer / But I'm not the only one
/ I hope someday you'll join us /
And the world will live as one.*

—"Imagine," by John Lennon

John Lennon's timeless lyrics from the song "Imagine" capture the spirit of what it means to move from ME to WE to US. These words echo the essence of murmuration; a collective vision in which individual contributions blend seamlessly to create something greater than the sum of its parts. The Beatles' legacy lives on, not just in their music, but in the way they showed the world what's possible when people come together with a shared purpose. These icons transformed the cultural landscape around them, and demonstrated the power of unified creative energies and convergence. This leads into a deeper discussion of the foundational concepts of fields.

THE ESSENCE OF FIELDS

As you learned in Chapter 3, the intuitive mind Connects ME with the external world. This realm harnesses intuition, spirituality, and other facets to paint a canvas of boundless possibilities for ME in multiple energy fields, including WE, US, and the universe. Recognizing these fields as forces that drive your personal growth and collective achievement, you realize that they are more than mere backdrops, they are vital participants in the journey. This interaction between the multiple energy fields not only shapes your individual and communal experiences but also embodies the essence of murmuration.

Remember, "Out beyond ideas of wrongdoing and right doing, there is a field. I'll meet you there." These timeless words from Rumi capture the profound nature of the energy fields that permeate your existence, where the personal and collective realms converge. They encompass ME, WE, and US. These *Human Fields of Energy (HFE)* form a sophisticated network of conscious striving toward potential. Existing in the ever-present moment, these fields extend beyond the physical body and are in a continuous mutual process with the environmental energy fields. They embody a collective consciousness shaped by different dimensions; physical, mental, emotional, and spiritual. These living fields contain your shared Beliefs, thoughts, and emotions.

Studies in living systems invite you to shift how you think about these energy fields. One of the formative thinkers in this area, strategist Norman Wolfe, shared his powerful insights in *The Living Organization* (2011). Wolfe tells you that everything is energy, and three "fields" of energy are present in every community of ME, WE, and US: the Activity Field, the Relationship Field, and the **Context Field**.

NAVIGATING THE ENERGY FIELDS

1. The Activity Field (ME)

Wolfe describes this as the Energy of Doing that originates within the individual: ME. It is characterized by cause and effect. It happens like this: If you intentionally decide to shift your mindset (the cause), the immediate effect is different thinking. The results of this field are observable behaviors, immediate and connected with mental ability or IQ.

The internal component of this field involves the mind, body, and spirit. It serves as your foundational energy, characterized by a dynamic and innovative flow, balanced symmetry, and gentle vibrations. It fosters sensitivity, discernment, and an inquisitive spirit, which are essential for personal growth, self-reflection, and actions.

For example, say you are a small business owner and you believe that you are not brave enough to speak in front of a room full of people. Your fear is overwhelming. However, you decide to change your mindset by saying to yourself, "I know I can speak in front of a room full of people." Perhaps, you go to a public-speaking class or to PSYCH-K®. The most important fact is that you have decided to shift your mindset, which has influenced your behaviors. The effect is that you are actively and consciously learning to do public speaking. In two months, you give your first public presentation to the Council on how the fees from the new parking meters are hurting your business. Your mind, body, and spirit have come together with the Energy of Doing to unlock an *Evolutionary Mindset*, which makes this chain of decisions and changes possible.

2. The Relationship Field (WE)

Relationship energy can multiply the sum of all the individual energy contributions. Wolfe says that this field is the Energy of Interaction that is generated by each ME that makes up the WE. This energy is communication. The results of this field can be verbal and/or nonverbal. These can resemble attraction/repulsion effects and have a potential impact on biological processes, as well as subtle, subjective experiences like changes in mood or energy levels.

When individuals unite to form collectives such as teams, a transformative energy field emerges. This field is shaped by the interactions among its members, and affects the group's dynamics and effectiveness. The Relationship Field contains the energy produced from one person interacting with another. In order to better understand this, Wolfe encourages you to think about the pairing of lyrics and instrumental music. When joined, they evoke something more stirring than either can alone. This communication is alive; it is a living thing. As noted by David Coghlan, Professor Emeritus at Trinity College Dublin and a leading expert in organization development and action research, this dynamic energy field undergoes continuous cycles of planning, action, and evaluation—essential processes for effective change.[80]

Now return to the above example. You made your presentation to City Council regarding your concerns over the new parking meters. The next morning, you received a call from another downtown business owner who wants to create a small group to collect information to support a change in the way the parking meters have been set up. This becomes the WE, the Relationship Field. Using Wolfe's analogy, the parking meter rules and regulations become the lyrics. They are the rules and directions of use, but someone must use them. Once people park and pay, the shopping, restaurant lounging, and wine-sipping begins, or in Wolfe's analogy, the music plays.

Basically, the communication between the business owners is the *Energy of Interaction*. It is using their evaluation, planning, and action skills and their emotional intelligence to determine what new course of actions they would like to suggest with the parking meters' rules and direction of use. Hopefully, their intentional course of action will positively affect the music, the people enjoying the downtown area.

3. The Context Field (Us)

This field is the *Energy of Meaning and Purpose*. Sharing stories is a means of exchanging energy. The results in this field are intuitive and can be experienced by all sharing in the experience through the senses. It is ever-evolving and Connected to the spirit or the heart. This energy field is where shared knowledge and mutual support enhance the overall safety and understanding of its members. It is a subject of ongoing research, particularly in studies of how starlings engage in murmuration to share vital survival information.

Returning to the example, the business owner (ME) and her new colleague determined, as a WE, to expand their group (WE) to involve other local owners (US). This field is the Energy of Meaning and Purpose, the Context Field. It encompasses the shared knowledge, mutual support, and understanding of all its members. They share vital information, continue to lobby their position, and are ready for a definitive change in the parking meter policy.

4. The Convergent Whole Field (The Fourth Field)

The Fields of Activity, Relationship, and Context merge to create *The Fourth Field*. Researcher Michelle Holliday calls this the **Convergent Whole Field,** where "divergent parts come together in relationship to form a convergent whole with new characteristics and capabilities."[81] To help you create a mental image for the concept of this energy field, Wolfe invites you to think of it as you would a container of water: The water takes the shape of the container; the container defines the shape of the water. It defines what is and is not possible in the other. Each field—Activity, Relationship, and Context—interacts within this container to shape and define what is possible within the collective whole.

The Convergent Whole Field is the outcome of all the other fields. It is the level not of ME, WE, or US, but of the society and result they create together. Here, Holliday says, you find the phenomenon of emergence, in which new capabilities and characteristics are created, in the same way the properties of water (wetness, fluidity) emerge from the convergence of hydrogen and oxygen.

The outcome of the Convergent Whole Field is that the City Council relaxed the parking fees and agreed to continue to study and reduce the fees in the future as the local businesses became increasingly healthy. It continues to be the phenomenon of emergence in which a new outcome is possible and preferable based on the community wisdom. It is murmuration.

PUTTING IT ALL TOGETHER

Now apply your foundational concepts to your understanding of these energy fields. How do the *ABC's of Murmuration* work in this context?

The Four-Path Journey of Embrace, Envision, Explore, and Engage encourages you to envision murmuration, the first step to mirror nature. This process Connects to the Context Field of meaning and purpose. What would this look and feel like to ME, to WE, to US? This envisioning is critical to create a mindset that is ready to embrace an *Evolutionary Mindset*.

Embracing an *Evolutionary Mindset* allows you to dream and move forward toward a successful outcome for all, but it must begin with ME. This is the Field of Activity in which the *ABC's of Murmuration* come into play:

AWARENESS: Attend to the now

BELIEFS: Adapt to new perspectives

CONNECT: Act as one

In the diagram below, both Embracing the *Evolutionary Mindset* and Envisioning murmuration are critical to move toward the Convergent Whole Field. Envisioning populates the information of *why* and *what to* (the meaning and purpose) and ME must then decide to have the *want to*, the motivation, and choose to develop the Energy of Doing by activating an *Evolutionary Mindset*. The motivation of a ME is mandatory to move forward. Focusing on these two paths provides the "future orientation" needed to move from the singular brilliance of ME to the supportive strength of WE, and finally to the collective wisdom and spirit of US—and lead to a legacy of profound change and unity.

The Map: ABC's of Murmuration

THE WALKWAYS	WALKWAY I WALKWAY II WALKWAY III				
THE FOUR-PATH JOURNEY	EMBRACE	ENVISION	EXPLORE	ENGAGE	EMERGE
	Evolutionary Mindset	Vision of Murmuration	Walk a New Way	Conscious Habits of Thriving	OUTCOME
THE ENERGY FIELDS	Activity Field	Relational Field	Context Field		CONVERGENT WHOLE FIELD
	Energy of Doing	Energy of Interaction	Energy of Meaning and Purpose		ENERGY OF COLLECTIVE WISDOM

This chart illustrates the ABC's of Murmuration, and maps out a journey through the Four Paths: Embrace, Envision, Explore, and Engage. Each phase is tied to individual and collective growth, and moves from adopting an Evolutionary Mindset to achieving a shared, collective wisdom. The energy fields further define the process by emphasizing the importance of doing, interaction, and purpose to support personal and group transformation. The result that emerges is a celebration of collective success and wisdom.

Each field interlinks to create a tapestry of energy that influences individual and collective experiences, and guides you through a journey of personal discovery and communal evolution.

INTEGRATING THE FOUR-PATH JOURNEY TO CREATE THE CONVERGENT WHOLE FIELD

Look once more at the familiar Four-Path Journey, which you've used as a guide throughout your exploration. This will help you Connect the concepts discussed to the Convergent Whole Field.

THE FOUR-PATH JOURNEY

EVOLVE *from* ME *to* WE *to* US

PATH I
Embrace
an *Evolutionary Mindset*
to make a path for genuine
alignment and harmony.

PATH II
Envision
Murmuration
With an inner eye,
imagine murmuration as
the vital light of change
and love in the world.

PATH III
Explore
and Walk a New Way
Actively navigate the ABC's:
AWARENESS:
Attend to the now
BELIEFS:
Adapt to new perspectives
CONNECT:
Act as one

PATH IV
Engage
in *Conscious Habits of Thriving*
STEP UP:
Initiate the first action
STEP BACK:
Allow others to STEP UP
STEP TOGETHER:
Embrace mutual trust
and respect

©2024 ABC's of Murmuration

The Four Paths play an integral role in shaping the Fourth Energy Field of Convergence. This journey isn't just a sequence of steps; it's a transformative process that cultivates the fertile ground from which the Fourth Field emerges. By evolving from ME to WE to US, envisioning collective cohesion, exploring new ways through daily actions, and engaging in conscious habits, you pave the way for a powerful synthesis of energy fields. Three fields—Activity, Relationship, and Context—prepare you to converge in the Fourth Field, where collective intelligence and unified efforts manifest in transformative outcomes. This is murmuration.

THE CONVERGENT WHOLE FIELD: THE FOURTH FIELD

Let's go deeper into the Fourth Field, where we have seen how the dynamic interplay between ME, WE, and US aligns with the external world. This field represents the convergence of individual and collective energies, fostering an environment ripe for innovation, learning, and growth. Envision a workspace where multiple energies synchronize in harmony—this Fourth Field is akin to a relational field where the interdependence of various elements transcends the sum of their parts, echoing the synergistic legacy of The Beatles' combined musical achievements, a legacy.

This field is an emergent, non-physical structure where your individual narratives, functioning as separate nodes, merge to form a larger, complex narrative system. It directs our focus towards phenomena that emerge from these interactions, redefining success through a collective achievement lens. It's a celebration of synergy and unity, where extraordinary outcomes across various fields are not just possible but expected.

In the Fourth Field, subconscious minds act as automated processors by swiftly responding based on entrenched Beliefs and perceptions. To fully harness this field's potential, it is crucial to evolve these automatic responses to align with your current intentions by transforming fear-based reactions into constructive actions.

Conversely, your conscious mind provides the capacity to make deliberate choices informed by collective intelligence and intuition. This enables you to transform individual desires into actions that benefit the whole, and to steer yours and others' collective journey toward desired outcomes. By fostering an Awareness of the present, you enable your conscious mind to influence the subconscious and facilitate decisions that resonate with your highest aspirations for the collective good.

EXPANSIVE KNOWING IN THE FOURTH FIELD

- **Subconscious Mind:** Acts as an automatic processor by steering behaviors based on entrenched Beliefs. To achieve alignment with your current goals and collective aspirations, these behaviors must evolve.
- **Conscious Mind:** Leveraging collective intelligence and intuition, the conscious mind facilitates deliberate actions that reflect your shared goals, and transforms individual desires into communal benefits.

The Fourth Field marks the apex of your collective journey, where the convergence of individual and group energies yields universal positive outcomes, unveils new opportunities, achieves collective excellence, and promotes mindful action. This field embodies the synthesis of your highest aspirations and concerted efforts, and showcases the transformative effects of your unified actions on both personal growth and community enhancement.

THE CONVERGENT WHOLE IN PRACTICE

Dr. Kathy Hagler (Facilitator)

The immediate and extraordinary success of a new community college illustrates how the needs of a community (the environment) ignited the energy fields of ME, WE, and US to achieve a successful outcome that forever changed the community. An individual college dean (ME) named Larry Barnhart displayed the *Servant Leadership* characteristics of Awareness, foresight, and stewardship as he STEPPED UP and recommended that his department expand. He worked at Boise State University's technical education department, and as he became aware of an extraordinary need for employees in the business sector and his department's burgeoning enrollment, Barnhart knew that his department could and should evolve into a stand-alone technical school, a community college. He drove the effort to make this possible and succeeded.

His initiative, his Energy of Doing, supplied the traction needed to attract others (WE). The Energy of Interaction, the Relationship Field, grew quickly and soon small teams were coming together and making key decisions. Very quickly the context, the Energy of Meaning and Doing, empowered each ME to operate interdependently, which enhanced the collective efficacy of WE. ***These effective teams then:***

- Collaborated to develop a plan
- Presented the plan for approval
- Created a sense of trust that launched a new community college that, 10 years later, has approximately 35,000 students enrolled.

This analysis not only showcases the practical application of theoretical concepts but also highlights the power of ME, WE, and US enhanced by facilitation, planning, and organized collaborative efforts to achieve transformative outcomes.

The Activity Field (ME)
The initiative began when Barnhart, dean of the technical education department, recognized the need to expand its programs to better serve the region. This vision of growth embodied the Activity Field, where direct action and individual initiative drove change.

The Relationship Field (WE)
Effective communication and collaboration were pivotal, as illustrated through "community conversations" that involved diverse community stakeholders from several counties. These dialogues facilitated collective decision-making, a hallmark of the Relationship Field.

The Context Field (US)
The shared recognition of Boise's need for a community college created a unified narrative among university leaders, local businesses, and the broader community. This collective understanding underscored the Context Field, and aligned community goals with strategic educational planning.

The Convergent Whole Field (Fourth Field)
The creation of the College of Western Idaho represents the outcome, the culmination of efforts from the preceding fields. This Fourth Field emerged from integrating active initiatives, collaborative relationships, and the overarching community context to illustrate how diverse energies can converge to create impactful educational institutions.

Global Impact
Now an independent entity, the College of Western Idaho offers a wide range of academic and vocational programs, and serves thousands of students and businesses, which exemplifies the successful Four-Path Journey of Embracing, Envisioning, Exploring, and Engaging with US, the community.

YOUR COLLECTIVE POTENTIAL

As you move forward, it's important to understand how your collective potential can transform your world. Here's how you can achieve this:

1. Seek Positive Universal Outcomes in a Convergent Whole Field

The greatest challenge facing humanity today is the feeling of powerlessness to affect change. Traditional ways of thinking, working, and behaving are no longer sufficient. To thrive and survive like the starlings, you need to adopt a new form of collective consciousness—the *ABC's of Murmuration*—to create universal transformative outcomes.

Transformative outcomes must manifest visible results, and encompass the full flow from ME to WE to US. This requires emphasizing the conditions that foster patterns of thinking, communicating, and Connecting; ultimately producing practical results. Unfortunately, the ME to WE to US dimensions have often been overlooked in the pursuit of transformative outcomes.

In organizations, culture (the US), is often studied and researched. However, everything—including internal company culture—all starts with ME. And each ME must have an *Evolutionary Mindset* (a mindset that is open to conscious choice) and also possess tools to stop limiting Beliefs so they are not subjected to the whims of the subconscious.

2. Expect Emergent Opportunities

Transformative outcomes emerge from the ability to sense and recognize new opportunities. This involves understanding the embodied internal and external knowledge of ME, WE, and US, and drawing on the Greek concept of "knowing with all your senses." This cumulative knowledge creates an US, a murmuration of collective intelligence.

Presencing—combining open-minded sensing with actualizing the emerging future—allows you to thrive like the starlings, which sense and create their future through murmuration. You gain this knowledge through an intimate relationship with nature. Elder Rick Hill of Six Nations explains that knowledge is tied to the land, and guides you through dreams, visions, and practices.[82]

An Indigenous paradigm views knowledge as belonging to the cosmos, with humans as interpreters. This perspective extends beyond humanity to nature and all life, and provides a broader context for understanding the Fourth Field.

3. Collective Thriving

Your journey from ME to WE to US forms a foundation of learning and information to create a path forward. This path is activated by a deep shift in energy that is necessary for collective excellence. Collective thriving moves from collective understanding of the meaning and purpose of the journey; to the interactivity required by teams; and finally to managing the emerging outcomes of your and their convergence.

4. Embrace Conscious Collective Behaviors

Presencing counters the separation of mind and world to assert their intertwined nature. Your field becomes known through interactions, forming an intimate relationship while taking on its own autonomous behavior. This field is not limited to specific interactions but exists within, between, and beyond you. You establish a connection to the world's call through both your inner and outer actions.

PRACTICAL STEPS TO EMBRACE THE FOURTH FIELD

1. **KNOW THAT YOU ARE NOT ALONE:** Recognize the collective support available.

2. **PERCEPTION FROM THE FIELD:** Experience a shift in how you perceive space, time, self, light, sensation, and warmth, beginning with ME.

3. **HEIGHTENED POSSIBILITIES:** Understand that potential futures previously out of your reach are now within the realm of possibility.

4. **WHOLE-IN-THE-PARTS AND PARTS-IN-THE-WHOLE:** Achieve alignment between individual and collective attention, intention, and agency.

5. **SUSTAINED PRACTICAL RESULTS:** Realize the potential of activating longer-term generative fields to achieve significant, practical outcomes that are shockingly effective.

By understanding and embracing these principles, you unlock the collective potential to create lasting, positive change, and demonstrate the transformative power of your shared journey.

THE MURMURATION OF STARLINGS: A MODEL FOR CONVERGENT WHOLE FIELD OUTCOMES

The phenomenon of starling murmuration powerfully demonstrates collective intelligence. Starlings congregate in massive roosts for safety and to share vital survival information, and embody a dynamic process of participatory sense-making. This interplay, essential to their communal understanding, results in breathtaking patterns across the sky, a vivid representation of the Fourth Field—the Convergent Whole Field of starlings.

The resulting murmuration is not just a gathering but a new entity, a complex interplay of individual and collective inputs that leads to mesmerizing patterns in the sky. These patterns are the physical manifestation of the Fourth Field—the culmination of shared environmental information and collective energy that defines the starlings' existence.

FINAL THOUGHTS: SOARING TO COLLECTIVE HARMONY

The hope is that the *ABC's of Murmuration* has provided you with new paths for personal and collective growth. By embracing the natural phenomenon of murmuration, you can reshape your mindset and unlock the transformative potential within yourself, your organizations, and your communities. The mission is to facilitate a shift in perspectives, embedding harmony into your culture. Just as starlings navigate the skies together, you strive to navigate the complexities in your workplaces and societies collectively.

By practicing the principles of the Four-Path Journey—Embrace, Envision, Explore, and Engage—you can tap into the power of the Convergent Whole Field, the Fourth Field, to create a future where harmony is the essence of your interactions. Embark on this transformative journey, celebrating diversity, fostering empathy, and building a culture in which everyone feels seen, heard, and valued. By evolving from ME to WE to US, you recognize the power of your collective efforts.

Your collective efforts will create a lasting impact, and radiate beyond your immediate spheres. The time is now. Spread your wings and soar together toward a future of harmony.

How-to Skills: see pages 313–316 for more information

Appreciative Inquiry
Art of Belonging
Holding Space
Jam Jar
Leaderful Behavior
Servant Leadership
The Three C's Framework
The xchange Approach

Global Thought Leaders: see pages 317–320 for more information

Bruce H. Lipton

EPILOGUE

COLLECTIVE WISDOM OF NATURE

The wisest and noblest teacher is nature itself.
—Leonardo da Vinci

THE ESSENCE OF MURMURATION (US): THE COMMUNITY

Surrounded by the majestic mountains of the Southern Appalachians, Hendersonville, North Carolina, is enveloped by what poet Carl Sandburg called "nature in its raw and natural state." Sandburg, who lived just up the road from our neighborhood on a goat farm, understood the profound wisdom that nature offers. Indeed, nature is a wise and noble teacher to our town and our community, Charlestown Place. We deeply appreciate our sleepy, idyllic corner of the world.

The sky is sanctuary to the starlings, and Charlestown Place is our sanctuary. When we observe the mesmerizing images of starlings in murmuration, we wonder: How do they do that? What could bring groups of people together like the starlings, and allow them to be more alive, more natural, and healthier than ever before? With immense curiosity, humility, and gentleness, we continue to watch as our neighborhood leaders STEP UP and plant small seeds of possibility to contribute to positive collective experiences for our community.

An often-unspoken reality of building and nurturing a community is the rule of The Three P's: People, Practices, and Place. There is a tacit understanding that when all three P's are aligned, a sense of oneness can be achieved. Reflecting back, we can see how self-organizing neighbors began to harvest the growing crop of potential experiences that our leaders had sown.

The people of Charlestown Place understood the essence of *Servant Leadership*: serving others with compassion and grace. Guided by an elected board of directors, the community embraced this natural structure, much like starlings in flight. Small groups began STEPPING UP, volunteering to contribute to the health and safety of the community. Teams such as the Landscape Committee, the Welcoming Committee, and the Finance Committee came together to create an environment that encouraged participation and growth. The Board recognized the importance of STEPPING BACK and allowing space for neighbors to create and share, which hastened the evolution from individual ME's to a collective WE, eventually achieving the majestic harmony of murmuration.

This structure slowly allowed others to evolve, to belong, and to desire participation and contribution. Ten years ago, Charlestown Place was still in its early stages, facing significant challenges. The community was disorganized, and residents felt disconnected. However, a turning point occurred when homeowners began to understand the importance of collective responsibility. As one resident noted, "People started STEPPING UP—they started understanding that it was their responsibility. It became clear that it was their home, their place." This realization marked the beginning of a new collective consciousness within Charlestown Place, where the community began to work together more cohesively, STEPPING UP as individuals while also learning when to STEP BACK.

ADAPTING THE TRAIL

Then it happened…just like in *Alice in Wonderland*, "The secret, Alice, is to surround yourself with people who make your heart smile. It's then, only then, that you'll find Wonderland."[83]

It was Christmas at Charlestown Place, and the neighbors gathered. Their hearts smiled as they connected. Gathering started happening again and again through the year. What made gathering special was that there was finally a place in the community spacious enough to host such events. We had People and Practices, and now we had Place. It was as if Santa and Mrs. Claus had moved in, opening their hearts and home to all. It's like Connecting the dots; there is no clear picture of what is possible until you Connect the people.

The concept of murmuration was becoming a reality in Charlestown Place, not just in how the community gathered but in how they interacted and supported one another. From organizing events like the chili cook-off and "Wine Down Wednesdays," to assembling a neighborhood library, to residents STEPPING UP to manage sidewalk maintenance, the community embodied the principles of murmuration: collective action and unity. These efforts symbolized the emotional and physical well-being of the community, which ensured that everyone felt included and valued.

MAKING YOUR PATH

We know that this is only the beginning. We believe in our community; we believe in ourselves and others. We know that neighbors will go out of their way to be present and to show up. We realize that fostering the self-organization we strive for requires collective humility. Being open to all neighbors' perspectives—even when we may not understand them at the moment—requires curiosity and a willingness to change as we move toward collective wisdom. Neighbors need an environment where they can express what needs to be said. It is inevitable that communities will face challenges that have never been addressed before. Above all, we need heart, patience, and goodwill. We need to understand that the well-being of our neighbors is crucial.

We've seen that people are better at learning and healing when they are Connected, and leverage each other's talents and grow together. When we Connect people in ways that foster a collective sense of belonging, we combine their energies, expanding both the individual and the community. Belonging is a powerful antidote to loneliness and illness. But the most wonderful part is this: An individual ME remains an individual even as they become part of US, part of the community. In the end, everyone wins.

Reflecting on the evolution of Charlestown Place, we see a community that has grown from chaos into something much stronger because residents learned to work together: to STEP UP when needed and STEP BACK to let others lead. This balance, this shared responsibility, is what transforms a group of individuals into a collective force, much like a murmuration of starlings STEPPING TOGETHER. The success of Charlestown Place serves as a testament to the power of collective action, adaptable leadership, and the enduring wisdom of nature's teachings.

Nature shows us how to consciously Connect and gather. It is unity in motion. It is the power of individuals coming together, of finding balance in collaboration. This magical display speaks volumes about belonging. As these birds take to the sky, merging into one magnificent fluid entity, they remind us of the power of unity growing in Charlestown Place.

AND THE STORY CONTINUES WITH HURRICANE HELENE

And then Hurricane Helene descended on Charlestown Place. The devastation she brought wasn't confined to our small community—it stretched far beyond, touching so many lives. As the storm raged, the stark reality of our isolation from the outside world began to sink in.

We watched helplessly through our windows as Helene unleashed her fury, battering our neighborhood. The eye of the storm passed eerily over us, offering a momentary silence that only deepened the dread of what was still to come. We sat, knuckles white, knowing the worst wasn't over. While the world witnessed the destruction from afar, we were immersed in it—trapped within the whirlwind that surrounded us. In those moments, we had no connection to anything beyond Charlestown Place.

But as the storm finally cleared and the first rays of sunlight peeked through the clouds, so did our neighbors, one by one. There they were, stepping out of their homes, ready to help, to listen, and to support each other. With the internet down and cell service spotty at best, neighbors began using our little neighborhood library as a gathering spot, offering up cash for those who hadn't been able to prepare. Some ventured out for groceries, picking up essentials for others. It was an extraordinary display of unity. Everyone STEPPED TOGETHER.

We were still without internet and reliable cell service, but we were among the fortunate ones. Out of 100 homes in our county that still had electricity and water, 52 were right here in Charlestown Place, or so we heard by word of mouth. In the surrounding mountains of western North Carolina, many people were still missing, stranded, or left with nothing. Rescue crews had arrived from far and wide, with the National Guard airlifting survivors to safety.

What we witnessed in the aftermath was much like the murmuration of starlings—individuals coming together to form something far greater than themselves. There was an unspoken collective will to protect one another, to rebuild, and to offer hope. Gatherings began. If there was a silver lining to the dark storm clouds of Helene, it was this: we were not alone. We were together.

HOW-TO SKILLS

1. Adaptability Quotient (AQ)®
The Adaptability Quotient (AQ) by AQai® measures an individual's or team's ability to adapt to changing environments. It focuses on how well someone can adjust behaviors and thinking in response to evolving circumstances. In the book, AQ is used to assess readiness for adaptability, to help teams thrive by being flexible and open to new solutions.

2. Appreciative Inquiry
Appreciative Inquiry is a methodology that focuses on identifying and amplifying what works well within a group or organization. By leveraging strengths and positive experiences, it inspires change, growth, and the pursuit of shared goals.

3. Art of Belonging
The practice of creating environments in which individuals feel seen, valued, and Connected. It emphasizes cultivating spaces of inclusion, trust, and shared purpose to foster a sense of belonging within groups or communities.

4. Body Scan
A mindfulness practice in which one focuses attention on different parts of the body to enhance awareness and relaxation.

5. Five Behaviors Model
A framework developed by Patrick Lencioni for improving team dynamics by focusing on five key areas: trust, conflict, commitment, accountability, and results.

6. Four Worlds of Adaptability
A model from AQai® that describes the four domains in which adaptability is critical: personal, interpersonal, organizational, and environmental.

7. Footlights of Consciousness
Footlights of Consciousness is a term used to describe the direct and immediate awareness of inner experiences, such as thoughts, feelings, and visual images. It was first used by William James in 1890 as a metaphor for how our focused attention is like a spotlight that influences behavior from the subconscious mind. It emphasizes the importance of being mindful of where your attention is directed to align actions with team goals.

8. Holding Space
The skill of creating a safe, non-judgmental environment that allows others to express themselves fully, process emotions, or navigate challenges, while offering support without directing or controlling the outcome.

9. Jam Jar
The *Jam Jar* represents how others perceive you based on your behavior—the "label" on the jar. This concept highlights the need for self-awareness in how your actions are viewed by others and the impact of those perceptions on team dynamics.

10. Laying New Snow
Laying New Snow is the practice of breaking away from old habits and forging new paths. It symbolizes mental flexibility and innovation, and encourages individuals and teams to embrace novel solutions and fresh approaches.

11. Leaderful Behavior

Leaderful Behavior involves taking initiative within a group by leading through encouragement, setting examples, and promoting shared leadership. It fosters a collaborative environment in which every team member has leadership potential, responsibility, and respect from other team members for their recommendations.

12. Living in Choice

Living in Choice emphasizes intentional, conscious decision-making rather than automatic reactions. It encourages individuals to take responsibility for their actions; to align with their values and contribute meaningfully to collective goals. This approach fosters personal and team empowerment.

13. Pause, Notice, and Choose (taught by xchange)

Pause, Notice, and Choose is a mindfulness practice that helps individuals pause to reflect, notice their thoughts and feelings, and consciously choose their next action. It's a skill for fostering self-awareness and ensuring intentional decision-making in teams.

14. SCARS Model

A framework for understanding and addressing the lasting impacts of past trauma or challenges on current behavior and attitudes, as seen in the book, *Art of Scars*.

15. Servant Leadership/Art of Servant Leadership

A leadership style where the leader prioritizes the growth, well-being, and development of their team members, and focuses on serving others and fostering collective success rather than exerting power or control.

16. Strategic Doing™
Strategic Doing™ is a framework for guiding teams to collaborate and solve complex problems by focusing on action-oriented questions, like "What can we do?" and "What will we do?" It emphasizes rapid adaptation and collective decision-making to align individual and team goals.

17. The Three C's Framework
A model for fostering collective intelligence, comprising Intellectual Capital (content/knowledge for individuals), Social Capital (connections within teams), and Communal Capital (creating belonging and security within a community)

18. The xchange Approach
The xchange Approach is a facilitation method that scales up curiosity and connection within groups. It fosters collective intelligence through the Transformation Triangle—which focus on Intellectual Capital (ME), Social Capital (WE), and Communal Capital (US). The method uses *Appreciative Inquiry* to inspire systemic change and a sense of belonging.

19. Zoom In and Zoom Out
Zoom In and *Zoom Out* is the ability to shift focus between specific details (*Zooming In*) and the bigger picture (*Zooming Out*). It helps teams analyze both micro and macro perspectives to make informed, balanced decisions.

GLOBAL THOUGHT LEADERS

DR. BRUCE H. LIPTON

Bruce H. Lipton, PhD, is an internationally recognized leader in bridging the realms of science and spirit. A stem cell biologist and bestselling author of three books including international best seller, *The Biology of Belief*, he was honored with the 2009 Goi Peace Award. Dr. Lipton has been featured as a guest speaker on hundreds of television and radio shows, and has delivered keynote presentations at numerous national and international conferences.

Bruce H. Lipton, PhD (brucelipton.com)

DUCCIO LOCATI

Duccio Locati, Director of PSYCH-K® Centre International, Director of Health and Wellbeing Program, and a PSYCH-K® Instructor, graduated from the Istituto Superiore di Osteopatia in Milan and earned his Bachelor of Science in Osteopathy from the University of Wales. He further honed his skills through postgraduate workshops in osteopathy across Europe and the United States. Driven by a passion for the connection between mind, body, and spirit, Locati expanded his expertise by completing a two-year course in Biological Medicine. A pivotal moment in his journey was discovering Dr. Bruce Lipton's work, which introduced him to PSYCH-K®. Recognizing its potential for transforming beliefs and perceptions at the subconscious level, Locati integrated PSYCH-K® into his practice, which enhanced his ability to help patients achieve deeper healing.

Duccio Locati (ieyes.org/en/about-me/)

DR. GARY CONE

Dr. Gary Cone founded the Center for Transpersonal Healing in Oklahoma City in 1992, which he renamed The Cone Center – Living in Choice in 2007. Over the past decade and a half, he has developed and applied the Energy Matrix Clearing System© (EMCS), a method for clearing energy blockages in the human biofield that contribute to dysfunction in the physical, mental, emotional, and spiritual bodies. EMCS is the cornerstone of his Energy Medicine and Energy Psychology practices.

Gary Cone (garycone.com)

JACK LOWE, JR.

Jack Lowe, Jr., began his career with TDIndustries in 1964, advanced to CEO and Board Chair in 1980, and eventually retired as CEO in 2004. Based in Dallas, TDIndustries is a national leader in mechanical and plumbing construction and facility services, with projects including the Dallas Cowboys' stadium, American Airlines Center, Arizona Cardinals' Stadium in Phoenix, The Ballpark in Arlington, Dallas Convention Center, Texas Instruments semiconductor plants, and the JCPenney headquarters. Lowe earned his BA and BSEE degrees from Rice University, graduating Magna Cum Laude, and also served in the U.S. Navy.

Jack Lowe, Jr. (tdindustries.com)

JON BERGHOFF

Jon Berghoff, the co-founder and CEO of xchange, is a trailblazer in the field of transformational group facilitation. Recognized as a collective-wisdom whisperer, Berghoff has guided global CEO summits, leadership conferences, and high-stakes gatherings for organizations such as Conscious Capitalism®, Women Presidents Organization, HeartMath, Arthur W. Page Society, NASA, Keller Williams Realty, and many others. His work has influenced more than 15,000 coaches, consultants, and change agents who now use *The xchange Approach* to redefine the potential unlocked through transformational learning experiences on a large scale.

Jon Berghoff (xchangeapproach.com)

DR. ROBERT A. COOKE

Robert A. Cooke, Ph.D., is the chief executive officer of Human Synergistics, an international company that specializes in leadership and organizational development. Dr. Cooke and his associates develop surveys and experiential exercises to measure and constructively change individual thinking and behavioral styles, group processes, and organizational culture. Their cross-level integrated diagnostic system enables consultants and leaders to promote organizational sustainability while improving teamwork and members' well-being, engagement, and effectiveness.

Robert. A Cooke, PhD (humansynergistics.com)

KATHY OPP

Kathy Opp is the CEO and owner of K2OHSolutions, LLC, and brings more than 30 years of experience as a seasoned business executive. She specializes in strategic direction, process improvement, culture assessment, change management, and leadership coaching. Opp previously served as president and executive director of the Western States Land Commissioners Association, and held various roles in state government and with Boise Cascade Corporation. She holds certifications in Organizational Culture Inventory®, *Strategic Doing*™, and Team Alchemy™, among others.

Kathy Opp (k2ohsolutions.com)

ROSS THORNLEY

Ross Thornley is the CEO and co-founder of AQai®, a company focused on adaptability assessments and coaching. With a diverse background in business and publishing, he has held key roles, including Art Director and Majority Owner at Odin Publishing, and contributed to companies like Nature's Panacea, tripleO performance solution, and Mug For Life Ltd. Passionate about empowering others to reach their full potential, Thornley leverages his work at AQai® to drive personal and professional growth. He is a strong advocate for continuous learning, and believes it to be essential for success in today's rapidly evolving world.

Ross Thornley (aqai.io)

PSYCH-K®—THE KEY TO SUSTAINABLE CHANGE

The authors have found that PSYCH-K® is a game-changer in cultivating an Integrated Mindset by transforming limiting Beliefs and adopting new perspectives. This powerful methodology blends elements of psychology, neuroscience, kinesiology, and spirituality to create profound shifts in self-perception and worldview. By engaging both the conscious and subconscious minds, PSYCH-K® helps to develop new neural connections to align your subconscious beliefs with your conscious goals. This transformation leads to more intentional, positive behaviors and a harmonious life, which ultimately contributes to collective wellbeing and unity.

WHAT IS PSYCH-K®?

- A non-invasive, interactive process of change with a proven record of success since 1988
- A powerful yet simple method to shift self-limiting and self-sabotaging subconscious beliefs into supportive and empowering ones
- A unique blend of contemporary neuroscience research and ancient mind-body wisdom
- A groundbreaking approach to change at the subconscious level, where 95 percent of our consciousness operates
- A method that transcends traditional techniques like visualization, affirmations, willpower, and positive thinking

- An approach that is effective in behavioral and habit change, wellness, stress reduction, and resolving areas of personal or professional conflict, resistance, and struggle
- A method that enhances the impact of what's already working while addressing the root cause of issues, not just symptoms
- A process that does not require reliving past pain to create present change
- A framework that proves beliefs can be transformed in a matter of minutes, no matter how long you've held them
- An approach that speeds up personal transformation and change

RESULTS OF USING PSYCH-K®

People who use PSYCH-K® often experience:

- A deep sense of inner confidence
- An openness, calmness, and ease with others based on compassion
- Greater alignment and internal congruency, which makes external challenges easier to navigate

Establishing internal congruency helps to smooth navigation of the external environment.

PSYCH-K® represents one of the most important, efficient, effective, and rapid change processes that is available on this planet today.

— H. Lipton, Ph.D.,
PSYCH-K® Online Facilitator's Conference 2014

PSYCH-K® is an elegant process that is utilized within private sessions or taught within specialized workshops. See ABCsofMumuration.com for additional details.

ABOUT THE AUTHORS

DR. KATHY J. HAGLER is a nationally recognized author, coach, speaker, and organizational consultant with 40 years of experience. As the founding partner of K2OHSOLUTIONS, she has become a leader in organizational transformation to enhance communication and interactions in work and learning environments. Her firm, originally named the Technology Exchange Center, was honored with the Best Non-Profit Award by Coretta Scott King for its innovative approach to collaborative learning across various sectors. Dr. Hagler is also the author of *Art of Scars*, a book that reflects her deep insights into growth and resilience.

A lifelong adventurer, she enjoys traveling, yoga, and music, and has been a touring pianist, former roller-skating champion, and Harley-Davidson rider. Originally from New Mexico, she now resides in the scenic mountains of North Carolina with her husband, Ken.

Learn more about Dr. Kathy Hagler and her lifelong passion for connectivity at KathyHagler.com

ROBIN L. GRAHAM is a results-oriented entrepreneur who helps people and organizations overcome barriers to high performance. Early in her career, she experienced success in corporate business and as an entrepreneur, but she knew deep down she was meant to do something bigger. Soon she identified this as a need to blend spirituality with business. Since 1994, Graham has been facilitating personal growth with PSYCH-K®, first helping herself and then others discover how to break through old limitations to experience greater confidence and success, both personally and professionally. She has delivered this pioneering, innovative approach to establish transformation with thousands of individuals in 22 countries across six continents. As of 2021, Graham has been the Director of Training for PSYCH-K® Centre International. She loves adventures, which includes travel, skiing, diving, and exploring.

Discover more about Graham's work at InnerActiveBeliefs.com

ACKNOWLEDGMENTS

Kathy Hagler and Robin Graham

CREATING THIS BOOK DEMONSTRATES ME TO WE TO US. *As individual writers, we discovered how to blend our perspectives and styles.*

A book is always a WE effort. We are honored and grateful to all who guided, supported, and gave insights to this creation.

We thank the global experts who gave their time and wisdom to us.

We thank the early readers who gave their thoughts, both supportive and areas of improvement.

We thank our editors on this journey. With the earliest version, Judie Harvey, and with insightful guidance for the final version, Sally McGraw.

We thank the amazing graphic designer, Vickie Swisher, for the book cover and the graphics that support the manuscript.

We are beyond grateful to Kristyn Davis and Marissa Burton for their project management and organizational expertise, shared-tasks responsibilities, precious willingness to adapt to each new change, insights of creating clarity, and for being awesome individuals.

Robin appreciates Kathy for being a wise bird. "Thank you to all my mentors, guides, clients, family, and friends who taught me, that I have learned from, and who have supported me. And to my late husband, Voss, who inspired me with his love, insights, laughter, and hugs. Thank you."

Kathy so appreciates Robin as a teacher, mentor, coach, and co-author. "My love and deep appreciation goes out to my angels, Gayla, Larry, John, and Moose. And to my wonderful friends on this earth! My life is full of love."

This book is now the US, and as a reader, you are part of the expanding collective field.

Let us spread our wings and soar together toward a future of harmony.

ENDNOTES

INTRODUCTION

1. Leonard Mlodinow, *Subliminal: How Your Unconscious Mind Rules Your Behavior* (New York: Pantheon Books, 2012), 87.
2. "Chapter 4," University of Pretoria, accessed September 16, 2024, https://repository.up.ac.za/bitstream/handle/2263/28706/04chapter4.pdf?sequence=5&isAllowed=y.

CHAPTER 1

3. "Starling Murmurations: Why Do Starlings Flock Together?" *Voice of Garden Bird*, last modified March 5, 2023, https://voice.gardenbird.co.uk/starlings-flock-murmuratons.
4. "Flights of Fancy," *American Scientist*, accessed September 16, 2024, https://www.americanscientist.org/article/flights-of-fancy.
5. Birds of a Feather: On Track with Seven Neighbors, Flock Together," *Princeton University Research*, last modified July 26, 2023, https://research.princeton.edu/news/birds-feather-track-seven-neighbors-flock-together.

CHAPTER 2

6. Olivia Guy-Evans, "Fight, Flight, Freeze, or Fawn: How We Respond to Threats," *Simply Psychology*, last modified November 9, 2023, https://www.simplypsychology.org/fight-flight-freeze-fawn.html.
7. W. B. Cannon, *Bodily Changes in Pain, Hunger, Fear, and Rage*. (New York: Appleton-Century-Crofts, 1915).
8. Guy-Evans, "Fight, Flight, Freeze, or Fawn."
9. Marret K. Noordewier, Daan T. Scheepers, and Leon P. Hilbert, "Freezing in Response to Social Threat: A Replication," *Psychological Research*, October 2020, https://www.ncbi.nlm.nih.gov/pmc/articles/PMC7478949.
10. Pete Walker, *Complex PTSD: From Surviving to Thriving: A Guide and Map for Recovering from Childhood Trauma* (Petaluma, CA: Azure Coyote Publishing, 2013).
11. Ross Thornley, interview by Dr. Kathy Hagler, September 8, 2023.
12. Daniel Friedland, *Leading Well From Within* (San Diego: SuperSmartHealth Publishing, 2016), as presented in The xchange Approach Conscious Leadership training modules, https://www.xchangeapproach.com.
13. Attributed to Lao Tzu, source unverified.

CHAPTER 3

14 Bruce H. Lipton and Steve Bhaerman, *Spontaneous Evolution: Our Positive Future and a Way to Get There from Here* (Carlsbad, CA: Hay House, 2009), 25.

15 Shinzen Young, *Break Through Pain*, March 2006.

16 Mlodinow, *Subliminal*, 34.

17 Tor Norretranders, *The User Illusion: Cutting Consciousness Down to Size* (New York: Penguin Books, 1999), 125. Originally published in 1991.

18 Daniel Goleman, *Emotional Intelligence: Why It Can Matter More Than IQ*. (New York: Bantam Books, 1995).

19 Thornley, interview by Hagler.

20 G.I. Gurdjieff, *Views from the Real World* (New York: E.P. Dutton, 1973).

21 Gary Cone, "EMCS Living in Choice," in *Living in Choice*. (Oklahoma City: The Cone Center, 2008), 7.

22 Carter Phipps, *Evolutionaries: Unlocking the Spiritual and Cultural Potential of Science's Greatest Idea* (New York: Harper Perennial, 2012), 304.

23 Jalal al-Din Rumi, *The Essential Rumi*, trans. Coleman Barks (New York: HarperOne, 1995).

CHAPTER 4

24 Dr. Bruce H. Lipton, interview by Robin Graham, February 27, 2024.

25 Bernard J. Baars, Stan Franklin, and Thomas Zoega Ramsoy, "Global Workspace Dynamics: Cortical 'Binding and Propagation' Enables Conscious Contents," *Frontiers in Psychology*, September 25, 2013, https://doi.org/10.3389/fpsyg.2013.00200.

26 Stephen R. Covey, *The 7 Habits of Highly Effective People* (New York: Free Press, 1990), 48.

27 Sonia Sotomayor, quoted in *BrainyQuote*, accessed September 13, 2024, https://www.brainyquote.com/quotes/sonia_sotomayor_610965.

28 Jack Lowe, interview by Dr. Kathy Hagler, personal communication, September 2023.

29 Charles Duhigg, *The Power of Habit: Why We Do What We Do in Life and Business* (New York: Random House, 2012).

30 Walter B. Cannon, *Bodily Changes in Pain, Hunger, Fear, and Rage: An Account of Recent Research into the Function of Emotional Excitement*, 2nd ed. (New York: D. Appleton and Company, 1929).

CHAPTER 5

31 Bruce H. Lipton, *The Biology of Belief: Unleashing the Power of Consciousness, Matter & Miracles* (Carlsbad, CA: Hay House, 2004), 137.

32 Duccio Locati, D.O., interview by Dr. Kathy Hagler, September 6, 2023.

CHAPTER 6

33 "Transformations That Work," *Harvard Business Review*, May-June 2024, https://hbr.org/2024/05/transformations-that-work; Boris Ewenstein, Wesley Smith, and Ashvin Sologar, "Changing Change Management," *McKinsey & Company*, July 2015, https://www.mckinsey.com/featured-insights/leadership/changing-change-management; "Mindsets Matter in Transformations: A Conversation with Jon Garcia," *McKinsey & Company*, accessed September 13, 2024, https://www.mckinsey.com/capabilities/rts/our-insights/mind-sets-matter-in-transformations-a-conversation-with-jon-garcia#.

34 Mahzarin R. Banaji, Max H. Bazerman, and Dolly Chugh, "How (Un)Ethical Are You?" *Harvard Business Review*, December 2003.

35 IBM. "Cost Benefit Analysis Guide for IBM Cloud Migration." IBM. Accessed September 13, 2024. https://www.ibm.com/downloads/cas/2EXR3WMA.

36 University of Washington Faculty, "Words and Your Brain," *University of Washington*, accessed September 16, 2024, https://faculty.washington.edu/chudler/words.html.

37 David Rock, *Your Brain at Work* (New York: HarperCollins, 2009), 54.

38 "Decision-making May Be Surprisingly Unconscious Activity" *Science Daily*. April 15, 2008. https://www.sciencedaily.com/release/2008/04/080414145705.htm.

39 Peter Senge, C. Otto Scharmer, Joseph Jaworski, and Betty Sue Flowers, *Presence: Human Purpose and the Field of the Future* (New York: Doubleday, 2004), 11.

40 Melinda S. Jensen, Richard Yao, Whitney N. Street, and Daniel J. Simons, "Change Blindness and Inattentional Blindness," *National Library of Medicine*, PubMed, John Wiley & Sons, Ltd., 2011, https://pubmed.ncbi.nlm.nih.gov/26302304.

41 Trafton Drew, Melissa L. H. Vo, and Jeremy M. Wolfe, "The Invisible Gorilla Strikes Again: Sustained Inattentional Blindness in Expert Observers," *Psychological Science* 24, no. 9 (2013): 1848-1853, https://doi.org/10.1177/0956797613479386.

42 Dan Pilat and Dr. Sekoul Krastev, "Why Do Some Ideas Prompt Other Ideas Later On Without Our Conscious Awareness?" *The Decision Lab*, accessed September 16, 2024, https://thedecisionlab.com/biases/priming.

43 Alia J. Crum, William R. Corbin, Kelly D. Brownell, and Peter Salovey, "Mind Over Milkshakes: Mindsets, Not Just Nutrients, Determine Ghrelin Response," *Health Psychology* 30, no. 4 (2011): 424-429, accessed September 16, 2024, https://mbl.stanford.edu/sites/g/files/sbiybj26571/files/media/file/2011_milkshakes_crum_et_al_health_psych.pdf.

44 Centers for Disease Control and Prevention. "Epigenetics, Health, and Disease." CDC, last reviewed April 20, 2023. https://www.cdc.gov/genomics-and-health/about/epigenetic-impacts-on-health.html.

45 Bruce H. Lipton, *The Biology of Belief: Unleashing the Power of Consciousness, Matter & Miracles* (Carlsbad, CA: Hay House, 2004), 146-147.

46 Gregg Braden, "The Science of Miracles," YouTube video, 1:32:51, posted by Gaia, March 7, 2016, https://www.youtube.com/watch?v=g-ct0ZsQP_A.

47 Bruce H. Lipton, *The Biology of Belief: Unleashing the Power of Consciousness, Matter & Miracles* (Santa Rosa, CA: Mountain of Love/Elite Books, 2005), 39-41.

48 Danah Zohar, *Rewiring the Corporate Brain: Using the New Science to Rethink How We Structure and Lead Organizations* (Stanford: Stanford Business Books, 1997), 3.

49 University of Rochester Medical Center, "Study Reveals Brain's Finely Tuned System of Energy Supply," *URMC Newsroom*, August 7, 2016, https://www.urmc.rochester.edu/news/story/study-reveals-brains-finely-tuned-system-of-energy-supply.

50 Paul D. MacLean, *The Triune Brain in Evolution: Role in Paleocerebral Functions* (New York: Springer, 1990).

51 Jennice Vilhauer, Ph.D., "How Your Thinking Affects Your Brain Chemistry," *Psychology Today*, April 10, 2023, https://www.psychologytoday.com/us/blog/living-forward/202304/how-your-thinking-affects-your-brain-chemistry.

52 Patrick R. Steffen, Dawson Hedges, and Rebecca Matheson, "The Brain Is Adaptive, Not Triune: How the Brain Responds to Threat, Challenge, and Change," *National Library of Medicine*, April 1, 2022, https://www.ncbi.nlm.nih.gov/pmc/articles/PMC9010774.

53 Pingli Wei, Caitlin Keller, and Lingjun Li, "Neuropeptides in Gut-Brain Axis and Their Influence on Host Immunity and Stress," *National Library of Medicine*, March 4, 2020, https://pmc.ncbi.nlm.nih.gov/articles/PMC7160382.

54 "The Brain-Gut Connection," *Johns Hopkins Medicine*, accessed September 16, 2024, https://www.hopkinsmedicine.org/health/wellness-and-prevention/the-brain-gut-connection.

55 Jill Bolte Taylor, "My Stroke of Insight," *TED Talks*, February 2008, https://www.ted.com/talks/jill_bolte_taylor_my_stroke_of_insight.

56 Jeffery L. Fannin, PhD, and Robert M. Williams, MA, "qEEG Reveals Interactive Link Between The Principles Of Business, The Principles of Nature and the Whole-Brain State" *NeuroConnections*, Fall 2011, https://psych-k.com/wp-content/uploads/2013/10/neuroConnectionsV7-copy.pdf.

57 Lipton, interview by Graham.

CHAPTER 7

58 Deepak Chopra, "Can You Ever Choose to Be Whole?" *Deepak Chopra*, March 13, 2023, https://www.deepakchopra.com/articles/can-you-ever-choose-to-be-whole.

59 "Birds of a Feather: Track Seven Neighbors to Flock Together," *Princeton University*, last modified February 7, 2013, https://www.princeton.edu/news/2013/02/07/birds-feather-track-seven-neighbors-flock-together.

60 George A. Miller, "The Magical Number Seven, Plus or Minus Two: Some Limits on Our Capacity for Processing Information," Psychological Review 63, no. 2 (1956): 81-97.

61 Wayne Hetherington, "The Number 7: Why It Is So Important," *agile42*, February 14, 2020, https://www.agile42.com/en/blog/number-7-team-size-agile.

62 "Birds of a Feather," *Princeton University*.

63 Joris Celis, "As Agile as a Flock of Birds," Indra Partners, February 22, 2017, https://www.indra-partners.com/2017/02/22/agile-flock-birds.

64 Modified from the SCARS Model in Dr. Kathy J. Hagler, ART of SCARS: Healing Organizational Culture, Climate, Character (2021).

65 Dan Siegel, *Mindsight: The New Science of Personal Transformation* (New York: Bantam Books, 2011), 27.

CHAPTER 8

66 Desmond Tutu, No Future Without Forgiveness (New York: Doubleday, 1999).

67 Phil Jackson, Eleven Rings: The Soul of Success (New York: Penguin, 2013), 16.

68 "Posthuman Ethics with Cary Wolfe and Karen Barad: Animal Compassion as Trans-Species Entanglement," Critical Animal Studies, March 17, 2014.

69 Max Ehrmann, *Desiderata* (1927).

70 Mayo Clinic, "Stress Symptoms: Effect on Your Body and Behavior," in collaboration with the American Psychological Association, January 25, 2023, https://www.mayoclinic.org/healthy-lifestyle/stress-management/in-depth/stress-symptoms/art-20050987.

CHAPTER 9

71 Ryunosuke Satoro, quoted in BrainyQuote, accessed September 16, 2024, https://www.brainyquote.com/quotes/ryunosuke_satoro_167565.

72 Cary Wolfe, "Posthuman Ethics with Cary Wolfe and Karen Barad: Animal Compassion as Trans-Species Entanglement," *Critical Animal Studies*, March 17, 2014.

73 Rumi, "Keep Walking," *A Cottage by the Sea*, accessed September 16, 2024, https://www.acottagebythesea.net/poems/keep-walking-by-rumi.

74 Ross Thornley, "AQai – The Home of Adaptability Assessments & Coaching," AQai, accessed September 16, 2024, https://www.aqai.io.

CHAPTER 10

75 Often attributed to Leonardo da Vinci, but actually from *I, Leonardo da Vinci*, episode of *The Saga of Western Man*, written, produced, and narrated by John H. Secondari, voice of Leonardo by Fredric March, American Broadcasting, 1966.

76 Ibid

77 Paraphrased from Rumi, Mystical Poems of Rumi, translated by A. J. Arberry (Chicago: University of Chicago Press, 1991).

78 Rumi, quoted in Goodreads, accessed September 16, 2024, Quote by Rumi: "Do not feel lonely, the entire universe is insi...".

CHAPTER 11

79 Mattie Stepanek, quoted in BrainyQuote, accessed September 16, 2024, https://www.brainyquote.com/quotes/mattie_stepanek_319300.

80 D. Coghlan, "Action Research: Exploring Perspectives on a Philosophy of Practical Knowing," Academy of Management Annals 5 (2011): 53-87.

81 Michelle Holliday, The Age of Thrivability: Vital Perspectives and Practices for a Better World (2019), https://www.michelleholliday.com.

82 Rick Hill, "Legacies: Conversations on Knowledge and the Land," Earth to Tables Legacies, accessed September 16, 2024, https://earthtotables.org/collaborators/rick-hill.

EPILOGUE

83 Popular anonymous quote, origins unclear, often incorrectly attributed to *Alice in Wonderland*.

www.ingramcontent.com/pod-product-compliance
Lightning Source LLC
Chambersburg PA
CBHW072147070526
44585CB00015B/1023